Kathy Boyle

# Official Guide to Programming with CGI.pm

## Praise for Lincoln Stein's CGI.pm

*I have been happily developing Web applications using the CGI.pm module for some time now...I love it!*

**Ken Filipps, Programmer/Analyst**

*I would like to compliment you on your work with CGI.pm. The work you have done with it is quite impressive and helpful.*

**Bobby Kleemann, Programmer, Aardvarkpet/911 Gifts**

*Keep up the good work. Your library is wonderful!*

**Bernhard Weisshuhn, Senior Programmer, Weisshuhn & Weisshuhn Kommunikationsmanagement**

*I'll start out by saying what a g*d I think you are for creating such useful PERL scripts. Thanks!*

**Steven Etzell, System Administrator, Mindframe, Inc.**

# Official Guide to Programming with CGI.pm

**Lincoln Stein**

WILEY COMPUTER PUBLISHING

John Wiley & Sons, Inc.
New York • Chichester • Weinheim • Brisbane • Singapore • Toronto

Publisher: Robert Ipsen
Editor: Carol Long
Assistant Editor: Kathryn A. Malm
Managing Editor: Brian Snapp
Electronic Products, Associate Editor: Michael Sosa
Text Design & Composition: Benchmark Productions, Inc.



This book is printed on acid-free paper. ♾

Published by John Wiley & Sons, Inc.
Published simultaneously in Canada.



***Library of Congress Cataloging-in-Publication Data:***
Stein, Lincoln D.,
Official guide to programming with CGI.pm / Lincoln Stein.
p. cm.
"Wiley Computer Publishing."
Includes index.
ISBN 0-471-24744-8
1. CGI (Computer network protocol) 2. Perl (Computer program language) 3. Web servers—Computer programs. I. Title.
TK5105.565.S74 1998
005.2'762--dc21 98-10724
CIP

Printed in the United States of America.
10 9 8 7 6 5 4 3

# Contents

# Preface

This is a complete guide to the Perl CGI.pm module, a package of routines that take the drudgery out of Perl CGI scripting and lets you concentrate on the fun part: creative programming. With CGI.pm you can create error-free HTML on the fly, write and process fill-out forms, design interactive clickable image maps, store and process cookies, handle file uploads, attach JavaScript and cascading style sheets to your documents, and maintain script state. With the help of other Perl modules, you can interface your CGI scripts to databases and other business applications. It works on almost all systems, including Windows, Macintosh, UNIX, OS/2 ,and even VMS. Best of all, CGI.pm is free. You will find it in the standard Perl 5.004 distribution. If you have a recent version of Perl on your system, CGI.pm is probably already installed and ready to use.

This book was born when I realized that the electronic version of the CGI.pm manual was getting out of hand. I wanted to add a tutorial section, more code examples, background information on the CGI protocol, and an expanded reference guide. However, at over 150K, the manual was already too long to read through while sitting in front of a computer screen, and it added noticeably to the size of the Perl distribution. This book contains all the information that you will find in the electronic manual, plus information that previously was only accessible to those courageous enough to mine the source code itself. I hope that those who use CGI.pm in their daily Web development work, will find the book a welcome supplement to the existing electronic resources. For those who have never heard of the CGI module, or have looked at it but are skeptical of labor-saving aids, I hope this book will convert them.

The book is divided into five chapters. Chapter 1 steps you through the process of downloading CGI.pm, installing it on your system, and configuring your Web server to use it. Chapters 2 and 3 are a combined tutorial and user's guide. Starting with simple scripts and working upwards in complexity, they take you through each of CGI.pm's main features. Working code examples show how each feature integrates into full CGI scripts, and may even give you ideas for your own applications. Chapter 2 covers the basics: generating HTML documents on the fly, processing fill-out forms, and creating multi-page documents. Chapter 3 covers advanced topics such as script debugging, state maintenance, cookies, frames, cascading style sheets, and fancy HTML formatting. Chapter 4 gives instructions for extending and modifying CGI.pm using Perl's object-oriented inheritance system. Chapter 5, the last chapter, is a complete reference guide to every CGI.pm function call, organized alphabetically. Appendix A lists the ten most frequently asked questions about CGI.pm. Appendix B provides information about the companion Web site.

All the code examples contained within this book, the complete source distribution of CGI.pm, and any errata and updates can be found at this book's companion Web site at www.wiley.com/compbooks/stein. If you have enough space on your desk for both book *and* computer, you can follow along as you read. Each of the source code examples is fully functional. Read through the source code, then jump to the site to watch it run. Better yet, download the source code from the companion site and run it locally on your own server. That way, you can experiment with the code by changing it and seeing the effect it has on the resultant pages—or use the examples as templates on which to base your own scripts.

## ACKNOWLEDGMENTS

This book would not exist without the encouragement and understanding of Carol Long, my editor at John Wiley & Sons, and the efforts of Kathryn A. Malm, the assistant editor. My greatest thanks go out to the members of the Perl community, whose constant (and sometimes overwhelming) bug reports, feature suggestions, code patches, and cross-platform differences have made CGI.pm robust and feature-full. There are too many of you to list by name, but those who stand out from the rest (for their persistence, if nothing else!) include Tom Christiansen, Timothy Bunce, Andreas Koenig, Douglas MacEachern, Randal Schwartz, Gunther Birznieks, Keith Oborn, Robin Houston and Marco Dings. Thank you all for your tireless help.

Lincoln Stein

Chapter One

# Getting Started with CGI.pm

Welcome to CGI.pm! This chapter will describe CGI.pm, tell you how to obtain it, and guide you through the process of installing and running CGI.pm on your system.

## What Is CGI.pm?

CGI.pm is a Perl library for writing World Wide Web CGI scripts simply and easily. It eliminates most of the tedium in CGI scripting, such as parsing parameter lists and generating syntactically correct HTML. CGI.pm lets you concentrate on more important issues, such as what your CGI pages should actually *do.* CGI.pm eases awkward tasks such as maintaining the state of a complex series of fill-out forms across a series of page requests. Difficult tasks, such as accepting uploaded files or managing cookies become downright pleasant. With CGI.pm and Perl you can create dynamic pages that change each time they're accessed, for example:

- Form-based interfaces to databases or legacy software
- Guestbooks

- User-feedback forms
- Page counters
- HTML page processors
- Site gatekeepers

The possibilities in Web page design are only limited by your imagination and programming skills.

CGI.pm was designed to work with Perl 5 or higher, and makes full use of Perl 5's object-oriented inheritance system. However, you do not have to use Perl 5's object-oriented features, and many people don't. CGI.pm works with UNIX, Windows95, Windows NT, OS/2, Macintosh, and even VMS systems, and with almost any Web server in use today.

## BACKGROUND

I wrote CGI.pm several years ago in order to help create my own CGI scripts. It has since become the standard Perl library for CGI scripting, and is constantly upgraded and improved. It is available for free, in full source code form, and can be redistributed without restrictions.

Before I wrote CGI.pm, I was scripting in the standard method. I'd create a fill-out HTML form by hand and point it at a Perl script so that the contents of the form were sent to the script when the user pressed the submit button. The Perl script, in turn, would parse out the contents of each of the fields, process them, and print the result. To make the parsing easier, I used Steve Brenner's excellent cgi-utils.pl, a Perl 4 library for CGI scripting. This was the scripting method suggested by existing HTML books, and it seemed to work fine.

After a few weeks, however, I realized that there was something seriously wrong with this scripting style. The main symptom of the problem was that the program resided in two separate places: in a fill-out form located in the HTML document tree, and in a Perl script located in the Web server's scripts directory. Whenever I changed something in the fill-out form, such as adding a new field or changing the label on a button, I had to remember to make the complementary change in the Perl script. Conversely, whenever I wanted to add a new feature to the script, I had to make changes to the fill-out form. The script and its form were having a long-distance relationship.

More seriously, however, the fill-out forms I created in HTML were dead. The text fields were blank, the checkboxes turned off, and the radio buttons were set to their defaults. The user interface was inconvenient as well. Most of the scripts I wrote were database interfaces. The user would fill out the query form, press the submit button, and view the results. If the results weren't exactly as desired, the user had to page back to the fill-out form, make some changes, and repeat the process. I wanted the interaction to be more conversational, so the user could fill out the form, press the submit button, and the results would appear *on the same page*. If the user wanted to try again, the form would be right there.

I soon realized that the solution was to have the Perl script generate the fill-out form. The form would point back to the script, so that when the form was submitted, the script could be called to process it. In retrospect, this solution was obvious. After all, I was already creating other types of HTML documents from within Perl. I could even combine the fill-out form with the script results by printing them both on the same page. By checking for the existence of certain fields, I could have the same script generate a series of forms, each different from the previous one, or put reasonable default values in form fields based on the user's previous inputs.

This solved the long-distance relationship problem, but raised a whole new set of issues. Because the fill-out form and its response now appeared on the same page, a peculiar phenomenon occurred whenever the user pressed the submit button. The script response appeared as expected, but the fill-out form was wiped clean, erasing all the user's previous entries. Clearly, this would not do. The values that the user entered in the form had to be maintained when the script recreated the form. But this meant writing special code to check every text field, every radio button, and every menu item before creating it so that I could write out the HTML that correctly recreated its former state.

For example, here's how I would make sure that a checkbox that was turned on when the form was submitted stayed on when I regenerated it:

```
if ($checkbox1 eq 'on') {
    print '<INPUT TYPE="CHECKBOX" NAME="checkbox1" CHECKED>';
} else {
    print '<INPUT TYPE="CHECKBOX" NAME="checkbox1">';
}
```

After a few weeks I became disenchanted with the whole scheme. It was too much work to keep track of the state of the fill-out form, particularly with complicated elements like lists containing multiple selections. At that point, inspiration struck. I realized that I could create a library to keep track of the fill-out form and call functions in the library to create the fill-out form elements. It would be the library's responsibility to recognize when I was asking it to create a form element that it had seen before and emit the HTML needed to ensure that the form's state was maintained.

Thus, CGI.pm was born. Actually, it started out as a Perl 4 library called cgi-utils.pl. Initially, it was no more than a parsing routine for processing the contents of fill-out forms, and a set of functions for creating text fields, checkboxes, radio buttons, menus, and the like. Conveniently, soon after I started work on this library, Perl 5 was released with its object-oriented features. I realized that the idea of a Perl object was a good match for the idea of a fill-out form "state." To use the library, you create a CGI object, then make calls to that object to generate the various parts of the fill-out form. When the form is submitted and its contents returned to the script, the library arranges for the new CGI object to contain the previous contents of the form. This allows the object to make the appropriate modifications to the HTML returned by the element-generating functions. I rewrote cgi-utils.pl to take advantage of Perl 5's features, renamed it CGI.pm, and released it to the world. The reaction was gratifying. Almost overnight, I began receiving e-mails from hundreds of people who had started using CGI.pm.

I wanted CGI.pm to be the one-stop answer to all Perl CGI scripting problems, so I added access to HTTP session information such as the host-name of the remote machine. I incorporated MIME type negotiation, and wrote routines for creating the standard information at the tops and bottoms of HTML pages. As Netscape began adding new features to HTML, CGI.pm's function calls grew to accommodate them. Soon, some of the function calls had as many as 6 different arguments. For example, to create a new checkbox named "checkbox1" with the label "Hi Mom!," the value "on," and an initial setting of "checked," you had to call a function named checkbox() like this:

```
use CGI;
$q = new CGI; # create the new CGI object
print $q->checkbox('checkbox1',1,'on','Hi Mom!');
```

People began to complain that they were having trouble remembering the order of all these arguments, so I rewrote CGI.pm to use named arguments, and the function calls became much easier to read:

```
$q = new CGI; # create the new CGI object
print $q->checkbox(-name=>'checkbox1',-label=>'Hi Mom!',
                   -value=>'on',-checked=>1);
```

After about a year of using CGI.pm, I still wasn't satisfied with how I saw other people using it. I realized that 95 percent of the time, people were creating only one CGI object and using it through to the end of the script. If you always use the same CGI object, then why force programmers to explicitly create it each time? This led to the concept of a "default" CGI object. If you didn't create an object yourself, CGI.pm would create it for you. Then you could call the object's functions without explicitly referring to the CGI object. Not only did this improvement make the scripts look cleaner, but it also reduced the typing, for example:

```
print checkbox(-name=>'checkbox1',-label=>'Hi Mom!',
               -value=>'on',-checked=>1);
```

I was very satisfied with the module at this point, but then Microsoft entered the browser wars. Internet Explorer and Navigator were locked in a fight that added features to the Web at a breathtaking rate. Cookies were introduced, then frames, file uploads, server push, and client pull. Java applets appeared, then JavaScript, ActiveX, VBScript, and cascading stylesheets. With each new innovation, CGI.pm grew larger and larger.

Soon users were complaining that CGI.pm took forever to load and run, and that their CGI scripts weren't keeping up with demand. In response, I overhauled the entire module, using the Perl autoloader in a clever—but incredibly obscure—manner to defer the loading of nonessential code routines until they were needed. With this innovation, I was able to reduce the time it takes to load CGI.pm to about 10 milliseconds; not much longer than the original cgi-utils.pl code.

The last major improvement I made to CGI.pm was to add support for all HTML tags, not just the ones involved in creating fill-out forms. This enables programmers to write this:

```
print start_html('Hi Mom'),
      h1('CGI Scripting is Easy with CGI.pm'),
      p({-align=>CENTER},'So elegant, don't you think?'),
      end_html;
```

instead of this:

```
print "<HTML><HEAD>";
print "<TITLE>Hi Mom</TITLE>";
print "</HEAD";
print "<BODY>";
print "<H1>CGI Scripting is Easy with CGI.pm</H1>";
print "<P ALIGN=\"CENTER\">So elegant, don't you think?</P>";
print "</BODY>";
print "</HTML>";
```

Which code would *you* rather scan for syntax errors?

This book covers CGI.pm version 2.38. As the Web continues to evolve, so will CGI.pm. No doubt version 2.39, or later versions, will support Dynamic HTML, XML, Channel Definition Forms, and any new developments Netscape and Microsoft introduce. Whatever complexities they come up with, CGI.pm will adapt to ease the learning curve. Check this book's companion Web site at www.wiley.com/compbooks/stein/ for the latest CGI.pm updates and current information.

# What You Need to Know Before Using CGI.pm

Although CGI.pm assists you in many ways, it can't teach you to program. In order to use CGI.pm effectively, you should have a basic knowledge of Perl, and the ability to write Perl scripts of simple-to-moderate complexity. It is better if you know how to use the special features of Perl 5; however, you do not need to understand object-oriented programming. In fact, you will not even hear about object-oriented programming techniques until Chapter 3, *Advanced Tricks.* If you don't know Perl, I strongly recommend starting with *Learning Perl*, by Randal Schwartz (O'Reilly & Associates, 1993). When you feel comfortable with Perl's core features, purchase *Programming Perl,* by Larry Wall, Tom Christiansen, and Randal Schwartz (O'Reilly & Associates, 1996) to learn about the new features in Perl 5. It is not necessary to read this book from cover to cover, but do peruse the sections dealing with array references and anonymous arrays, since many of CGI.pm's nicest features take advantage of these data structures. Also strongly recommended is *Effective Perl Programming,* by Joseph Hall with Randal Schwartz (Addison-Wesley, 1998), an invaluable compendium of Perl tricks and techniques.

You should know how to write HTML documents, and understand how to build a fill-out form using the <FORM> tag. You will not need to know all the subtleties of creating fill-out form elements, such as the many variants of the <INPUT> tag or the difference between single-element and multi-element <SELECT> tags, since CGI.pm shields you from these details. If you are unfamiliar with HTML, you might want to read my previous book, *How to Set Up and Maintain a Web Site*, by Lincoln Stein (Addison-Wesley, 1996), or start out with *HTML 4.0 Sourcebook*, by Ian Graham (John Wiley & Sons, 1998).

Finally, you will need access to a Web server on which you have scripting privileges. Without access to a Web server, there is no way to install fully interactive CGI scripts—although you can still write scripts that generate fancy HTML faster and more error free than you could by hand. If you have Web pages on an Internet Service Provider's (ISP) system and are unsure whether you have scripting privileges, check with the ISP to see what to do to install and run CGI scripts.

# Finding CGI.pm

If Perl 5.004 or later is installed on your system, you already have CGI.pm. CGI.pm has been a standard part of the Perl 5 distribution since the 5.004 release. To check your system, open up the Perl 5 library directory (usually /usr/local/lib/perl5 on UNIX systems, or C:\perl5\lib on Windows95/NT systems) and look for a file named CGI.pm. There should also be a subdirectory named CGI in the library directory that contains the files Push.pm, Carp.pm, Cookie.pm, Apache.pm, and Fast.pm. If any of these files are absent, your installation is incomplete and you will need to follow the directions for downloading CGI.pm in the following section. Even if CGI.pm is already installed, you may want to download the most recent version from the companion Web site at www.wiley.com/compbooks/stein.

## DOWNLOADING THE CGI.PM DISTRIBUTION

You can download the most recent CGI.pm distribution from CPAN (Comprehensive Perl Archive Network). CPAN is a network of FTP (File Transfer Protocol) sites scattered around the world. To find the site nearest you, point your Web browser at www.perl.com/CPAN, and follow the links to modules/by-module/CGI/. There you will find the latest copy of the CGI.pm distribution in compressed tape (tar) archive form. This is the form most suitable for UNIX users. To uncompress this archive, you will need the gzip and tar programs that are standard tools on most UNIX machines. If you are using a Windows or Macintosh system, you probably won't have these programs handy. Connect to CGI.pm's home site at www.wiley.com/compbooks/stein and follow the links to the archive format most suitable for your system. Windows users will probably want to download the ZIP archive, while Macintosh users will want the StuffIt format.

CGI.pm requires Perl version 5.003, patchlevel 7 or higher. If you try to use CGI.pm with an earlier version of Perl, an error will result and CGI.pm will refuse to run. CGI.pm uses certain Perl features that only appeared in later versions. You'll find the most recent version of Perl in source and binary form in CPAN. Go to CPAN's top page, www.perl.com/CPAN/, and look in the src and/or ports directory for the distribution most appropriate for your operating system.

Unpack the CGI distribution using gzip, tar, ZIP, or StuffIt. For UNIX users, the appropriate command is:

```
lstein> zcat CGI.pm-2.38.tar.gz | tar xvf -
```

In this and all other examples, the **bold** font indicates what you type at the keyboard. The output from the computer is shown in a light monospace font. Replace the 2.38 version number in this command with whatever is current at www.wiley.com/compbooks/stein.

Windows and Macintosh users should use the graphical interface of the WinZip or StuffIt utilities to get the distribution extracted and unpacked. If you do not have one of these programs, you can find them at www.shareware.com, a site that maintains a large searchable index of freeware and shareware programs. Using its search engine, find the FTP archive site nearest you and download the appropriate utility.

When the distribution is unpacked, you should have a directory containing these files and directories:

- ***Announce*** Recent announcements and late-breaking news about CGI.pm.
- ***CGI.pm*** The source code for the main CGI.pm module.
- ***CGI/*** A directory containing the source code for modules related to CGI.pm, such as the server push and cookies modules.
- ***cgi_docs.html*** Documentation for the library in HTML format.
- ***cgi-lib_porting.html*** Information for those who are using Steve Brenner's Perl cgi-lib.pl library to maintain legacy scripts written in Perl 4. This file contains instructions for porting cgi-lib.pl scripts to CGI.pm, as does Chapter 3 of this book, *Advanced Tricks*.
- ***examples/*** A directory containing a number of example CGI scripts that demonstrate how to use certain CGI.pm features. You are welcome to take these scripts and use them as the basis for your own scripts. In fact, you'll find several of them used as code examples in later sections of this book.
- ***Makefile.PL*** A Perl MakeMaker template for creating Makefiles.
- ***Manifest*** A listing of all files that are supposed to be in the distribution.
- ***README*** News and installation directions.

In order to start using CGI.pm, you will need to copy the main module and its helpers into your system's Perl library directory. On UNIX systems, it is best to let the MakeMaker program do the installation for you. This program—part of the standard Perl distribution—automates the process of installing the CGI.pm libraries. To invoke MakeMaker, enter the CGI.pm distribution directory and type the text shown in bold at the command line prompt as follows:

```
lstein> perl Makefile.PL
Checking if your kit is complete...
```

```
Looks good
Writing Makefile for CGI
```

This step creates a Makefile that contains the correct Perl library paths and other information. The next step is to invoke the Make program.

```
lstein> make
cp CGI/Carp.pm ./blib/lib/CGI/Carp.pm
cp CGI/Fast.pm ./blib/lib/CGI/Fast.pm
cp CGI/Push.pm ./blib/lib/CGI/Push.pm
cp CGI.pm ./blib/lib/CGI.pm
cp CGI/Cookie.pm ./blib/lib/CGI/Cookie.pm
cp CGI/Apache.pm ./blib/lib/CGI/Apache.pm
cp CGI/Switch.pm ./blib/lib/CGI/Switch.pm
Manifying ./blib/man3/CGI::Fast.3
Manifying ./blib/man3/CGI::Carp.3
Manifying ./blib/man3/CGI::Push.3
Manifying ./blib/man3/CGI.3
Manifying ./blib/man3/CGI::Switch.3
Manifying ./blib/man3/CGI::Apache.3
Manifying ./blib/man3/CGI::Cookie.3
```

Make does two things: It copies CGI.pm and the other modules into a staging directory known as blib, and it creates manual pages for each of the modules. The last step is to install the modules into the main system Perl5 library directory. You do this by typing make install:

```
lstein> make install
Installing /usr/local/lib/perl5/site_perl/./CGI/Carp.pm
Installing /usr/local/lib/perl5/site_perl/./CGI/Fast.pm
Installing /usr/local/lib/perl5/site_perl/./CGI/Push.pm
Installing /usr/local/lib/perl5/site_perl/./CGI/Cookie.pm
Installing /usr/local/lib/perl5/site_perl/./CGI/Apache.pm
```

```
Installing /usr/local/lib/perl5/site_perl/./CGI/Switch.pm
Installing /usr/local/lib/perl5/site_perl/./CGI.pm
Installing /usr/local/lib/perl5/man/man3/./CGI::Fast.3
Installing /usr/local/lib/perl5/man/man3/./CGI::Carp.3
Installing /usr/local/lib/perl5/man/man3/./CGI::Push.3
Installing /usr/local/lib/perl5/man/man3/./CGI.3
Installing /usr/local/lib/perl5/man/man3/./CGI::Switch.3
Installing /usr/local/lib/perl5/man/man3/./CGI::Apache.3
Installing /usr/local/lib/perl5/man/man3/./CGI::Cookie.3
Writing /usr/local/lib/perl5/site_perl/i586-linux/auto/CGI/.packlist
Appending installation info to /usr/local/lib/perl5/i586-linux/5.004/perllocal.pod
```

This last step copies the contents of the staging directory and the manual pages to the correct locations in the main Perl5 library directory. Depending on the configuration of your system, and whether you have older versions of CGI.pm installed, you may see slightly different messages.

You will very likely have to be running as the superuser ("root" on UNIX systems, or Administrator on Windows NT systems) in order to accomplish the last installation step. This is because many systems are set up to forbid ordinary users from writing into system library directories. If you are using a system that does not have the concept of a superuser, such as Macintosh or Windows95, you won't have to worry about this. If you are working on a UNIX, Windows NT, or VMS system and do not have superuser access, you can install CGI.pm in a private directory of your own; your home directory, for example. To do this, modify the first step to look something like this:

```
lstein> perl Makefile.PL INSTALLDIRS=site \
             INSTALLSITELIB=/home/lstein/lib
```

Replace the reference to /home/lstein/lib with the directory in which you want to install the module. When you make and make install, the files will be copied to the location you indicated.

**TIP**

**If you install CGI.pm in a private directory, Perl may not be able to find it without some help from you. To provide this help, put the line use lib /home/lstein/lib at the top of each of your scripts (right underneath the #!/usr/bin/perl line) replacing the directory name with whatever is appropriate. Many programmers make the mistake of putting CGI.pm in the Web server scripts directory. This is not necessary because CGI.pm is a library file, not an executable file that will ever be run directly as a CGI script.**

If you are on a Windows NT, 95, or Macintosh system, the make program may be available and you will have to do the installation by hand. This is very easy if you know the location of the Perl5 library directory on your system. On Windows systems, enter the CGI.pm distribution directory, and execute the following commands from the NT/DOS command-line prompt:

```
C:\TEMP\CGI.pm-2.37\> copy CGI.pm C:\Perl\lib
C:\TEMP\CGI.pm-2.37\> mkdir C:\Perl\lib\CGI
C:\TEMP\CGI.pm-2.37\> copy CGI\* C:\Perl\lib\CGI
```

This assumes that Perl5 has been installed in such a way that its library directory is in C:\perl5\lib. Change these commands appropriately for your system's configuration.

On Macintosh systems, just drag the CGI.pm file and the entire CGI directory into the Perl5 library folder. There is no standard location for the Perl5 library folder on the Macintosh system. Find the folder that contains other .pm files and move the CGI.pm file there.

**TIP**

**You can install into a personal directory on Windows and Macintosh systems also, but be sure to include "use lib <directory>" at the top of each script so that Perl knows where to look for the CGI module.**

Because CGI.pm doesn't require a compile phase, there is no major drawback to copying the files directly into Windows and Macintosh systems rather than using the MakeMaker and make steps recommended on UNIX systems. The only real difference is that the manual pages won't be created automatically. This is not a real problem since basic Windows and Mac systems don't have a built-in manual page viewer. If you'd like to read the manual pages on these systems, you can convert them into HTML files by running the pod2html program, which accompanies some, but not all, ports of Perl. On Windows systems, type:

```
C:\TEMP\CGI.pm-2.37\> pod2html.pl *.pm CGI/*.pm
```

This will create a series of HTML files named CGI.html, CGI::Push.html, CGI::Cookie.html, and so forth. You can view them with your favorite HTMl browser by launching the browser and choosing File/Open from the menubar. On Macintosh systems, drag the CGI.pm file and the contents of the CGI subdirectory into the pod2html "droplet" to create the HTML files in place.

Alternately, you can just read the contents of the .pm files with your favorite text editor. Aside from a small amount of formatting information, the manual documentation is completely human readable.

To confirm that CGI.pm has been correctly installed, type the following at the command line:

```
lstein> perl
use CGI qw/:standard/;
print h1("Aye aye Captain!");
^D
<H1>Aye aye Captain!</H1>
```

(The notation ^D means control-D. That is, press the control and D keys simultaneously. On UNIX systems, this is a signal that you have finished typing in the script and are ready to have Perl evaluate it. On Windows systems, type ^Z, control-Z, instead). If CGI.pm is installed correctly, the bit of HTML code shown above will print out.

# Web Server Configuration

If your site's Web server is already configured to run Perl CGI scripts, then there is nothing more for you to do. Advance to the tutorial in Chapter Two, *CGI.pm Basics*. If not, some extra configuration may be necessary before the Web server and Perl will work comfortably together. The details depend both on your operating system and on the particular Web server software you use.

On most UNIX servers, no extra configuration should be necessary. Any Perl script that is placed in the server scripts directory (usually named cgi-bin) will be correctly recognized and will run. You may skip the next few pages and start scripting! On Windows and Macintosh operating systems, however, you must associate Perl script files with the Perl interpreter so that the Web server knows what to do when a Perl script is requested.

On Windows systems, the Perl installation script should have associated files ending with .pl with the Perl interpreter, perl.exe. This makes it possible to launch text files containing Perl scripts from the command line or by double-clicking them in a directory window. Test this now by creating a small file named foo.pl containing the following code:

```
#!perl
use CGI qw/:standard/;
print h1("Man the torpedoes and full speed ahead!");
```

When you type the name of this file in a command window, it should print out the phrase between the <H1> and </H1> tags, much as the example at the end of the previous section did. If this doesn't work as expected, go back and rerun the Perl install script.

What you do next depends on which Web server your site uses. In the case of some servers, such as the O'Reilly & Associates WebSite server, and the Purveyor server, you're all done. If the Windows command shell recognizes .pl files as belonging to perl.exe, then the Web server will correctly recognize the association.

Things aren't quite as simple with other servers, however. In particular, the Microsoft Internet Information Server (all versions) requires that you add some information to the system registry to tell the server what to do when a remote user requests a Perl script. To associate Perl scripts with perl.exe, you must go through the following steps:

1. Start the registry editor, Regedt32.exe, from the command line.
2. Using the expanding outline, navigate to the key: HKEY_LOCAL_MACHINE\SYSTEM\CurrentControlSet\Services \W3SVC\Parameters\ScriptMap
3. Choose Edit/Add Value from the menubar.
4. A dialog box named Add Value will appear. In the field labeled Value Name, type in **.pl** and select a data type of REG_SZ from the popup menu.
5. A dialog box named String Editor will appear. Type in **C:\Perl\bin\perl.exe %s %s** and press OK. Make the appropriate changes if perl.exe is installed at a different location on your system.
6. Close the registry editor.

If you are using the ActiveWare port of Perl5 (available at http://www .activeware.com/), there are actually two different versions of Perl that you can use with the Microsoft Internet Information Server. One, perl.exe, is a standalone Perl interpreter that runs as a separate program from the server itself. This is the interpreter that is associated with .pl files in the steps given previously. The second version of Perl is implemented as a dynamically loadable (.dll) library, C:\Perl\bin\perlis.dll. In theory, this version of Perl will load and run faster than the standalone version. In practice, it does not seem to work very well, and I recommend that you stick with the standalone interpreter. If you would like to experiment with the .dll version, please read the ActiveWare release notes that accompany the package.

MacPerl, the Macintosh port of Perl, uses Macintosh file types to associate Perl scripts with the Perl interpreter application. This allows you to run Perl scripts by double-clicking on them, or even to process files by dragging and dropping them onto Perl script icons. Additional work is necessary in order to get Perl to work with the Web server, however. This is because Macintosh servers use an AppleScript-based protocol for communicating with server scripts rather than the standard CGI protocol.

Users of the WebSTAR and MacHTTP servers who wish to use the MacPerl port of Perl5 should download and install Matthias Neeracher's PCGI AppleScript adapter. PCGI fools Perl (and CGI.pm as well) into thinking that it is running in a standard UNIX/Windows CGI environment. Nearly all of CGI.pm's features work correctly on the Macintosh, including such esoterica as frames, cookies, and server push. The only exception is file upload, which is reportedly unreliable in the current version.

# If You Run into Trouble

CGI.pm has been tested successfully with hundreds of combinations of Web server software and operating systems. However, each system has its own quirks, and it is virtually impossible for software to keep up with the rapidly changing world of the Web.

Among the things that CGI.pm tries to do when it starts up is to guess the operating system and use this as the basis for setting various run-time options. Occasionally, CGI.pm may guess incorrectly and set options that are inappropriate for your operating system and/or Web server. This is most likely to happen if you are using an obscure operating system such as AmigaOS, or a Web server that does things in an unusual way. If this happens, there is a simple way to force CGI.pm's setup choice. Here are the steps:

1. Open up the CGI.pm file with the text editor of your choice.
2. Find the subroutine named initializeGlobals(). It is located near the top of the file.
3. Toward the beginning of the subroutine, add one of the five following lines:

```
$OS = 'WINDOWS';
$OS = 'MACINTOSH';
$OS = 'VMS';
$OS = 'OS2';
$OS = 'UNIX';
```

If your operating system is not on this list, you'll need to experiment a bit to find which of these five settings will work.

File uploads are also a potential system incompatibility issue, because uploads are spooled to a temporary directory before being made available to your script. The location of the temporary directory differs from system to system, and CGI.pm does its best to find it. CGI.pm will find the temporary directory on all standard UNIX, Windows, Macintosh, OS/2, and VMS systems, but may fail with an obscure operating system. If you are having trouble with file uploads, you may need to force CGI.pm's temporary directory choice. Open the CGI.pm file with a text editor, and find the forbidding text that reads:

```
# HARD-CODED LOCATION FOR FILE UPLOAD TEMPORARY FILES.
# UNCOMMENT THIS ONLY IF YOU KNOW WHAT YOU'RE DOING.
# $TempFile::TMPDIRECTORY = '/usr/tmp';
```

Uncomment the third line (by removing the # mark in front of it), and change the path of the temporary directory to whatever is appropriate for your system (for instance, C:\Temporary).

If you have tried these things and are still unable to run CGI.pm, there are several support options. First, check the Frequently Asked Questions section at the end of this book. It contains answers to frustrated programmers' ten most frequently asked questions about CGI.pm. A similar list, updated for the current version, can be found in the latest CGI.pm distribution, and at this book's companion Web site. If you don't find a satisfactory answer, you can make a posting to the Usenet newsgroup comp.lang.perl.modules. Be sure to scan through the newsgroup before you post; chances are fair that someone else has had a similar problem. If this is unsuccessful, you can write directly to me at lstein@w3.org. I will do my best to respond to your request promptly. If you suspect a bug, please let me know and it will be fixed in the next version of the module. If you request a feature, I'll take it into consideration. If enough other people request the same feature, chances are it will also make its appearance.

## OTHER MODULES OF INTEREST

If you do a lot of CGI scripting, there are several other Perl modules that can make your work easier. The following is a brief list of the ones I recommend. You can find them all on CPAN at the URL given previously.

- ***DBI/DBD*** DBI is a Perl interface to relational databases. Separate DBD (database driver) modules allow you to access a number of commercial and noncommercial databases, including Sybase, Oracle, mySQL, and Illustra. This is one of the easiest ways to hook up your organization's database to the Web.
- ***GD.pm*** GD.pm is a Perl interface to Thomas Boutell's libgd library. With it, you can create your own GIF images on the fly from within a CGI script.
- ***LWP*** LWP (Library for Web Programming) is an excellent toolkit for writing *client-side* programs. With this set of modules, you can write your own Web crawling robots, turn HTML into fancy ASCII text or PostScript, and mirror pages from remote sites.
- ***Mod_perl*** mod_perl is a Perl interpreter embedded inside the Apache Web server. With this module installed, Perl CGI scripts run much faster because there is no significant delay for the Perl interpreter to start up.
- ***Win32::ODBC*** This is an interface to Windows ODBC-compliant databases. With this module, your script can talk to any database that comes with an ODBC driver, such as Microsoft Access or Microsoft SQL Server.

# Chapter Two

# CGI.pm Basics

The easiest way to learn CGI.pm is to use it. This chapter shows you the basics by starting simple and gradually growing complex. Later chapters will teach the theory behind CGI scripting.

In order to run the examples in this chapter, you'll need to have:

1. Perl version 5.003 or higher
2. The CGI.pm module installed in the Perl library directory
3. Access to a Web server's scripts directory

If you don't have one or more of these things, see Chapter 1, *Getting Started with CGI.pm*, for help!

The examples in this chapter are available at this book's companion Web site at John Wiley & Sons. Load URL www.wiley.com/compbooks/stein and follow the links to the source code examples.

# Displaying a Plain Text File

The first four examples create plain text files on the fly and display them. They're as simple as CGI scripts get. Start your favorite text editor, and type in the following code:

```
#!/usr/bin/perl
# Script: plaintext.pl
use CGI ':standard';
print header('text/plain'),
"Nothing to it!";
```

**TIP**

**The top line of the file tells UNIX systems where to find the Perl executable file. In this and all subsequent examples, change this line to the correct path to Perl. Windows users can safely ignore this advice, since Windows uses file associations to associate documents with their applications.**

Most Web servers require that CGI scripts be saved to a particular scripts directory. On UNIX systems, this directory is often named cgi-bin. On Windows systems, it may be called cgi-bin, scripts, or even cgi-standard. Identify this directory and save the file to it using the name script1.pl. If you are on a UNIX system, you will need to make the file executable (by typing **chmod +x script1.pl**). You should also make sure that the script is world readable (chmod o+w script.pl in UNIX, or by changing the access control list to allow reading by everyone in Windows NT).

First test the script from the command line. Type the following:

```
zorro> perl plaintext.pl ""
```

If all goes well, the script will run and print out the following two lines of text:

```
Content-type: text/plain
Nothing to it!
```

We will cover the meaning of this text later.

If you get an error message, go back and confirm that Perl is installed correctly, that the PATH variable includes the location of the Perl executable, and that the CGI library is installed.

Now you are ready to run the script from the Web server. Open up a Web browser and point it at the URL of the script. This may be slightly different from server to server, but on most servers, you'll enter something similar to www.yoursite.com/cgi-bin/plaintext.pl.

The browser will ask the server to fetch your script's URL, the server will launch and run the script, and the script will return the document shown in Figure 2.1.

**TIP**
**If the browser displays an error message, go back and check that the permissions of the script allow everyone to read and execute it. The Web server runs as an unprivileged user, and occasionally its privileges will deny the server permission to access a file that you can read under your own user account. If you still get an error, go to the *Troubleshooting* section later in this chapter.**

Figure 2.1 When plaintext.pl runs, it creates this Web page.

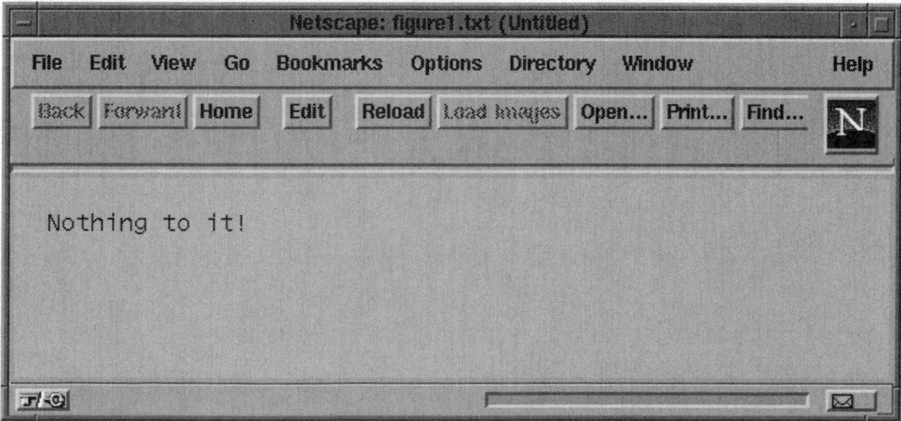

Let's look at the script in detail:

```
use CGI ':standard';
```

This line loads the CGI.pm module, then imports its standard function definitions into your script. You can now use the standard CGI functions without prefixing them with the CGI:: namespace. In other words, you can refer to header() instead of CGI::header().

```
print header('text/plain'),
      'Nothing to it!';
```

This code is a Perl print() statement that prints out two strings. The first string is a call to the CGI.pm header() function, which returns a valid HTTP header. HTTP headers contain a variety of information that is meaningful to the Web server, the Web browser, or both. The important code here is the line that gives the browser the MIME type of the document to expect; in this case, text/plain. This results in the output of the header line "Content-type: text/plain."

The second string is the phrase "Nothing to it!" This becomes the contents of the document, often called the *body*. The document content is separated from the header by a blank line automatically provided by CGI.pm.

You can extend this example to create any sort of plain text document. All print() statements after the header will appear on the page. All formatting, including line breaks, will be preserved exactly as if the script was printing to a dumb terminal. Plaintext2.pl, listed below, creates a small poem, and Figure 2.2 shows its screenshot.

```
#!/usr/bin/perl
# Script: plaintext2.pl
use CGI ':standard';
print header('text/plain');
print "Jabberwock\n\n";
print "'Twas brillig, and the slithy toves\n";
```

Figure 2.2 Plaintext2.pl and plaintext3.pl create multiple formatted lines of text.

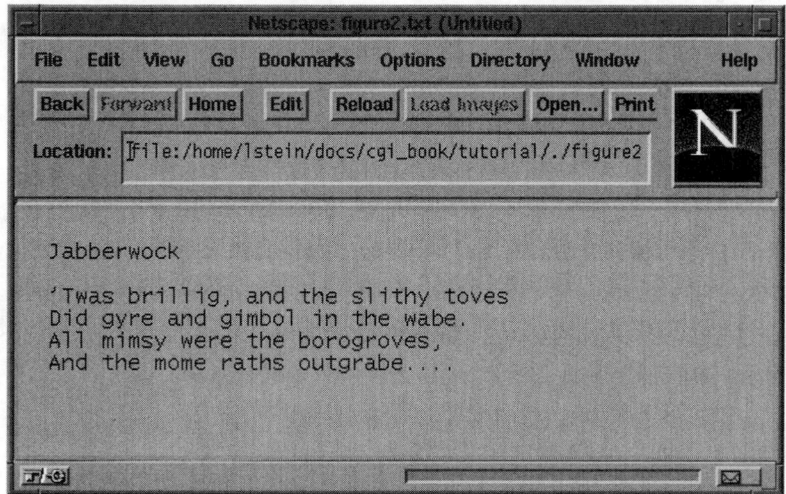


```
print "Did gyre and gimbol in the wabe.\n";
print "All mimsy were the borogroves,\n";
print "And the mome raths outgrabe....\n";
```

Plaintext3.pl returns the same results, but uses Perl's cleaner "here is" notation to avoid redundant print() statements. The example also shows that the text returned by header() is just a string that can be manipulated like any other string.

```
#!/usr/bin/perl
# Script: plaintext3.pl
use CGI ':standard';
$header = header('text/plain');
print <<END_OF_TEXT;
$header
Jabberwock

'Twas brillig, and the slithy toves
Did gyre and gimbol in the wabe.
```

```
All mimsy were the borogroves,
And the mome raths outgrabe....
END_OF_TEXT
```

The text produced by a CGI script doesn't have to be hard-coded within the script. If you prefer, you can pull the text out of a file or other external source. Plaintext4.pl gets its text from a specified file and displays it after starring out all four letter words using a regular expression match and substitution (see Figure 2.3). This shows you a simple example of how CGI.pm can be used as a document filter.

```
#!/usr/bin/perl
# Script: plaintext4.pl
use CGI ':standard';
$FILE = '/usr/tmp/press_release.txt';
open (FILE,$FILE) || die "Can't open $FILE: $!\n";
print header('text/plain');
while (<FILE>) {
      s/\b(\w)\w{2}(\w)\b/$1**$2/g;
      print;
}
close FILE;
```

**TIP**

**When CGI.pm scripts are run from the command line, they will stop and wait for you to type some CGI parameters before continuing. This is one of the debugging features described in the next chapter. Press Control-D (^D) on UNIX systems, or Control-Z (^Z) on Windows systems, to signal you have nothing to enter, or modify your script to use the -noDebug flag:**

```
use CGI ':standard','-noDebug';
```

**This feature is only available in CGI.pm versions 2.38 and higher.**

Figure 2.3 Plaintext4.pl removes four-letter words from text files before displaying them.

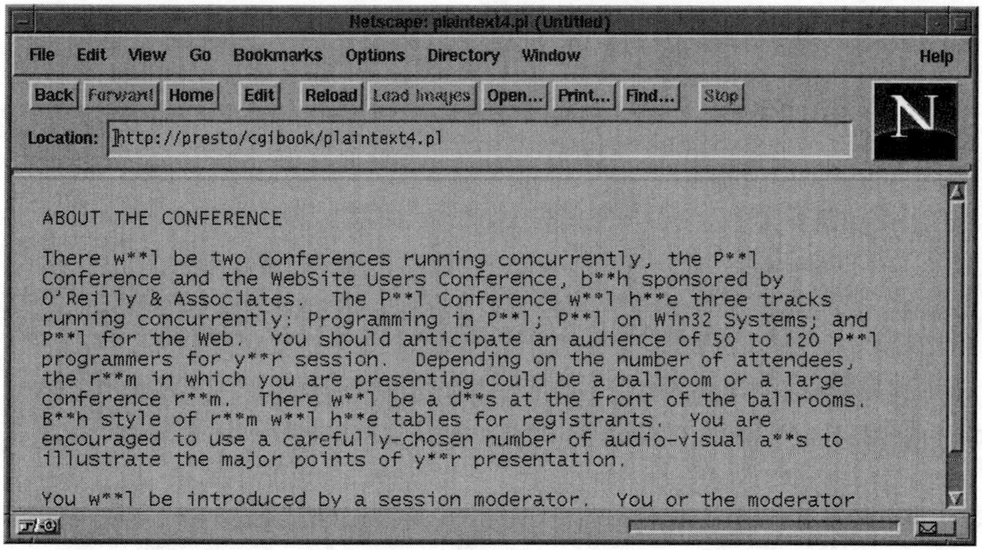

# Creating an HTML Page

The previous examples were not very interesting, they could have easily been written with static text files. The power of CGI scripting, however, is in its ability to create dynamic documents that change each time they're accessed. The next example creates a Web page that displays the current local time and date. Each time the page is reloaded, the page is updated. To make things fun, we will create a full-blown HTML document using the following code:

```
#!/usr/bin/perl
# File: time1.pl
use CGI ':standard';
$current_time = localtime;

print header,
      start_html('A Virtual Clock'),
      h1('A Virtual Clock'),
```

```
"The current time is $current_time.",
hr,
end_html;
```

Save this script with the name time1.pl and install it in the server's scripts directory. When you fetch the script's URL, the result should look something like Figure 2.4. Every time you reload the URL, the time will be updated.

**TIP**

**If the time doesn't update when you reload the script, try changing your browser's cache settings so that it checks the document every time it loads. Chapter 3, *Advanced CGI,* gives more advice on dealing with browser caching problems.**

How does this script work? Again, it starts by importing CGI.pm's standard set of function definitions. Next it fetches the current time using Perl's built-in localtime() function, and stores it in the variable $current_time.

The rest is a long print() statement. As before, we call header() to return the HTTP header. In the previous examples, we had to specify the MIME

**Figure 2.4 Time.pl updates the Virtual Clock when the URL is reloaded.**

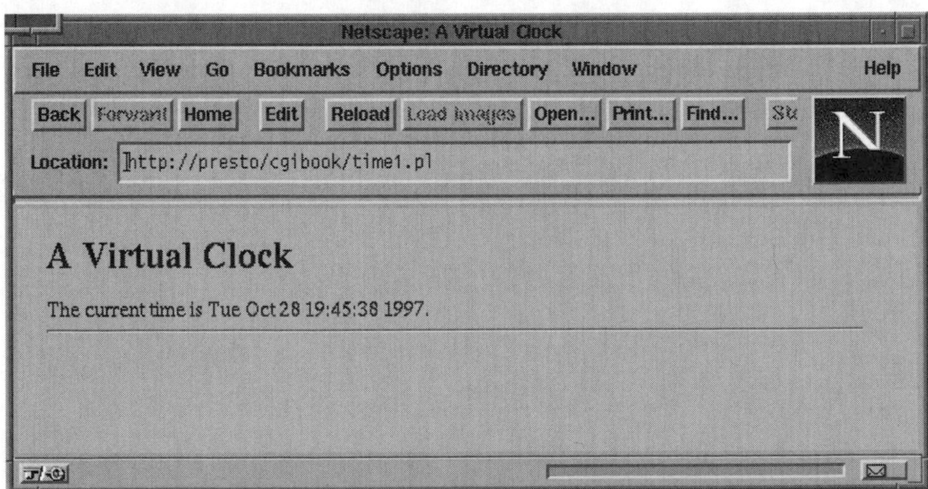

type of the document; here, we don't specify it at all. Because HTML documents are so common, header() defaults to type text/html if the function isn't given an explicit MIME type. It is fine to replace the function call with header('text/html') if you prefer.

The balance of the print() statement creates the document, and makes heavy use of CGI.pm's HTML shortcuts.

```
start_html('A Virtual Clock')
```

This call returns a string containing the entire HTML preamble, including the <HEAD>, <TITLE>, <BODY> tags, and the SGML DTD (Standard Generalized Markup Language Data Type Definition) that some Web publishing systems rely on. Start_html()'s argument becomes the title of the document.

```
h1('A Virtual Clock')
```

This returns an HTML level 1 header tag surrounding the text "A Virtual Clock." As is common, the first header is the same as the document title, but this is not a requirement. In addition to the h1() function, CGI.pm defines h2(), h3(), h4() and other functions corresponding to all other standard HTML tags.

**TIP**

**CGI.pm predefines functions for all tags in HTML 3.2, and the more common Netscape and Microsoft extensions. Since the HTML specifications are changing rapidly, CGI.pm may not always be up-to-date with the latest extensions. When the HTML 4.0 standard is ratified, CGI.pm will be updated to handle all the HTML 4-specific tags. Untill then, see Chapter 3, *Advanced Tricks*, for an easy way to add your own HTML tag definitions. Adding a new tag is as easy as typing its name.**

Continuing on through the source code, we encounter this line:

```
"The current time is $current_time."
```

This string incorporates the current local time from $current_time. It is inserted into the HTML page without modification. As in other HTML documents, line breaks, tabs, and other formatting will be ignored, and the browser will word wrap the string. To insert preformatted text, just place it in inside a call to pre(), which will put the text in an HTML preformatted section (<PRE>...</PRE>).

```
hr
```

This returns an <HR> tag, creating a horizontal rule.

```
end_html
```

This ends the HTML document by returning the </BODY> and </HTML> tags.

Many programmers, including myself, often forget to end their documents with this tag. Fortunately, most browsers will display the page properly even without a proper ending.

If you were to run the previous line of script from the command line, the output would be similar to the contents of Figure 2.5. As you can see, a small amount of Perl code has expanded to a larger amount of HTML. We will continue to see substantial savings in keystrokes in later examples.

If you do not want to use CGI.pm's HTML shortcuts, you can still print your own HTML. In fact, there may be times when it is easier to embed HTML tags directly in a string. Use whatever method is most convenient. Time2.pl creates exactly the same output as the previous example, but creates some of the HTML tags directly, and uses CGI.pm for others.

```
#!/usr/bin/perl
# File: time2.pl
use CGI ':standard';
$current_time = localtime;
```

**Figure 2.5 HTML output from time1.p.**

```
Content-type: text/html
<!DOCTYPE HTML PUBLIC "-//IETF//DTD HTML//EN">
<HTML><HEAD>
<TITLE>Virtual Clock</TITLE>
</HEAD>
<BODY>
<H1>Virtual Clock</H1>
The current time is 07:23:18 30 September 1997 EDT."
<HR>
</BODY>
</HTML>
```

```
print header,
      start_html('A Virtual Clock');
print <<END_OF_TEXT;
<H1>A Virtual Clock</H1>
The current time is $current_time.
<HR>
END_OF_TEXT
print end_html;
```

# Creating a Page with Fancy HTML Tags

The examples in the last section use CGI.pm's HTML shortcuts to create simple <TAG></TAG> pairs. How do you create tags that contain attributes, such as the SRC attribute of an <IMG> tag?

The answer is simple. Just give the shortcut function an associative array containing the attributes you want to place inside the tag. Time3.pl is just like the previous versions, except that it includes a small inline image of a clock, as shown in Figure 2.6, and a hypertext link pointing to the site's homepage.

```
#!/usr/bin/perl
# File: time3.pl
use CGI ':standard';
$current_time = localtime;

print header,
      start_html('A Virtual Clock'),
      img({-src=>'/images/clock.gif',-alt=>'A Clock'}),
      h1('A Virtual Clock'),
      "The current time is $current_time.",
      hr,
      a({-href=>'/'},"Go to the home page."),
      end_html;
```

The interesting parts of this script are the third and next to last lines of the print() statement where we invoke the img() and a() functions.

Figure 2.6 A fancier version of the virtual clock produced by time3.pl.

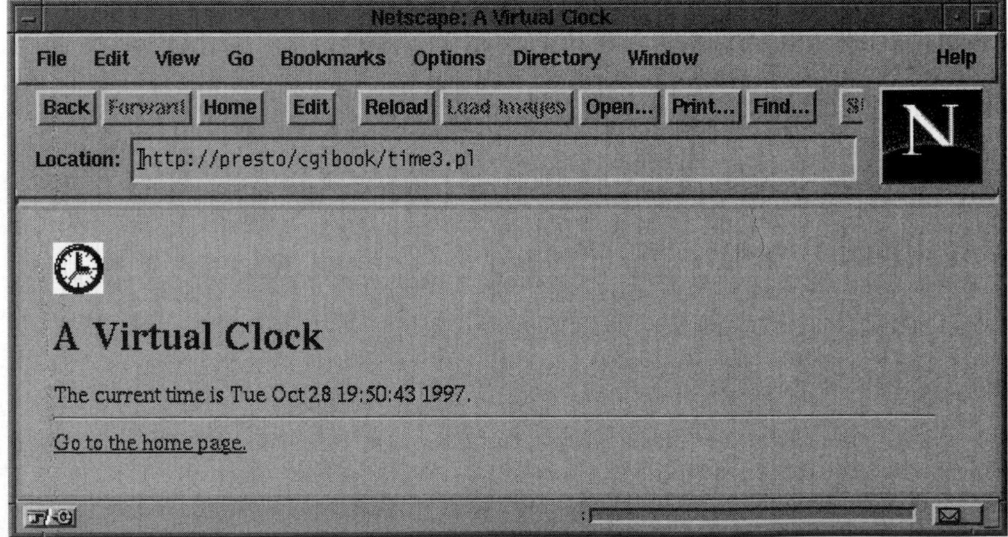

```
img({-src=>'/images/clock.gif',-alt=>'A Clock'})
```

This function creates an <IMG> tag. It has one argument, a reference to an anonymous hash, created using a pair of curly brackets. The hash has two keys, -src and -alt, corresponding to the <IMG> tag's SRC and ALT attributes. When this function is invoked, it creates a tag that looks like the following:

```
<IMG SRC="/images/clock.gif" ALT="A Clock">
```

The next line of code

```
a({-href=>'/'},"Go to the home page.")
```

creates a hypertext anchor (<A>) tag containing an HREF attribute pointing to the top page of the Web site. (We could just as easily have pointed to a full URL on a remote Web site.) As before, the first argument is an anonymous hash reference containing attribute name/value pairs. Unlike the call to img(), however, this is followed by a second argument that becomes the tag content. The output of the function looks like this:

```
<A HREF="/">Go to the home page.</A>
```

You might be wondering what happens if you pass an HTML shortcut function lists of arguments, for instance:

```
a({-href=>'/'},'Go','to','the','home','page.')
```

Surprisingly, the result is exactly the same as the previous version. When you give an HTML shortcut several strings, it concatenates them all together with spaces between them. Although this might seem unusual, it is actually very handy for nesting tags to create complex formats. Consider the following:

```
a({-href=>'/'},'Go to the',strong('home'),'page.')
```

**TIP**

**If you are not used to Perl 5, you may be unfamiliar with *variable references.* A reference is a pointer to another variable and is most frequently used to pass complex data structures, such as entire lists or hashes (associative arrays) to a subroutine. You can create a reference to an existing variable by putting a backslash in front of its name. For example, foo(\@abc,\%def) is a call to a subroutine named "foo" in which its arguments are references to the list @abc and the hash %def. You can also make anonymous references on the fly using square brackets ([]) for list references, and curly brackets ({}) for hash references. For example, foo(['two','little','piggies'],{'go'=>'to bed'}) again calls the function foo(), but this time using two anonymous references. You will find a much lengthier explanation in the Perl reference manual page.**

This returns HTML that emphasizes the word *home* by putting a pair of <STRONG> tags around it like this:

```
<A HREF="/">Go to the <STRONG>home</STRONG> page.</A>
```

The next example, vegetables1.pl, uses this feature to create an ordered list.

```
#!/usr/bin/perl
# Script: vegetables1.pl
use CGI ':standard';
print header,
      start_html('Vegetables'),
      h1('Eat Your Vegetables'),
      ol(
            li('peas'),
            li('broccoli'),
            li('cabbage'),
            li('peppers',
                ul(
                      li('red'),
                      li('yellow'),
                      li('green')
                  )
            ),
            li('kolrabi'),
```

```
            li('radishes')
        ),
    hr,
    end_html;
```

This example produces HTML containing two lists: an outer numbered list (peas, broccoli, and so on), and an inner bullet list describing three different varieties of bell pepper, as in Figure 2.7. The relevant part of the output looks like this (line breaks have been inserted for readability):

```
<OL>
    <LI>peas</LI>
    <LI>broccoli</LI>
    <LI>cabbage</LI>
    <LI>peppers
        <UL>
            <LI>red</LI>
            <LI>yellow</LI>
            <LI>green</LI>
        </UL>
    </LI>
    <LI>kolrabi</LI>
    <LI>radishes</LI>
</OL>
```

**Figure 2.7 A nested list produced with the ol() and li() functions.**

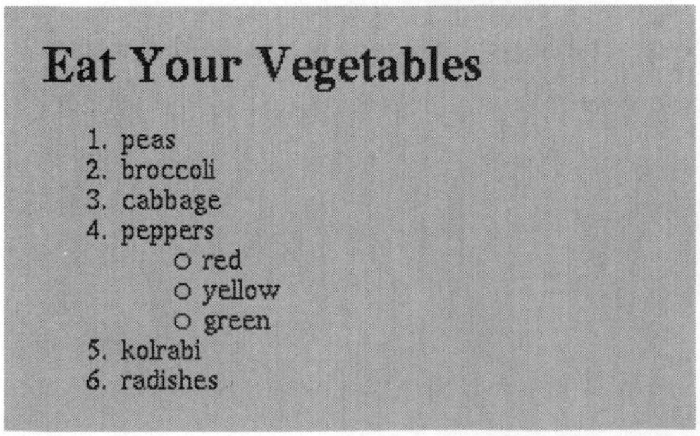

Eat Your Vegetables

1. peas
2. broccoli
3. cabbage
4. peppers
   - red
   - yellow
   - green
5. kolrabi
6. radishes

Occasionally, the automatic addition of a space between neighboring strings is *not* what you want. This most frequently comes up when doing precise formatting of side-by-side images, or hypertext links that contain images. Because CGI.pm uses array interpolation to concatenate strings together, you can change the automatic space to another character, or suppress it entirely, by changing the value of the magic $" variable. The following short example demonstrates this technique:

```
{
   local($") = '';
   print a({-link=>'top'},strong('I'),'n the beginning.');
}
```

This puts an <A> anchor around the text "In the beginning" and makes the initial character bold. By placing this section within a Perl block (with the curly brackets) and making $" local to that block, we ensure that the change to the variable doesn't have a global effect on the script.

Even though the HTML shortcuts are already saving keystrokes, there's something a bit unsatisfying about the vegetables1.pl script. It seems a little redundant to call li() nine times when what you really want to say is "turn everything in this list into a line item." The *distributive* feature of HTML shortcuts makes this possible. Instead of giving an HTML shortcut a simple list, give it a *reference* to a list, and the corresponding tag will be distributed across the members of the list like a multiplication operation in arithmetic. To understand what this means, consider this expression:

```
li(['peas','broccoli','cabbage'])
```

Notice that the list of three vegetables is enclosed by square brackets creating an anonymous array reference. When Perl evaluates this reference, the resulting HTML is:

```
<LI>peas</LI>
<LI>broccoli</LI>
<LI>cabbage</LI>
```

This means that you can compose the list in vegetables1.pl more concisely this way:

```
ol(
     li([ 'peas',
          'broccoli',
          'cabbage',
          'peppers' .
          ul(
             li(['red','yellow','green'])
            ),
          'kolrabi',
          'radishes'
        ])
)
```

Notice that the word *peppers* is concatenated to the sublist using the Perl dot (.) operator, rather than using a comma. Concatenating the words this way puts peppers and its sublist on the same level of the outer ordered list. Otherwise, peppers and its sublist would have been treated as separate items.

It is not necessary to use an anonymous array; you can easily define the vegetables as named lists (or read them from a vegetable database), make references to them with the backslash operator (\), and then pass the references to ol() and ul():

```
@peppers = ('red','yellow','green');
@veggies = ('peas','broccoli','cabbage',
          'peppers' . ul(li(\@peppers)),
          'kolrabi'.'radishes');
print ol(
     li(\@veggies)
     );
```

## HTML SHORTCUT SUMMARY

The variety of ways to call HTML shortcuts may seem bewildering, but you will soon get accustomed to using them. Table 2.1 will help get you started by summarizing all the possible ways to call HTML shortcuts.

## HTML 3.2 SHORTCUTS

For historical reasons, only shortcuts that generate HTML 2.0 tags are available if you load CGI.pm using the standard feature set. However, CGI.pm does support more advanced tags, including all those defined in the HTML 3.2 standard and the most frequently used HTML extensions recognized by Netscape and Microsoft browsers.

To use HTML 3.2 shortcuts, modify the "use CGI" line to look like this:

```
use CGI qw/:standard :html3/;
```

**Table 2.1 HTML Shortcut Calling Styles**

| When called with | The output is | Example In | Example Out |
|---|---|---|---|
| no arguments | the start tag only | p() | <P> |
| list of arguments | start tag, arguments, end tag | p('Do', 'camels', 'sweat?') | <P>Do camels sweat?</P> |
| first argument an associative array | start tag with attributes, plus arguments and end tag, if provided | p({-align=>CENTER}, 'Do','camels','sweat?') | <P ALIGN="CENTER">Do camelssweat?</P> |
| reference to a list of arguments | tag distributed across all arguments | p({-align=>CENTER}, ['Do','camels','sweat?']); | <P ALIGN="CENTER">Do <P ALIGN="CENTER"> camels</P> <P ALIGN="CENTER"> </P>sweat?</P> |

This imports both the standard set of shortcuts (":standard") and the HTML 3.2 shortcuts (":html3"). In case you are unfamiliar with this notation, the qw/.../ is Perl5's way to turn all the words between the // delimiters into a list. It is functionally equivalent to:

```
use CGI ':standard',':html3';
```

Which syntax to use is a personal choice.

Once HTML 3.2 shortcuts have been imported, you can create tables, text with super- and subscripts, and change the font style and color. It is a challenge to create HTML tables by hand, but the distributive nature of CGI.pm shortcuts eases the process. Here is a simple example that shows the code used to create the screenshot in Figure 2.8:

```
print
    table({-border=>''},
    caption(strong('When Should You Eat Your Vegetables?')),
    Tr({-align=>CENTER,-valign=>TOP},
        [
            th(['','Breakfast','Lunch','Dinner'])),
            th('Tomatoes').td(['no','yes','yes'])),
            th('Broccoli').td(['no','no','yes'])),
            th('Onions').td(['yes','yes','yes']))
        ]
      )
    );
```

Things to notice about this script:

- We indicate that the table's BORDER attribute is turned on with -border=>'' rather than with -border alone. As with any Perl associative array, keys must always be paired with values, even if the values are empty. If you make the common mistake of leaving off

Figure 2.8 CGI.pm can produce HTML 3 tables.

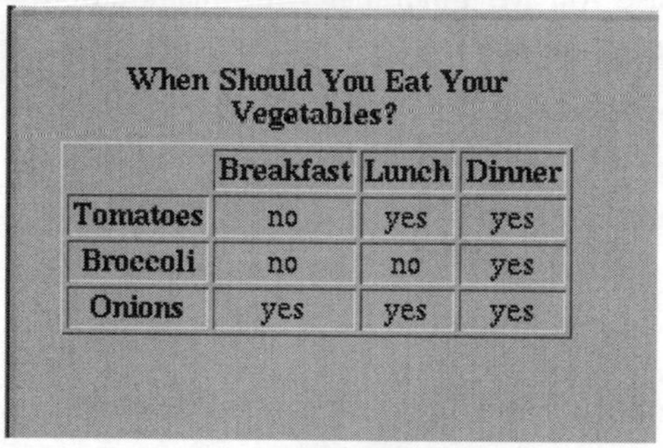

**When Should You Eat Your Vegetables?**

| | Breakfast | Lunch | Dinner |
|---|---|---|---|
| Tomatoes | no | yes | yes |
| Broccoli | no | no | yes |
| Onions | yes | yes | yes |

the value, the script will not behave the way you expect, and Perl will complain about an "odd number of array elements."

- The Tr() function, which creates a table row, has an uppercase initial character rather than being all lowercase like the HTML shortcuts you've seen before. This is because the lowercase version conflicts with Perl's built-in tr operator (which translates characters in strings). In addition to Tr(), there are a few other instances (most of which are not frequently used) where the capitalization is different from what you'd expect. Chapter 5, *Reference Guide*, lists all the exceptions.
- Because we pass them array references, the Tr() and td() functions repeat the <TR> and <TD> tags across their arguments. Not only is this very efficient for typing, but it causes each tag's attributes to be repeated. This means we do not have to retype the ALIGN and VALIGN attributes for each of the table rows.

The HTML output from this script fragment looks like this after newlines and tabs have been inserted for readability:

```
<TABLE BORDER>
    <CAPTION><STRONG>When Should You Eat Your
        Vegetables?</STRONG>
    </CAPTION>
```

```
  <TR ALIGN=CENTER VALIGN=TOP>
     <TH></TH><TH>Breakfast</TH><TH>Lunch</TH><TH>Dinner</TH>
  </TR>
  <TR ALIGN=CENTER VALIGN=TOP>
     <TH>Tomatoes</TH> <TD>no</TD> <TD>yes</TD> <TD>yes</TD>
  </TR>
  <TR ALIGN=CENTER VALIGN=TOP>
     <TH>Broccoli</TH> <TD>no</TD> <TD>no</TD> <TD>yes</TD>
  </TR>
  <TR ALIGN=CENTER VALIGN=TOP>
     <TH>Onions</TH> <TD>yes</TD> <TD>yes</TD> <TD>yes</TD>
  </TR>
</TABLE>
```

The next example, htmlize1.pl, shows how to use the table shortcuts to automatically convert a boring, text-only table into a more interesting HTML table. Unlike the previous examples, it does not run as a CGI script. It takes a text table on standard input, converts it to HTML, and prints the result on standard output.

The script expects a tab-delimited table in this format:

```
caption on the top line
colhead1   colhead2  colhead3   colhead4...
rowhead1   data      data       data...
rowhead2   data      data       data...
rowhead3   data      data       data...
rowhead4   data      data       data..
```

Here is the code:

```
#!/usr/bin/perl
#Script: htmlize1.pl
use CGI qw/:standard :html3 -noDebug/;
```

```
# get the caption
chomp($caption = <>);

# get the column headers
chomp($colhead = <>);
@col_head = split("\t",$colhead);

# Get the data into an array.
# The first item in each array is the header, the rest is
# the data cells
while (<>) {
     chomp;
     ($rowhead,@data) = split("\t");
     push(@rows,th($rowhead).td(\@data));
}

# Print out the table
print table({-border=>''},
          caption($caption),
          TR([th(\@col_head),@rows])
     );
```

This script starts out importing the standard and HTML3 functions from CGI.pm. Next it reads the caption and the column heads from the first two lines of the input (in a real application, we would error check here to make sure that these lines look OK). Next we enter a loop to read the rest of the table. For each line, we fetch the first column and place it in a variable named $rowhead. Other columns are placed in an array named @data. We then build a new row of the eventual HTML table by placing a <TH> tag around the column header, and <TD> tags around each element of @data. This row is pushed onto an array called @rows. Notice how the table data is concatenated onto the row header; this keeps it on the same row.

When we have finished building the table rows, we print out the table all at once by distributing the <TR> tag across the column headers and the row.

Figures 2.9 and 2.10 show the same table before and after automatic conversion to HTML. You can run this script as a standalone application as the first step in converting legacy tabular data into nicely formatted HTML, or you can incorporate the code into an on-the-fly converter for CGI scripts.

**Figure 2.9 A plain, tab-delimited text table.**

```
Should You Eat Them?
                Green    Red      Yellow
Peppers         yes      yes      yes
Apples          yes      yes      yes
Brocolli        yes      no       no
Oranges         no       no       yes
Lemons          no       no       yes
Mushrooms       no       no       no
Kale            yes      no       no
Peaches         no       no       yes
```

**Figure 2.10 The same table after conversion to HTML by htmlize.pl.**

Should You Eat Them?

| | Green | Red | Yellow |
|---|---|---|---|
| **Peppers** | yes | yes | yes |
| **Apples** | yes | yes | yes |
| **Brocolli** | yes | no | no |
| **Oranges** | no | no | yes |
| **Lemons** | no | no | yes |
| **Mushrooms** | no | no | no |
| **Kale** | yes | no | no |
| **Peaches** | no | no | yes |

## Getting User Input

All of the previous examples have been one-way affairs. The script runs, creates some text, and exits. This is useful, but CGI.pm's real power is to facilitate a script's ability to capture user information, process it, and produce custom pages.

To understand the next few examples, you must know a little bit about how the CGI protocol passes user parameters from the Web page to the script. If you've spent any time on the Web, the URLs that invoke CGI scripts will look familiar. CGI scripts can be invoked without any parameters:

```
http://some.site/cgi-bin/hello_world.pl
```

To send parameters to a script, add a question mark to the script name and follow this with whatever parameters you want to send:

```
http://some.site/cgi-bin/index_search.pl?CGI+perl
http://some.site/cgi-bin/order.pl?catalog=3921&quantity=2
```

Although the text that follows the question mark is arbitrary, the previous examples show the two most commonly used styles for parameter passing. The first shows the *keyword list* style in which the parameters are a series of keywords separated by + signs. This style is now only used in some very old CGI scripts and won't be mentioned again. The second example shows a named parameter list in which a series of name=value pairs are separated by ampersands. This style is used internally by browsers to transmit the contents of a fill-out form. Each element in a fill-out form, whether a text field, a push button, a checkbox, or a popup menu, has a name; when the form is submitted, the element name becomes the parameter name, and the contents of the element, for example, the text of the currently selected menu item, becomes the parameter value.

With the benefit of fill-out forms, the CGI script and the user can engage in an open-ended conversation, as shown in Figure 2.11. When the

Figure 2.11 Fill-out forms allow CGI scripts to conduct an interactive dialogue with the user.

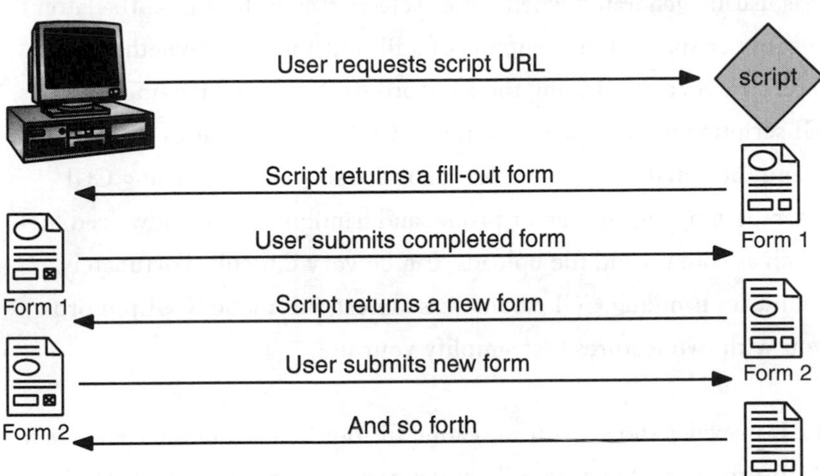


CGI script is first called, it generates a fill-out form and presents it to the user. The user completes the form and submits it. The script, in turn, processes the form and generates a page containing a *new* form for the user's inspection. This process can continue indefinitely.

The CGI script's URL and its parameters are subject to arcane URL escaping rules. Whitespace, control characters, and most punctuation characters are replaced by a percent sign and the hexadecimal code for the character. For example, the space between the words *John Doe* must be passed to a CGI script like this:

```
http://some.site/cgi-bin/find_address.pl?name=John%20Doe
```

The problem with processing script parameters is that, for various historical reasons, the rules for fetching and translating the parameters are complex. Sometimes the script parameters are found in an environment variable. In other cases, the parameters can be recovered from the command-line (@ARGV) array, or even passed via standard input. Sometimes you must recognize the URL escape sequences and translate them, and in other cases, the server may have already done the translation. Which rules apply depend on whether your script is generated by a GET or POST request (the former is usually generated when a user selects a hypertext link; the latter when a browser submits the contents of a fill-out form), or whether the parameters are formatted using the keyword list or named parameter styles.

CGI scripting without the benefit of a CGI library requires that you understand the details of the CGI protocol. Parsing and processing CGI parameters is annoying and error prone, and handling certain advanced features, such as cookies and file uploads, can be very difficult. Fortunately, CGI.pm makes handling CGI parameters almost automatic. CGI.pm provides you with two features that simplify your life:

1. It provides shortcuts for creating fill-out forms and their elements.
2. It provides a function call named param() for retrieving the values of CGI parameters.

Let's take the virtual clock example from earlier in this chapter and rework it so that the remote user can control it. Listing 2.1 gives the source code for time4.pl, and Figure 2.12 shows its appearance in a browser. The script prints out the current date and time as before, but now it also creates a small control panel that the user can manipulate to adjust the appearance of the clock. The user can select between displaying a 12- or 24-hour (military) format, and can turn parts of the date on and off.

Virtual2.pl recognizes the following named parameters:

- ***type***—the type of time to display, either 12-hour or 24-hour.
- ***time***—whether or not to display the current time at all. A value of 1 (or any nonzero value) causes the script to include the time in the formatted time/date string. A value of 0 (or any false Perl value such as an empty string or undef) suppresses the time.
- ***day***—whether to display the day of the week.
- ***month***—whether to display the current month.
- ***day-of-month***—whether to display the day of the month.
- ***year***—whether to display the year.

Figure 2.12 A user-customizable clock.

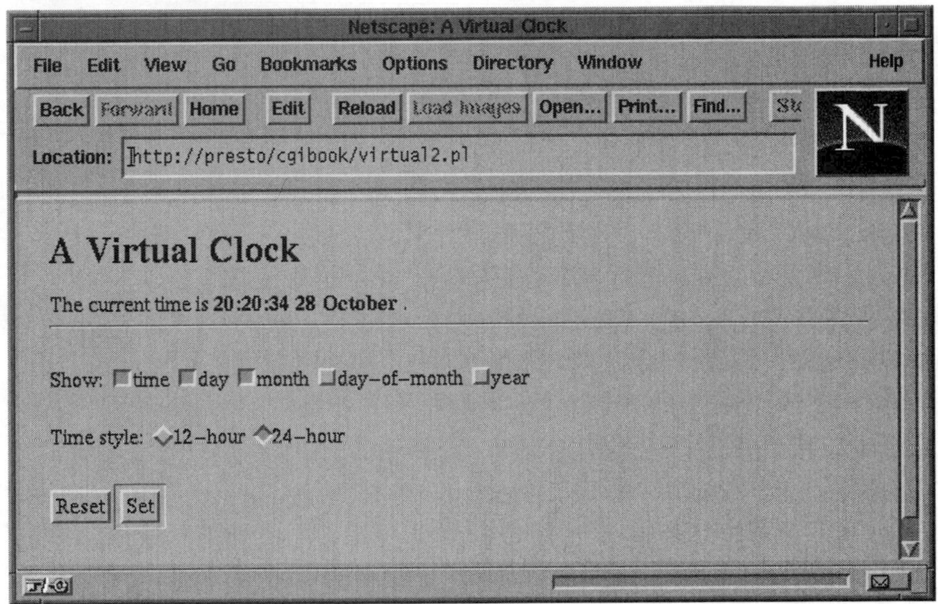


Although the script is usually controlled from its internally generated form, you can control the script directly by passing it parameters in its URL. For example, the URL:

```
http://your.site/cgi-bin/virtual2.pl?time=24-hour&time=1&month=1
```

will cause the script to display the month and time in 24-hour format.

The revised virtual clock script is longer than the previous one, so line numbers will be used to refer to its various parts.

Let's walk through the script step by step.

Lines 1 to 6 load the CGI module and import the standard function definitions. We then load the POSIX module, which provides handy time and date manipulation utilities, among other things. We're only interested in the strftime() function, a utility that creates timestamps in a variety of formats. Explicitly importing this one function gives the script a slight performance boost.

**Listing 2.1 The time4.pl script creates a user-customizable digital clock.**

```
#!/usr/bin/perl
#script: time4.pl

use CGI ':standard';
use POSIX 'strftime';

# print the HTTP header and the HTML document
print header,
  start_html('A Virtual Clock'),
  h1('A Virtual Clock');
print_time();
print_form();
print end_html;

# print out the time
sub print_time {
  my($format);
  if (param) {
    $format = (param('type') eq '12-hour') ? '%r ' : '%T ' if param('time');
    $format .= '%d ' if param('day');
    $format .= '%B ' if param('month');
    $format .= '%A ' if param('day-of-month');
    $format .= '%Y ' if param('year');
  } else {
    $format = '%r %A %B %d %Y';
  }
  $current_time = strftime($format,localtime);
  print "The current time is ",strong($current_time),".",hr;
}
```

```
30
31 # print the clock settings form
32 sub print_form {
33   print start_form,
34      "Show: ",
35      checkbox(-name=>'time',-checked=>1),
36      checkbox(-name=>'day',-checked=>1),
37      checkbox(-name=>'month',-checked=>1),
38      checkbox(-name=>'day-of-month',-checked=>1),
39      checkbox(-name=>'year',-checked=>1),
40      p(),
41      "Time style: ",
42      radio_group(-name=>'type',
43                  -values=>['12-hour','24-hour']),
44      p(),
45      reset(-name=>'Reset'),
46      submit(-name=>'Set'),
47      end_form;
48 }
```

Lines 7 to 13 print out the standard header, and start the HTML page. The script then calls two subroutines that are defined later in the script, print_time, to display the customized time and date, and print_form(), to create the fill-out form that adjusts the display. The script ends the HTML page and exits.

Lines 15 to 29 define the print_time() subroutine responsible for fetching the user's preferences and formatting the time and date appropriately. There are two ways the script might be called: when the remote user clicks a link that points at it, or when the user presses the submit button of its fill-out form. In the first case, the script will have no CGI parameters to process, and will create a reasonable default format to use for the time and date. In the second case, the script will create a format string based on the user's instructions.

The key to accessing script parameters is the param() call. Call param() with the name of a CGI parameter to return the parameter's value. Call param() with no arguments to obtain a list of all the parameter names passed to the script. Line 18 begins an if-else statement. We make a call to param() with no arguments. If the script is being called for the first time, param() returns an empty list, so we create a default format (12-hour clock, all the fields turned on). Otherwise, we call param() several more times to retrieve the values of the CGI parameters that we expect. Using these values, we build up a time format specifier to pass to the strftime() function by concatenating the various options one piece at a time.

Strftime() takes two arguments: The first is a format string that describes what the time and date look like. The second is the time to format (in seconds from some arbitrary date that is operating-system dependent). The format contains ordinary characters intermixed with a variety of special codes—%r for the time in 12-hour format, %T for 24-hour format, %Y for the current year, %d for the day, %B for the month, %A for the day of the month, and many others. It returns the time formatted according to the format string. For instance, strftime("Today is %d!",localtime) will return "Today is Monday!"

---

**TIP**

**You can find out more about the strftime() function by consulting your system's manual pages, or any book on the standard C programming libraries, such as *The C Programming Language, 2nd edition* by Brian Kernighan and Dennis Ritchie (Prentice-Hall, 1988).**

---

Lines 27 to 28 call strftime() with the format string and the local time, and save the result into $current_time. We then print out the formatted time and a horizontal rule.

Lines 31 to 48 are where the print_form() subroutine is defined. To create the fill-out form, we make calls to a number of functions that we haven't previously encountered. Unlike the HTML shortcuts, which have the same names as the HTML tags they produce, the functions that produce fill-out form elements have names that more aptly describe what they do. Instead of names like

<INPUT> and <SELECT>, the CGI.pm form functions have names like checkbox(), textfield(), popup_menu(), and button(). These functions are very feature-rich—some can take as many as a dozen optional arguments! For this reason, all the functions involved in producing fill-out forms are called using lists of named arguments, much like the attribute lists in HTML shortcuts. Each fill-out form element recognizes a slightly different set of arguments, but most of the arguments are the same. For example, -name is used to name an element in a fill-out form so that it can be referred to later; -value sets a default value to display in text fields and other elements that users can type into.

Like HTML shortcut functions, each of the CGI.pm functions involved in fill-out forms produces a fragment of HTML that we string together into one long print statement. We start with a call to start_form(). This creates an HTML <FORM> tag with its attributes set to reasonable defaults. Among other things, the defaults arrange for the contents of the fill-out form to be returned to our script when the user presses the submit button. This is a handy feature, because it lets the same script that produced the form also process it. All fill-out form elements must be contained between calls to start_form() and end_form().

After the start_form() call we make a series of calls to checkbox(). Checkbox() produces a fragment of HTML similar to this:

```
<INPUT TYPE="checkbox" NAME="checkbox name">checkbox name
```

When displayed by a browser, the result is a checkbox with a human-readable label printed to its right.

We make a total of four calls to checkbox(). The first checkbox, named time, allows the user to turn the display of the current time on and off. Day toggles the display of the day of week; month, the month display, and so on. Each call to checkbox() uses two of the function's several named arguments. The -name argument, required by every fill-out form element, gives the checkbox a name so that it can be referred to later. In the case of checkboxes, the name is also used for its human-readable label. The -checked argument controls whether the checkbox is initially turned off (the default) or turned on. In the case of this script, we want all the checkboxes to be turned on at first, so we specify -checked=>1. If we want the checkbox to be turned off, we would specify -checked=>0. (In Perl, 0, the empty string, and undef are all false, anything else is true.)

**TIP**

**The name and/or value of form elements often serve double duty, as the user-readable labels printed on the form, and as the name of the parameter passed to the CGI script. However, you are free to choose separate names and labels. See Chapter 5, *Reference Guide,* for the details on how to do this.**

We now create a pair of radio buttons to control whether the clock displays 12-hour time or 24-hour (military) time. The radio buttons are linked, so selecting one deselects the other. We can create any number of linked radio buttons with a single call to radio_group(). Like the previous call, radio_group() expects a -name argument, but in this case, the name refers to all members of the group. The name in this case is type. The -values argument defines the labels for all the radio buttons in the cluster, whose value is an anonymous list. In this case, the list is only two elements long. The HTML that this bit of code produces looks like this:

```
<INPUT TYPE="radio" NAME="type" VALUE="12-hour" CHECKED>12-hour
<INPUT TYPE="radio" NAME="type" VALUE="12-hour">25-hour
```

We now create a pair of buttons: one to be pressed if the user has changed the settings of the controls and now wishes to reset them to their original states, and another to submit the contents of the form to the script. We create the first button by calling reset(). It is a very simple function that takes only a single -name argument. This becomes the label that is printed on top of the button. In a similar way, we create the submission button by calling submit().

Last, we call end_form() to create the </FORM> tag that defines the end of the fill-out form. Do not forget to call this, or the fill-out form may behave strangely.

If you play with this script on this book's companion Web site, you might notice something interesting. Each time you change the settings on the fill-out form and press the Set button, the script regenerates the fill-out form with the settings exactly the way you left them. If a checkbox was turned off, it stays off. If you select 24-hour mode, the appropriate radio button remains selected. In other words, the settings of the fill-out form are sticky.

This may seem like simple and natural behavior for a fill-out form, but in fact, it requires some interesting tricks on the part of CGI.pm. Each time you call one of the fill-out form element functions, CGI.pm checks the current CGI parameters and modifies the HTML it produces. Consider the line

```
checkbox(-name=>'day',-checked=>1)
```

The -checked argument can be considered a *suggestion* to CGI.pm. When called, the function checks the current CGI parameters for an existing parameter named day. If none exists, it uses the value of the -checked argument and produces a fragment of HTML with the CHECKED attribute turned on. If, on the other hand, a day parameter already exists, then checked() ignores the value of -checked and uses whatever the previous state of the checkbox was, whether checked or unchecked.

---

**TIP**

**Although the sticky behavior of fill-out forms is often what you want, there are times when you will want to override the stickiness and force a form element to display the way you program it to. Use the -override argument to do this:**

```
checkbox(-name=>'day',-checked=>1,-override=>1)
```

---

Start_form() accepts several optional arguments, some of which we'll see in the next chapter, and others in Chapter 5, *Reference Guide*. The only argument you are likely to use regularly is -action, which controls the script that gets called when the user presses the submit button. If no -action argument is provided, the browser will submit the contents of the fill-out form to the same URL that generated the form. This is desirable if the same script is responsible for generating and processing the form. However, you can change this behavior by providing -action with the absolute or relative URL of a script to handle the fill-out form:

```
print start_form(-action=>'/cgi-bin/another_script.pl');
```

Actually, the script that produces the form and the one that processes it don't even have to be on the same Web server:

```
print start_form(-action=>'http:'/another.site/a_script.pl');
```

When you design your scripts, keep in mind that there is always the possibility that someone else will design a custom form to invoke your script. Your script should not make any assumptions about the CGI parameters that are sent to it.

# More Fill-Out Form Elements

The previous example shows how to create checkboxes, radio buttons, and the standard submit and reset push buttons. In addition to these features, you can create popup menus, scrolling lists of choices, text fields of various sorts, and elements that prompt the user to upload an entire file from disk.

The next chapter provides a detailed look at each of the functions for producing fill-out form elements and their various options. In this section, we will preview some of the most commonly used functions.

## TEXT INPUT

You can create a one-line field for entering text using the textfield() function. The following code fragment creates a field whose name is fruit, whose default value is kiwi, and whose width is 40 characters long.

```
textfield(-name=>'fruit',-value=>'kiwi',-size=>40);
```

Text fields are useful for short fields, such as names, dates, e-mail addresses, and search strings. If you need to accept longer texts, use textarea() instead. It creates a larger, multiline field complete with horizontal and vertical scrollbars. You can control how large the text area will be, and whether the user's input will automatically word-wrap or not. The following example creates a 10 row by 50 column word-wrapping text area with the name "fruit poetry."

```
textarea(-name=>'fruit poetry',
         -value=>'no fruit is an island',
         -rows=>10,
         -columns=>50,
         -wrap=>'physical');
```

If you'd like to prompt the user to enter some sensitive information that you don't want displayed on the screen (like a password), use password_field(). It looks and acts just like textfield(), but the user's keystrokes are displayed in the browser as stars. The next bit of code creates a password field named "fruit password" with a default value of "open sesame."

```
password_field(-name=>'fruit password',
                -value=>'open sesame',-size=>40);
```

There is also a "hidden" type of text field that can't be edited by the user, and in fact, isn't even displayed. Its name and value are passed back to your script, unaltered, when the user presses the submit button. Hidden fields are useful for scripts that need to store information between invocations. The script can stash a reminder to itself in one or more hidden fields. When the form is submitted and the script is run again, it can restore its state from the values stored there. Hidden fields are created using the hidden() function. A hidden field can be single or multivalued, as in the following examples:

```
hidden(-name=>'display',-value=>'off');
hidden(-name=>'colors',-value=>['red','orange','magenta']);
```

Like checkboxes and other form elements, text input fields are "sticky." If CGI.pm finds a preexisting CGI parameter with the same name as the text field, the old parameter will have priority over the -value argument. Hidden fields also obey this rule.

An interesting feature of all the text input fields is that you can omit the -value argument entirely. The field will be filled in with the previous value of the like-named CGI parameter.

```
print hidden(-name=>'display');
```

You will see this feature used to good effect in scripts that need to save state information.

---

**TIP**

**Because form elements never contain other HTML tags, the shortcuts that generate them do not need to distinguish tag attributes from tag content. This is why you can call textfield(-name=>'fruit',-value=>'no fruit is an island') without using curly braces around the attributes. If you prefer, you can use curly braces here as well, as in textfield({-name=>'fruit',-value=>'no fruit is an island'}).**

---

## EXCLUSIVE CHOICES

If you want the user to select among several choices, each mutually exclusive of the other, you can use a group of radio buttons or a popup menu. Radio groups are useful when there are only a few choices to select from, and when there is enough room on the form to display all the buttons without getting crowded. A prime example is the radio group that selects between 12- and 24-hour time in the virtual clock script. Popup menus are useful for displaying a large number of choices, or when screen space is at a premium.

Radio groups and popup menus are created using functions named radio_group() and popup_menu(), respectively. The two functions are used almost identically. The following lines of code show a choice of vegetables, first with a radio group and then with a popup menu. Figure 2.13 shows how they're displayed in the browser.

Figure 2.13 A radio group and popup menu created by CGI.pm form-creation functions.

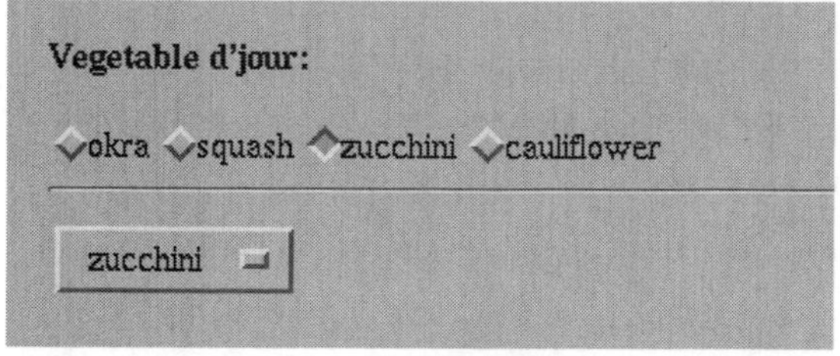


```
print strong("Vegetable d'jour:"),
  radio_group(-name=>'vegetable',
             -value=>['okra','squash','zucchini','cauliflower'],
             -default=>'squash');
  popup_menu(-name=>'vegetable',
            -value=>['okra','squash','zucchini','cauliflower'],
            -default=>'squash');
```

Because radio groups and popup menus are multivalued, the -value argument takes a reference to an array rather than a simple scalar value. The -default argument indicates which item should be selected when the page first displays. (If -default isn't provided, the first item on the list is selected.) As before, -name gives the CGI parameter generated by the radio group or popup menu a name. In these examples, when the form is submitted, you can find out which item was selected by calling param('vegetable').

You can change the way that radio groups and popup menus display in several ways. One is to change the text of the button or menu item without changing the value of the CGI parameter that is passed back to your script. This is done with the -labels argument, which points to an associative array that maps the value of the element to its label. For example, to display "oranges," "peaches," "apples," "nectarines" next to the radio buttons instead of the vegetable names, you would call radio_group() in the following way:

```
radio_group(-name=>'vegetable',
           -value=>['okra','squash','zucchini','cauliflower'],
           -labels=>{okra=>orange,squash=>peaches,
```

```
                    zucchini=>apples,cauliflower=>nectarines},
              -default=>'squash');
```

Despite the deception, when the user selects the second button in the radio group, the value returned by param('vegetable') is still squash.

CGI.pm gives you the option of formatting the buttons in radio groups into orderly rows and columns. To do this, give the radio_group() function a -rows or -cols argument, indicating the number of rows or columns you desire, as shown in the following snippet:

```
radio_group(-name=>'vegetable',
              -value=>['okra','squash','zucchini','cauliflower'],
              -default=>'squash',-cols=>2);
```

The HTML returned will now incorporate an invisible table that aligns the buttons. Figure 2.14 shows how the radio group looks when we request two columns.

## INCLUSIVE CHOICES

If you need to present the user with multiple options that are not mutually exclusive, you can use a group of checkboxes or a scrolling list of choices. Again, the decision rests on how much screen space you have to spare. The two elements are created by checkbox_group() and scrolling_list(), respectively, as shown in the following script:

Figure 2.14 This radio group has been placed in an invisible table to line up the elements.

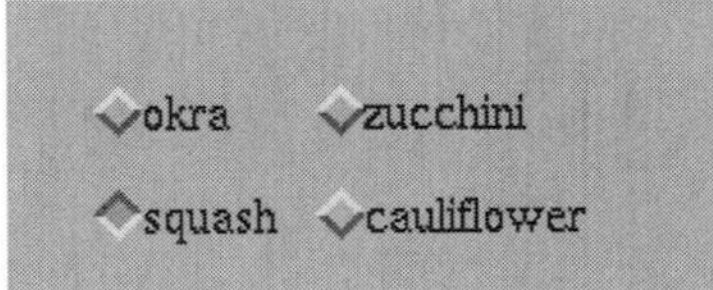

```
print strong("Contents of your ratatouille:"),
  checkbox_group(-name=>'vegetables',
                 -value=>['okra','squash','zucchini','cauliflower'],
                 -default=>['squash','okra']),
  scrolling_list(-name=>'vegetables',
                 -value=>['okra','squash','zucchini','cauliflower'],
                 -default=>['squash','okra'],
                 -multiple=>1);
```

Figure 2.15 shows the difference between the amount of space consumed by a checkbox group and an equivalent scrolling list.

The arguments accepted by the two functions are almost identical. The -name argument gives the CGI parameter a name so that it can be retrieved when the form is submitted, and -value points to a list reference containing the values of the list items or buttons. Unlike radio_button() or popup_menu(), however, the -default argument is allowed to point at an array reference, reflecting that multiple items can be selected simultaneously.

The -multiple argument applies only to scrolling lists. If set to true (nonzero), the user can select several items on the list simultaneously. If -multiple is absent or zero, the scrolling list will act like a popup menu and only allow the user to select a single item at a time.

**Figure 2.15 A checkbox group and a scrolling list.**

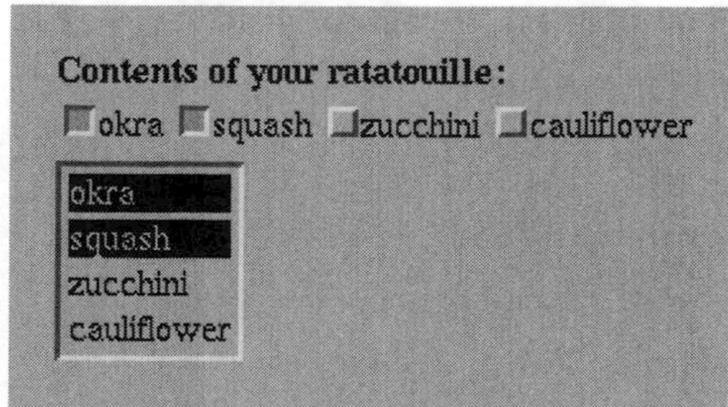

**TIP**

**Checkbox_group() and radio_group() actually return the list of buttons as an array. You can capture this array and manipulate it in various ways. For example, you might store the individual buttons in an HTML table or sort them alphabetically by name.**

To retrieve the selection from either a checkbox group or a scrolling list, call param() in an array context as follows:

```
@ratatouille_contents = param('vegetables');
```

You can adjust the appearance of checkbox groups and scrolling lists in various ways. Both functions recognize the -labels argument, allowing you to display a label different from the value that is returned in the CGI parameter. Checkbox_group() responds to -rows and -cols arguments by arranging its buttons on a grid. Scrolling_list() recognizes a -size argument, which sets the number of items to display. Without this argument, the user's browser will choose a default height that depends on the browser software and the operating system it is running on.

## BUTTONS

There are three standard types of push buttons: submit, reset, and default. Submit() creates a button that submits the contents of the form to the script. Like other form elements, submit buttons have names and values. The following code fragment creates a submit button with the name "action" and the value "Eat Vegetables":

```
print submit(-name=>'action',-value=>'Eat Vegetables');
```

The -value parameter serves double duty as the label that is printed on the button and the value of the CGI parameter that is returned to the script. You can have several submit buttons in the same form, each with different names or values. For example, you might have several buttons named "action," one with the value "Eat Vegetables," another with the value "Plant Vegetables," and a third with "Bury Vegetables." By calling param('action'), you can figure out which button the user pressed and take action accordingly, as in the following script:

```
if (param('action') eq 'Eat Vegetables') {
    print "yum yum";
} elsif (param('action') eq 'Plant Vegetables') {
    print "Old McDonald had a farm...";
} elsif (param('action') eq 'Bury Vegetables') {
    print "Dum dum da-dum, dum da-dum da-dum da-dum";
} else {
    print "Eat your vegetables!";
}
```

If you don't provide a -value argument, the button will use its name for the user-readable label. If you do not provide -name or -value arguments, the button will display a label reading "Submit Query." If you really want the button to be blank, you can provide an empty string (" ") for its value.

The second standard type of push button is the reset button. Reset buttons, created with the reset() function, undo all changes the user makes to the form and revert it to a pristine state. Unlike submit buttons, reset buttons don't cause the form to be submitted and never result in any CGI parameters being passed to your script. Reset() recognizes only one argument: -name. This becomes the label printed on the button, for example:

```
print reset(-name=>'Clear');
```

If you don't provide a name, the button will display "Reset."

The last standard push button is a default button, which is only available if you use CGI.pm. This button wipes out all the state information stored in "sticky" forms and resets all the form elements to their defaults. It does this by sending your script a message telling it to ignore the current CGI parameters and to act as if the script is being called for the first time. To generate a defaults button, call defaults(). Use -name to set the button's user-readable label, or accept the standard label, "Default." For example:

```
print default(-name=>'Clear Entirely');
```

In addition to the standard buttons, there are two special ones. The image_button() creates a clickable image map, or is used when you want an inline image as a button. There is also a button() function used to generate push buttons that execute JavaScript functions in browsers that recognize that language. You'll find more information about both of these buttons in Chapter 3, *Advanced Tricks*.

---

**TIP**

**By default, the text and labels of form elements are escaped according to HTML rules, allowing you to safely use "<CLICK ME>" as a button label. Unfortunately, it also interferes with your ability to incorporate special HTML characters, such as Á into your fields. To turn off automatic escaping, call the function autoEscape() with an argument of 1.**

---

# More About the Param() Function

The param() function can be used to retrieve the names and values of CGI parameters passed to your script. The param() function is easy to use, but it is actually more complex than it seems.

We have learned that you can call param() without any arguments to retrieve the names of all the CGI parameters passed to the script, and that you can call param() with the name of a parameter to retrieve that parameter's value. This makes it easy to loop through all the CGI parameters, even if you do not know what to expect in advance, for example:

```
foreach $name ( param() ) {
      $value = param($name);
      print "The value of $name is $value\n";
}
```

Calling param() without any arguments is also the usual idiom to decide whether the script has been called before:

```
prompt_for_input unless param();
```

What might not be immediately obvious is that there is not always a one-to-one correspondence between CGI parameter names and values. Often, a single named parameter appears several times on the parameter list. This happens when the same name is used for multiple checkboxes, or when the user selects multiple entries in a scrolling list. The user can simply call your CGI script with a URL like this one:

```
http://some.site/cgi-bin/order?item=squash&item=onion&item=carrot
```

How do you recover multiple values with param()? The answer is easy. If param() is called in a scalar context (by assigning its result to a scalar variable or attempting to perform some operation on it that only makes sense for single-valued variables), the function will return a single value. If param() is called in an array context (by assigning its result to a list or attempting to perform some operation on it that makes sense for multivalued variables), it will return a list of all parameters of that type. If you expect the parameter item to be single-valued, you can call param() this way:

```
$item = param('item');
```

If, instead, you expect item to be multivalued, you can call param() like this:

```
@items = param('item');
```

name= param( value)



What happens if a parameter is single-valued, but you try to assign the output of param() to an array? As you might expect, the result is a one-item list containing the value of the parameter. The reverse case, which happens when you assign a multivalued parameter to a scalar variable, is not quite so obvious. Veteran Perl programmers might expect the result to be a scalar that holds the size of the multivalued array. However, in the case of CGI.pm, the result is the first element of the array. This gives you more flexibility in designing user interfaces. If a list was originally implemented as a single-valued, pull-down menu, and you later change it to a multivalued scrolling list, the script that processes the list will continue to work without requiring major modification.

Here are some examples to help nail down the concept. Let's assume the following CGI parameters:

| Name | Value(s) |
|---|---|
| fruit | banana |
| vegetable | squash,onion,parsnip |

Here is the result of calling param() in various contexts:

| | |
|---|---|
| $a = param('fruit') | *$a is "banana"* |
| $a = param('vegetable') | *$a is "squash"* |
| @a = param('fruit') | *@a is ("banana")* |
| @a = param('vegetable') | *@a is ("squash","onion","parsnip")* |

Although not frequently used, param() recognizes a named-argument calling style. You can retrieve a particular CGI parameter by passing its name to the -name argument:

```
$fruit = param(-name=>'fruit');
```

This syntax can also be used to set the values of CGI parameters. When CGI.pm first loads, it retrieves the CGI parameters and stores them in an internal data structure. Whenever you request a particular parameter, CGI.pm is able to retrieve it rapidly. You can replace existing CGI parameters or add new ones using one of these two forms:

```
param(-name=>'fruit',-value=>'nectarine');
param(-name=>'fruit',-value=>['nectarine','orange','kumquat']);
```

The first form is used for setting a single-valued parameter; the second to create a parameter with multiple values. Setting CGI parameters in this way has no immediate effect on the appearance or contents of the page. The effect will only be felt later in the script when the modified value is retrieved through another call to param(). "Sticky" fill-out forms are also affected. For example, if you were now to create a text field named fruit, it would be displayed using the value of nectarine regardless of the -value argument.

A less verbose way to set the value of CGI parameters uses this syntax:

```
param('fruit','nectarine','orange','kumquat');
```

This call sets the CGI parameter named fruit to the multiple values nectarine, orange, and kumquat. It has exactly the same effect as the -name, -value syntax. Programmers who want to minimize their typing (the author included) tend to use this syntax.

# Outputting More than One Page

In all of the examples we've seen so far, the script has run, output a single page, and exited. Even in the examples that use a fill-out form for user input, both the form, the document, and its values appear on the same screen. Because of the way the Web works, scripts can only create a single page each time it runs, but this doesn't mean that one script can't produce a document with multiple pages. With a little ingenuity, you can create scripts that produce different pages each time they run.

The simplest example is a question/response style script. The script outputs two pages, the first prompting the user to provide some information, and the second using the information from the first page to create a page of results.

With a very small modification, the virtual clock script can be modified to use the question/response style. The changes involve lines 11 and 12 of Listing 2.1. Simply change them to read like this:

```
if (param) {
     print_time()
} else {
     print_form();

}
```

This bit of code calls param() to retrieve the list of CGI parameters. If it is non-empty, we know that the user has submitted the fill-out form, so we generate and display the time. If no parameters are present, we know the script is being called for the first time, and a fill-out form is generated.

In a more complex application, you might need to generate several different pages from the same script. A straightforward way to do this is to choose a single-named CGI parameter that selects among the different pages. A popular trick is to create multiple submission buttons, each with the same name (e.g., action) but a different value. When the user presses the button, the script takes different actions based on the value of the action parameter.

Listing 2.2 shows a trivial script that displays different messages depending on what button the user presses. The buttons are regenerated at the bottom of the page each time it is displayed, saving the user the trouble of paging back. Figure 2.16 displays the results of running this script.

**Listing 2.2 This script generates a different page depending on the button pressed.**

```
1 #!/usr/bin/perl
2 use CGI qw/:standard/;
3 @advice = (
4       'A stitch in time saves nine.',
5       'Look both ways before crossing the street.',
6       'Chew completely before swallowing.',
7       'A penny saved is a penny earned.',
8       'Fools rush in where angels fear to tread.'
9       );
10 print header,
11   start_html("Good Advice"),
12   h1("Good Advice");
13 $action = param('action');
14
15 if ($action=~/Message (\d+)/) {
16    $message_no = $1-1;
17    print strong($advice[$message_no]);
18 }
19 print start_form;
20 foreach (1..5) {
21    print submit(-name=>'action',-value=>"Message $_");
22 }
23 print end_form,end_html;
```

Listing 2.2 creates five buttons named action distinguished by the values Message 1 through Message 5 (lines 19 to 23). The script fetches the contents of the action parameter, and uses it to retrieve and display the message the user selected (lines 15 to 18). If the value of action is undefined, then the script is being called for the first time and the script does nothing.

Figure 2.16 This page displays a different piece of advice for every button pressed.

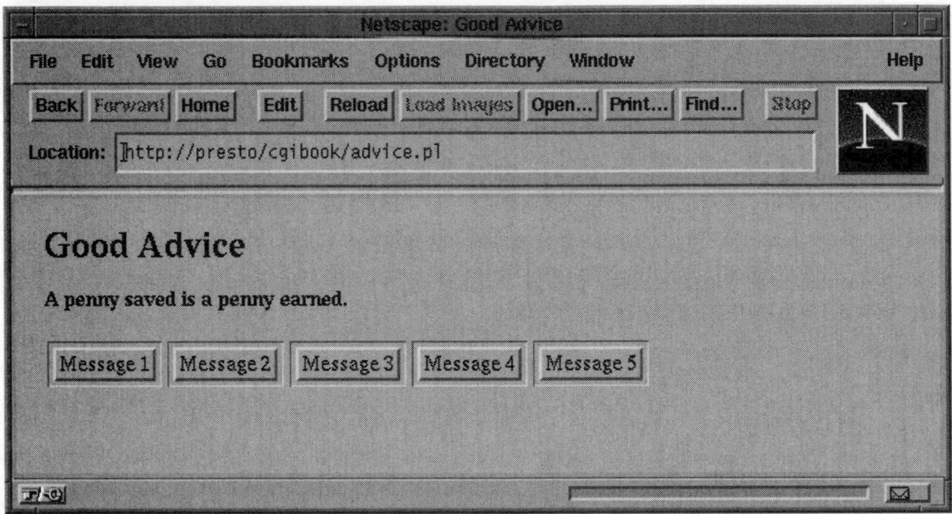


# A Multipart Form

As Web-based applications become more complex, the simple query/response paradigm begins to break down. Some scripts need to display several different pages based on user input, and even conduct extended conversations with the user. Consider, for example, a complex, multipage form, such as the loan application shown in Figure 2.17. The script generates page 1 of the form, which the user fills out and submits. The script now generates the second page of the form, possibly altering its appearance based on the answers to the first page. This process continues until all of the pages have been completed. The challenge to the CGI software developer is to maintain continuity during this process. To the user, the interaction with the script appears to be a single continuous session, unaware that the script is launched anew each time the user submits one of the fill-out forms. The variables or memory structures that the script created when it generated the previous pages are no longer available. The script must somehow store the information from all the previous pages so as to keep track of the user's previous answers.

Figure 2.17 A page from the loan.pl script.

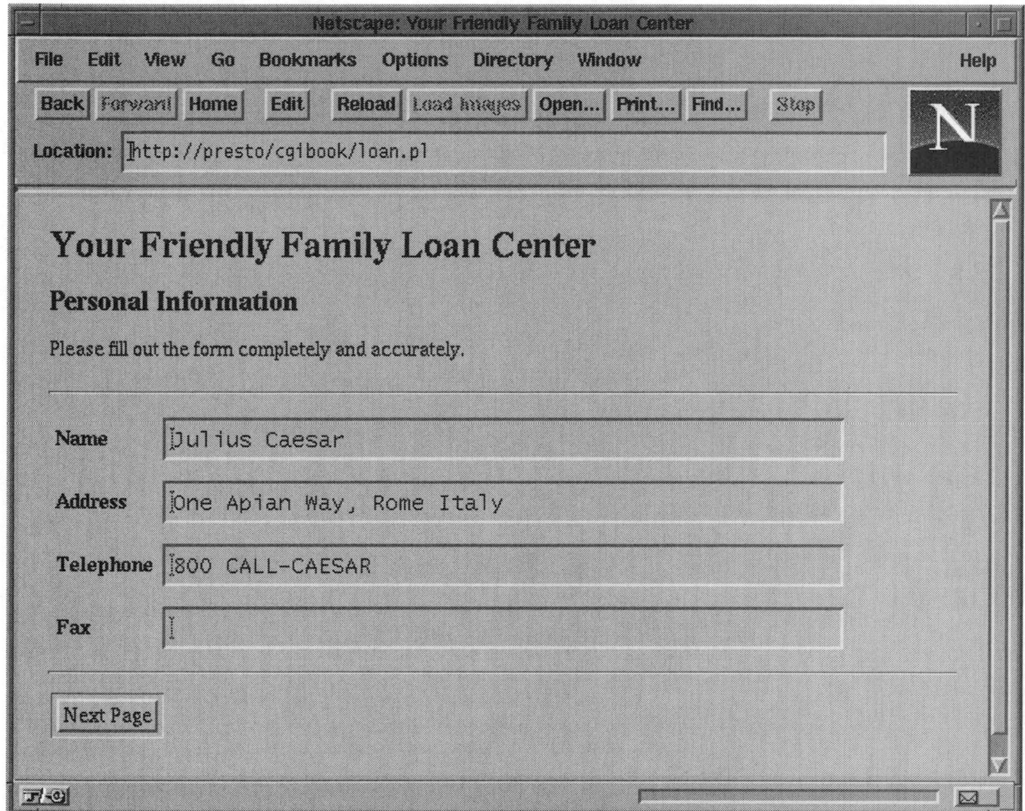


Listing 2.3 gives the loan.pl script, a program that collects credit information. The program creates a series of pages. Page 1 collects personal information, including name and address. Page 2 collects information on the user's references. Page 3 collects information on the user's assets, including house, car, and savings account. Page 4 displays a "review" page in which all the collected information is displayed before submitting it to the bank as shown in Figure 2.18. The last "confirmation" page displays a note from the bank telling the user that she will be hearing from a loan officer soon. At any point, the user is free to page back and forth between pages by pressing buttons labeled Next Page and Previous Page. The appropriate information is automatically recovered and placed in that page's fill-out form.

Figure 2.18 The confirmation page displayed by loan.pl.

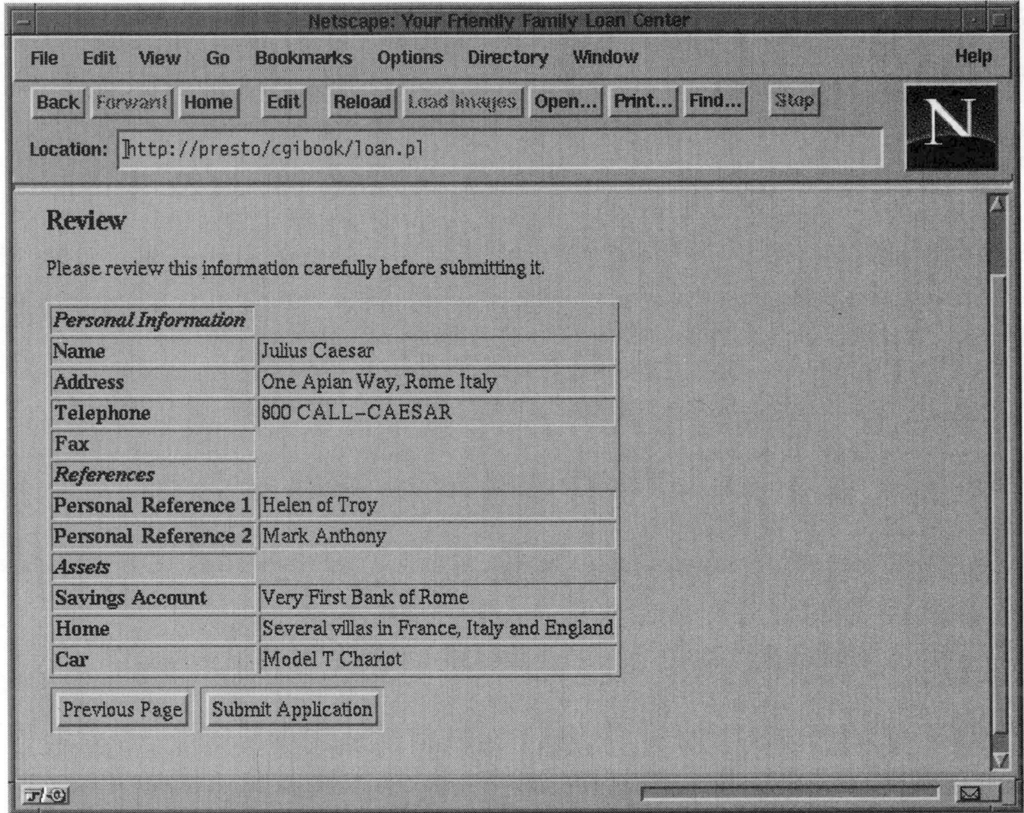


The trick used in this program is to store the cumulative state information within fill-out forms. Some information is made visible to the user in text fields, while other information is made invisible by storing it in hidden input tags.

Listing 2.3 Loan.pl creates a multipage form.

```
#!/usr/bin/perl

# script: loan.cgi
use CGI qw/:standard :html3/;
```

```
# this defines the contents of the fill out forms
# on each page.
@PAGES = ('Personal Information','References','Assets','Review','Confirmation');
%FIELDS = ('Personal Information' => ['Name','Address','Telephone','Fax'],
           'References'        => ['Personal Reference 1','Personal Reference 2'],
           'Assets'              => ['Savings Account','Home','Car']
         );
# accumulate the field names into %ALL_FIELDS;
foreach (values %FIELDS) {
    grep($ALL_FIELDS{$_}++,@$_);
}


# figure out what page we're on and where we're heading.
$current_page = calculate_page(param('page'),param('go'));
$page_name = $PAGES[$current_page];

print_header();
print_form($current_page)         if $FIELDS{$page_name};
print_review($current_page)       if $page_name eq 'Review';
print_confirmation($current_page) if $page_name eq 'Confirmation';
print end_html;

# CALCULATE THE CURRENT PAGE
sub calculate_page {
    my ($prev,$dir) = @_;
    return 0 if $prev eq ‘’;     # start with first page
    return $prev + 1 if $dir eq ‘Submit Application’;
    return $prev + 1 if $dir eq ‘Next Page’;
    return $prev - 1 if $dir eq ‘Previous Page’;
}
```

*Continued*

**Listing 2.3 Loan.pl creates a multipage form.** ***(Continued)***

```

# PRINT HTTP AND HTML HEADERS
sub print_header {
    print header,
      start_html("Your Friendly Family Loan Center"),
      h1("Your Friendly Family Loan Center"),
      h2($page_name);
}

# PRINT ONE OF THE QUESTIONNAIRE PAGES
sub print_form {
    my $current_page = shift;
    print "Please fill out the form completely and accurately.",
          start_form,
          hr;
    draw_form(@{$FIELDS{$page_name}});
    print hr;
    print submit(-name=>'go',-value=>'Previous Page')
     if $current_page > 0;
    print submit(-name=>'go',-value=>'Next Page'),
          hidden(-name=>'page',-value=>$current_page,-override=>1),
          end_form;
}

# PRINT THE REVIEW PAGE
sub print_review {
    my $current_page = shift;
    print "Please review this information carefully before submitting it. ",
          start_form;
    my (@rows);
    foreach $page ('Personal Information','References','Assets') {
```

```
        push(@rows,th({-align=>LEFT},em($page)));
        foreach $field (@{$FIELDS{$page}}) {
            push(@rows,
            TR(th({-align=>LEFT},$field),
               td(param($field)))
            );
            print hidden(-name=>$field);
        }
      }
      print table({-border=>1},caption($page),@rows),
        hidden(-name=>'page',-value=>$current_page,-override=>1),
        submit(-name=>'go',-value=>'Previous Page'),
        submit(-name=>'go',-value=>'Submit Application'),
        end_form;
}

# PRINT THE CONFIRMATION PAGE
sub print_confirmation {
    print "Thank you. A loan officer will be contacting you shortly.",
          p,
          a({-href=>'/'},'Home Page');
}


# CREATE A GENERIC QUESTIONNAIRE
sub draw_form {
    my (@fields) = @_;
    my (%fields);
    grep ($fields{$_}++,@fields);
    my (@hidden_fields) = grep(!$fields{$_},keys %ALL_FIELDS);
    my (@rows);
    foreach (@fields) {
      push(@rows,
```

Continued

**Listing 2.3 Loan.pl creates a multipage form.** ***(Continued)***

```
100             TR(th({-align=>LEFT},$_),
101                td(textfield(-name=>$_,-size=>50))
102               )
103             );
104      }
105      print table(@rows);
106
107      foreach (@hidden_fields) {
108          print hidden(-name=>$_);
109      }
110  }
```

The idea of this script is that the form on each page is self-generating. Instead of creating each form by hand, as in the past, we define the fields that belong to each page and a subroutine to turn the fields into a series of labels of text fields (lines 3 through 15). After importing CGI.pm, we make several global definitions. The list @PAGES defines the names of each of the pages, "Personal Information," "References," and so on. The hash list %FIELDS defines which fields of the credit questionnaire to present on each page. For example, the "Personal Information" page contains the fields "Name," "Address," "Telephone," and "Fax." (In a real world application, the list of fields would probably be read from a disk file or database.) Two pages are not associated with any fields. They are the "Review" page that presents a summary of results to the user, and the final "Confirmation" page. Lastly, we create a convenience hash named %ALL_FIELDS that holds the definitive list of all the fields.

The first task is to ascertain which page of the multipart form we should display (lines 17 and 18). We determine this by retrieving a CGI parameter called page that holds the number of the page the user last viewed, and another parameter called go, which contains the name of the submit button that the user presses (for example, "Next Page"). We pass this information to the calculate_page() subroutine, which contains the logic to return the correct current page number. We store the page number in the $current_page variable, then use it to find the name of the page by indexing into the @PAGE array.

Lines 20 to 24 create the HTTP and HTML headers with a call to the subroutine print_header(), passing it the name of the current page. Next come a series of conditional statements. If the page contains fields, then we make a call to print_form() to create a generic fill-out form. Otherwise, if the page name is "Review" or "Confirmation," we call print_review() or print_confirmation() respectively to create the review page and confirmation pages. Having done this, we end the HTML page and exit.

Lines 27 to 34 define the calculate_page() function. The subroutine takes the number of the previous page ($prev), the value of the "go" button ($dir for direction), and returns the current page to be displayed. The logic is simple; if there is no previous page (its value is the empty string), then the script is probably being called for the first time. We return a value of 0, indicating the first page. Otherwise, if the value of "go" is either "Submit Application" or "Next Page," it indicates that the user wants to move forward. We return the number of the previous page plus one. If the value of "go" is "Previous Page," we return the previous page minus 1.

In Lines 37 to 43, print_header() prints out the HTTP and HTML headers. This uses the header(), start_html(), h1(), and h2() calls that you've already seen.

Lines 91 through 104 define the print_form() subroutine, which turns a series of field names into a series of text fields in a fill-out form. Print_form() starts a fill-out form, then calls draw_form() with the list of the fields that should appear on this page of the questionnaire. Draw_form() turns each of the provided fields into a user-editable text field. Fields that aren't mentioned in the argument list, but belong elsewhere in the questionnaire, are stashed away in hidden fields, as we will soon see.

Print_form() now creates two submit buttons named "go," one labeled "Previous Page" and the other labeled "Next Page." The first button is suppressed if the script is displaying the first page, since there is no previous page in this case. We also print out a hidden field named "page" that contains the value of the current page. This field will not be visible on the page that the user sees, but it will be submitted along with the form when the user presses either of the submit buttons.

Notice that we used -override to force the hidden field to take the value of the current page. If we didn't provide this argument, then hidden() would print out the preexisting value of the CGI page parameter, which might be left over from a previous page.

Jumping ahead, look at the definition of draw_form() (lines 91 though 110). We see that the first thing this subroutine does is subtract the list of fields to display, @fields, from the list of all questionnaire fields, %ALL_FIELDS. The result is stored in the array @hidden_fields. (If you have never seen the Perl trick of using grep() to subtract one list from another, this is a good example.) We turn the visible fields into form input elements with textfield(), using a table to line them up next to their labels. We print out the table in line 105. In lines 107 to 109, we write out the hidden fields by making a series of calls to hidden().

Lines 60 through 81 define print_review(), the subroutine responsible for creating a nicely formatted summary of the user's credit application. Using CGI.pm's table shortcuts, print_review() creates a single long table that lists each of the questionnaire fields, sorted by the page on which they appear. Print_review() then makes a call to draw_form() with no fields listed. This has the effect of creating no editable fields, but instead, writes the entire list of fields out as hidden elements, invisibly saving the state of the questionnaire. Next, the subroutine writes out a hidden field containing the value of the current page and the two submit buttons.

Lines 83 to 88 print the confirmation page; a friendly message and a link to the homepage. Actually, nothing is done with the questionnaire values, but in a real application they would be recovered with param() and entered into the loan application processing system somehow.

At the bottom of our fill-out form we create two hypertext links. The first labeled "Home page" is a simple link that takes us to the site's entry page, /. The second labeled "Start over," is more interesting. Selecting this link clears out all the saved CGI parameters and takes the user back to the first page of the empty form, to start over. We could implement this link by hard-coding the URL of our script, but this might cause the link to fail if we ever renamed or moved the script. A more dependable solution is to call the CGI.pm url() function to fetch the URL of the script at run time.

A related function, self_url(), behaves much like url(). In addition to retrieving the script's URL, it appends to it a question mark (?) and the entire contents of the current CGI parameter list. When the link is selected, the script will be reinvoked with all its CGI parameters intact, saving state information in much the same way that hidden fields do, without resorting to a fill-out form. We will use this technique in the next example.

# A Guestbook Script

The next example, listed in Listing 2.4, is a complete guestbook script. When first called, the script prompts the user to enter her name, e-mail address, and optional information. When the user presses the button labeled Sign Guestbook, her information is checked for completeness. If the information passes the check, the script displays a second page, which asks the user to confirm that the information is correct. If she likes, she can press a button to go back to the previous page and change the fields. Otherwise, she can press another button to write the new guestbook entry to disk. In this case, the script displays a confirmation notice, then displays the current contents of the guestbook. A button labeled "View Guestbook" on the first page gives the user the option of jumping immediately to the guestbook display without signing it, as shown in Figure 2.19.

Like the previous example, the script uses an action parameter to distinguish between the first time the script is called, and requests to manipulate the guestbook in various ways. The parameter can have any of three values; "Sign Guestbook," to capture the user's information and display the confirmation page; "Confirm," to indicate that the user is happy with the information and wants to save it; and "View Guestbook," to view the current

Figure 2.19 Previous entries displayed by the guestbook script.

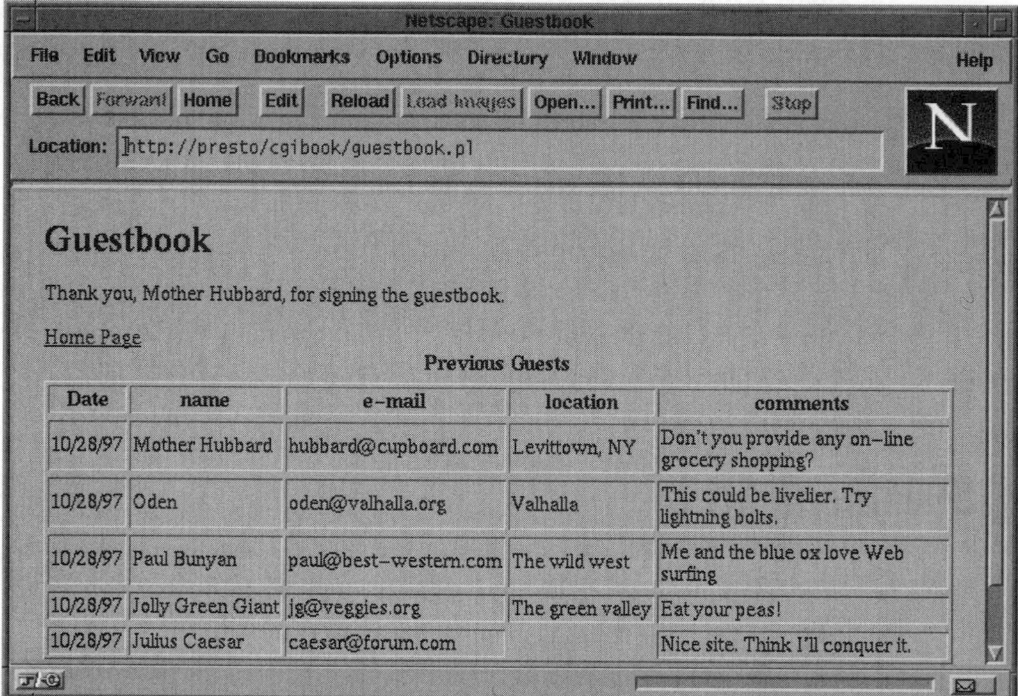


guestbook file. Anything else (or a blank value) causes the script to display the first page.

If the user wants to view the guestbook directly without going through the fill-out form, she can create a link with a URL like the one shown below. The script doesn't care whether the action parameter comes from the fill-out form or the script's URL.

```
<A HREF="/cgi-bin/guestbook.pl?action=view"> View the guestbook</A>
```

This is a long script, but it is worth working through. In addition to illustrating how to create a multipage form, this script also shows some of the details of writing scripts that create and manipulate data files. The source code for the script is provided in Listing 2.3.

**Listing 2.4 A Guestbook Script.**

```
#!/usr/bin/perl
use CGI qw/:standard :html3 :netscape/;
use POSIX 'strftime';

@REQUIRED = qw/name e-mail/;
@OPTIONAL = qw/location comments/;
$TIMEOUT = 10;  # allow up to 10 seconds for waiting on a locked guestbook
$GUESTBOOKFILE = "./guestbook.txt";
%ENTITIES = ('&'=>'&amp;', '>'=>'&gt;', '<'=>'&lt;', '\"'=>'&quot;' );

print header,
    start_html('Guestbook'),
    h1("Guestbook");

$_ = param('action');

 CASE: {
     /^sign/i and do    { sign_guestbook(); last CASE; };
     /^confirm/i and do { write_guestbook() and view_guestbook(); last CASE; };
     /^view/i and do    { view_guestbook(); last CASE; };
     # default
     generate_form();
 }

sub sign_guestbook {
    my @missing = check_missing(param());
    if (@missing) {
        print_warning(@missing);
        generate_form();
        return undef;
```

*Continued*

**Listing 2.4 A Guestbook Script.** ***(Continued)***

```
    }
    my @rows;
    foreach (@REQUIRED,@OPTIONAL) {
        push(@rows,TR(th({-align=>LEFT},$_),td(escapeHTML(param($_)))));
    }
    print "Here is your guestbook entry.  Press ",
          em('Confirm')," to save it, or ",em('Change'),
          " to change it.",
          hr,
          table(@rows),
          hr;

    print start_form;
    foreach (@REQUIRED,@OPTIONAL) {
        print hidden(-name=>$_);
    }
    print submit(-name=>'action',
                 -value=>'Change Entry'),
          submit(-name=>'action',
                 -value=>'Confirm Entry'),
          end_form;
}

print end_html;

sub check_missing {
    my (%p);
    grep (param($_) ne '' && $p{$_}++,@_);
    return grep(!$p{$_},@REQUIRED);
}

sub print_warning {
```

```
    print font({-color=>'red'},
          'Please fill in the following fields: ',
          em(join(', ',@_)),
          '.');
}

sub generate_form {
    print start_form,
     table(
        TR({-align=>LEFT},
          th('Your name'),
          td(textfield(-name=>'name',-size=>50))
        ),
        TR({-align=>LEFT},
          th('Your e-mail address'),
          td(textfield(-name=>'e-mail',-size=>50))
        ),
        TR({-align=>LEFT},
          th('Your location (optional)'),
          td(textfield(-name=>'location',-size=>50))
        ),
        TR({-align=>LEFT},
          th('Comments (optional)'),
          td(textarea(-name=>'comments',-rows=>4,
                      -columns=>50,
                      -wrap=>1))
        )
     ),
     br,
     submit(-name=>'action',-value=>'View Guestbook'),
     submit(-name=>'action',-value=>'Sign Guestbook'),
     end_form;
}
```

*Continued*

**Listing 2.4 A Guestbook Script.** ***(Continued)***

```
sub write_guestbook {
    my $fh = lock($GUESTBOOKFILE,1);
    unless ($fh) {
       print strong('Sorry, an error occurred: unable to open guestbook file.'),p();
       Delete('action');
       print a({-href=>self_url},'Try again');
       return undef;
    }
    my $date = strftime('%D',localtime);
    print $fh join("\t",$date,map {CGI::escape(param($_))} (@REQUIRED,@OPTIONAL)),"\n";
    print $fh "\n";
    print "Thank you, ",param('name'),", for signing the guestbook.\n",
      p(),
      a({href=>"/"},'Home Page');
    unlock($fh);
    1;
}

sub view_guestbook {

    print start_form,
          submit(-name=>'Sign Guestbook'),
          end_form
          unless param('name');

    my $fh = lock($GUESTBOOKFILE,0);

    my @rows;
    unless ($fh) {
```

```
        print strong('Sorry, an error occurred: unable to open guestbook file.'),br;
        Delete('action');
        print a({-href=>self_url},'Try again');
        return undef;
    }
    while (<$fh>) {
        chomp;
        my @data = map {CGI::unescape($_)} split("\t");
        foreach (@data) { $_ = escapeHTML($_); }
        unshift(@rows,td(\@data));
    }
    unshift(@rows,th(['Date',@REQUIRED,@OPTIONAL]));
    print table({-border=>''},
            caption(strong('Previous Guests')),
            TR(\@rows));
   print p,a({href=>"/"},'Home Page');
    1;
}

sub escapeHTML {
    my $text = shift;
    $text =~ s/([&\"><])/$ENTITIES{$1}/ge;
    return $text;
}

sub LOCK_SH { 1 }
sub LOCK_EX { 2 }
sub LOCK_UN { 8 }

sub lock {
    my $path = shift;
    my $for_writing = shift;
```

*Continued*

**Listing 2.4 A Guestbook Script. *(Continued)***

```

    my ($lock_type,$path_name,$description);
    if ($for_writing) {
        $lock_type = LOCK_EX;
        $path_name = ">>$path";
        $description = 'writing';
    } else {
        $lock_type = LOCK_SH;
        $path_name = $path;
        $description = 'reading';
    }

    local($msg,$oldsig);
    my $handler = sub { $msg='timed out'; $SIG{ALRM}=$oldsig; };
    ($oldsig,$SIG{ALRM}) = ($SIG{ALRM},$handler);
    alarm($TIMEOUT);

    open (FH,$path_name) or
       warn("Couldn't open $path for $description: $!"), return undef;

    # now try to lock it
    unless (flock (FH,$lock_type)) {
       warn("Couldn't get lock for $description (" . ($msg || "$!") . ")");
       alarm(0);
       close FH;
       return undef;
    }

    alarm(0);
    return FH;
}
```

```
188
189 sub unlock {
190     my $fh = shift;
191     flock($fh,LOCK_UN);
192     close $fh;
193 }
```

The script begins by importing the CGI module and several sets of subroutines. In addition to the standard HTML shortcuts, we import the HTML3 shortcuts in order to get access to tables, and the Netscape-specific shortcuts in order to get access to the nonstandard font() function. In actuality, "Netscape-specific" is something of a misnomer, since recent versions of Internet Explorer support most, if not all, of Netscape's HTML extensions. We also import the strftime() function from POSIX, which is used later for date-stamping the user's guestbook entry.

Lines 4 through 9 define some constants. We specify some guestbook fields that the user is required to fill-out (name and e-mail) and others that are optional (location and comment). These are stored in the global variables @REQUIRED and @OPTIONAL, respectively. We give the path name of the guestbook file, relative to the script. We also define a timeout for guestbook file-locking operations. As we will see, it is important for CGI scripts to lock files before writing to them in case another CGI script tries to access the file simultaneously. The $TIMEOUT variable defines how many seconds the script will wait on a locked file.

Later in the script, we filter HTML tags out of users' guestbook entries. It is here that we define the characters that are likely to be misinterpreted as HTML and the escape codes to substitute for them (HTML character entities).

Lines 10 to 12 print out the HTTP header and begins the HTML document. All pages have the same title and level-1 header, so it makes sense to print this only once. This would also be a good place to put other constant elements such as a logo, navigation bar, or a link back to the homepage.

Lines 16 to 21 choose between pages to display. They take advantage of a Perlish trick to create a Pascal-like case statement. The value of the action parameter is recovered using param() and stored in the $_ variable. Next the script executes a code block named CASE. The block contains a series of pattern matches on $_. Whenever a pattern is successfully matched, the code executes another code block that ends with the statement "last CASE." This causes the script to jump immediately to the end of the CASE block.

The first pattern match is for an action parameter beginning with the word *sign*, usually produced when the user presses the "Sign Guestbook" button on the first page. If a match is found, the script calls a subroutine named sign_guestbook() to redisplay the user's information and ask for her confirmation. Next we look for a pattern beginning with the word *confirm*. This is generated from the confirmation page when the user presses the "Confirm Entry" button. The script calls write_guestbook() to write the new entry to disk, followed by view_guestbook() to display the current guestbook to the user. The two subroutine calls are linked by a logical *and*, in case an error occurs while writing to disk (a disk-full error, for example), the script will abort all further processing. If the "action" parameter begins with the word *view*, then we jump immediately to view_guestbook(). Otherwise, if "action" is undefined or something we don't recognize, the script generates the first page.

Lines 68 through 94 define the generate_form() subroutine, which creates the fill-out form on page 1. It creates a series of text fields named "name," "e-mail," "location" (for the user's locality), and comments. In order to align the headings with the text fields, we put them both into a small two-column table. This is the general trick for getting form elements to line up. After creating the fields, we generate two "action" buttons, one named "View Guestbook" and the other "Sign Guestbook."

Lines 24 through 51 generate the confirmation page. The script first makes a call to check_missing(). This subroutine checks that all the required fields are present, and returns a list of the missing ones. If some fields are absent, the script prints out a warning message by calling the print_warning() subroutine. It then calls generate_form() again to regenerate the fill-out form so that the user can make the necessary changes, and returns without doing any further processing.

If all the required information is present, the script displays the confirmation. We again use the trick of lining up elements by placing them in a table. First we build up an array of table rows in which the first column is a field name and the second column is the current CGI parameter (lines 32 to 34). Then we incorporate the entire array into a table (lines 35 to 40). An important detail is the call to escapeHTML() on line 33. If the user happens to enter a character that is special in HTML, such as <, >, &, or ", our display might become disordered. EscapeHTML() replaces these characters with their HTML entities, <, >, and so on.

In lines 42 to 50, we create a small form containing two buttons named action. The first, labeled "Change Entry," lets the user go back to the previous page and edit her information. The second, labeled "Confirm Entry," takes the user onward to the last page. Here we encounter a small problem. When we go onward to the next page, or backward to the previous one, we must remember the current CGI parameters. But when the user submits the form, the script will be started over again from scratch, losing the parameters. We finesse this problem by using the hidden() function to incorporate a set of hidden fields into the form. We loop through each of the required and optional fields, and call hidden() with the field name. There is no need to set the value explicitly, because hidden() is smart enough to look in the CGI parameters for the field's current value.

Lines 55 to 59 create the check_missing() function. It quickly matches up the CGI parameters with the list of required fields and returns any fields that aren't present. If you have never seen the Perl idiom for comparing two lists using grep(), lines 57 and 58 are worth studying.

Lines 62 to 66, print_warning(), take the list of missing parameters and turns them into an HTML warning message calling the font() function to change the text color to red.

Lines 96 through 112 are where the user's information is actually written to disk inside the subroutine write_guestbook(). Unlike other guestbooks, this script doesn't create an HTML page directly. Instead it appends the user's information to a tab-delimited text file. Each row of the file is a new guestbook entry. The first column is a date stamp, the second column is the user's name, the third column is the user's e-mail address, and so on.

First we attempt to open the guestbook file for writing by calling the lock() function. It is important to lock the file before writing to it, because there is a very real possibility that when two different users try to use the guestbook script at the same time, one copy of the script will overwrite the changes made by the other. Lock() takes two arguments, the name of the file to open, and a flag indicating whether it should open the file for writing. If successful, the lock() function returns a filehandle to the guestbook file. If unsuccessful, it returns undef, in which case we print an error message and exit.

There is an interesting advantage in the way we generate the error message. It contains a link labeled "Try again." If the user selects it, she will be returned to the first page of the guestbook script with all the fields of the form already filled in. The script could have implemented this functionality using hidden fields as before, but in this case, we use a slightly different technique to create a state-preserving link. The CGI.pm function self_url() will return a URL which, when fetched, reinvokes the script with all its CGI parameters intact (it does this by incorporating them all into the query string part of the URL). However, if we try to use the unmodified output of self_url() in a hypertext link, it will not do quite what we want; the action parameter would still be there, and the script will redisplay the current page rather than the first one. So we first call the CGI.pm function Delete() (with a capital D) to remove "action" from the CGI parameter list. We then create a hypertext link with the a() function, and point its HREF attribute at the string returned by self_url().

In lines 104 to 109, we write the new entry into the guestbook file. First we obtain the current date by calling strftime() with a format that returns the date in MM/DD/YY form. Then we join the date and the guestbook fields together with tabs, and write them out as a single line to the guestbook file. The important detail here is the possibility that the user has already entered a tab in one of the fields. Since this will confuse our file format, we replace tabs with spaces on line 105.

We unlock the file by calling unlock(), which closes the file, and we return a nonzero value to indicate that the function completed successfully.

Lines 114 through 142 define the view_guestbook() subroutine, called to display the current guestbook. Again, we lock the guestbook file and print an error if unsuccessful. This time the second argument to lock() is 0 (false), indicating that we need read-only access to the file.

On lines 130 to 135, we fetch the contents of the guestbook file line by line, turn the lines into table rows, and push them onto an array. Notice how the script uses unshift() rather than push() to assemble the array. This has the effect of reversing the order of the lines, so that newer guestbook entries appear towards the top. After this loop, we unshift the top-most row to create headings for each of the columns. We turn the entire array into a table, print it out, and return.

Lines 144 to 148, the escapeHTML() subroutine, changes characters that have special meaning in HTML into safe entities. The heart of the subroutine is a substitution in which each of the special characters is replaced with its entry in the %ENTITIES hash.

Lines 150 through 193 define the functions lock() and unlock(). They are front ends to the lower-level POSIX flock() call. We first define constants for the flock(): LOCK_SH for a shared lock (which a program should call when it wants read-only access to a file), LOCK_EX for an exclusive lock (which a program calls when it wants write access), and LOCK_UN to unlock a file.

Next comes the definition for lock(). Lock() will attempt to obtain a lock on the named file. If some other program already has a lock, the function will wait until the other program releases the lock. Lock() would be a simple function if not for one detail. If the other program never releases the lock, the function might wait forever while the remote user stares at a blank browser window, which is unacceptable. To avoid this, we arrange for the system to interrupt flock() and send our script an alarm signal ("sigALRM") if the timeout period expires before flock() returns.

In lines 154 to 163, the script sets up a few variables. First we check whether the caller wants to open the file for writing or read only, and set the values of $lock_type, $path_name, and $description accordingly. Note that in order to open the file for writing we prepend ">>" to its path, causing it to be opened for appending.

We will need to create a subroutine to receive the alarm signal. On line 166, we create a signal handler named $handler by defining a small anonymous routine that does nothing but set the value of a variable called $msg to the string "timed out." We then set this routine as the signal handler for sigALRM by assigning it to the appropriate entry in Perl's signal handler list %SIG, and start the countdown by calling alarm() with the desired timeout period.

While the timer is counting down, we attempt to open the file. If successful, we pass the filehandle to flock(), specifying the appropriate lock type (LOCK_EX for read/write access, LOCK_SH for read-only access). Flock() will return a true value for success, or zero for failure. In the latter case, we print out an error message, clean up, and return an undefined value. Otherwise, we reset the alarm and return the filehandle.

Unlock() is much more simple. We just retrieve the filehandle and call flock() with the LOCK_UN option. We finish by closing the file.

**TIP**

**This script should work on all UNIX versions of Perl and any port where the flock() and alarm() functions are available. However, some Perl ports, for example the one for Windows95, do not implement one or both of these functions. In this case, you can either ignore file lock altogether (not the best idea, but safe on a server that isn't too heavily loaded), or implement a different type of locking. A popular technique is to check for the existence of a lock file before opening the file. If the file is present, then you know some other program is working with the file, and your script should wait until the lock file disappears. If the lock file is absent, create it before opening up the guestbook file, and be sure to delete it after you are through.**

# Displaying a Random Picture

Until now, we have used CGI.pm to create HTML documents from scratch. What if you do not want to create a new document, but instead want to select among several existing documents in an intelligent fashion? The CGI protocol was designed to allow this using the redirect instruction. The browser calls your script, and your script immediately redirects it to a new URL. The browser fetches the new URL and displays it. In most cases, the user won't even notice the double take.

To generate a redirect instruction, just call redirect() instead of header(), as in the following example:

```
#!/usr/bin/perl
use CGI qw/:standard/;
print redirect('http://some.site/some/path');
```

---

**TIP**

**When using redirect() you should not call header() or generate any HTML. The Web server will take care of adding some explanatory HTML for the few older browsers that don't understand the redirect instruction.**

---

The argument for redirect() can be a complete URL at someone else's site (including ftp: and gopher: URLs), or a partial URL, such as /pictures/logo.gif, which a browser will interpret to indicate a document at your own site.

In the next example, we use the redirect() function to our advantage to achieve a common Web effect, displaying a new inline image each time the user loads a page. The script relies on there being a directory at your site that contains a few dozen (or a few hundred) different images, all approximately the same size and shape. When the script runs, it calls a random number generator to select one of the images and returns its URL. Listing 2.5 gives the code for this example, random_pict1.pl.

The script begins by defining the location of the document root where the Web document hierarchy starts, and the location of the directory containing the pictures relative to the root. Next it obtains a listing of all the images in the directory by first calling chdir() to make the directory the current working directory, and then uses a <> typeglob to find all files with .jpg or .gif extensions [if you've never seen this use of the angle operators before, you can find it described in *Programming Perl,* by Larry Wall, Tom Christiansen and Randal Schwartz (O'Reilly & Associates, 1996)].

**Listing 2.5 Selecting a random picture time1.pl.**

```
#!/usr/bin/perl
# script: random_pict1.pl
use CGI qw/:standard/;
$DOCUMENT_ROOT = '/usr/local/web/htdocs';
$PICTURES = 'pictures';
chdir "$DOCUMENT_ROOT/$PICTURES"
    or die "Couldn't chdir to pictures directory $!";
@pictures = <*.{jpg,gif}>;
$lucky_one = $pictures[rand(@pictures)];
die "Failed to pick a picture" unless $lucky_one;
print redirect("$PICTURES/$lucky_one");
```

Having obtained the list of images, we need to pick one using the rand() operator. If something goes wrong at this point (for example, there are no pictures in this directory), we may get an empty name, and we error out. If there is no error, we create a URL by combining the name of the picture with the relative path of the pictures directory, and return it to the browser with redirect().

To use this script to generate random inline images, you create a normal HTML page and insert it into a <SRC> tag like this one:

```
<IMG SRC="/cgi-bin/random_pict1.pl" ALT="[Random Picture]">
```

Each time the user visits the page, a different image will appear. This is the way that many banner-ad generators work.

**TIP**

**If you are experimenting with the random_pict.pl script, you may need to press Shift-Reload in order to prevent browser cacheing from redisplaying the same picture each time.**

There is only one problem with this script. The locations of the document root and the directory containing the pictures are hard coded. If you move the script to a different server, or reconfigure the location of the document root, the script will no longer work.

There is, however, an elegant solution to this problem. Instead of hard-coding the location of the pictures directory, pass it to the script at run time as additional path information. To understand what additional path information is, consider this URL:

```
http://your.site/cgi-bin/random_pict2.pl/pictures
```

This is a conventional CGI URL with an extra path added to its end. When the Web server sees a URL like this, it scans through it from left to right until it finds a valid CGI script, the random_pict2.pl script. The server stops processing at this point and calls the script, passing along the additional path information, in this case, /pictures.

Two functions allow you to retrieve the additional path information. Path_info() fetches the information as is without further processing. In this case, path_info() would return /pictures. Path_translated(), in contrast, returns the additional information after translating it from URL form into a physical path. In this case, path_translated() would be /usr/local/web/htdocs/pictures (depending, of course, on the location of the document root). We can use these two functions to advantage in a more elegant version of the random picture script, random_pict2.pl, as shown in Listing 2.6.

The script is now fully portable because it uses path_translated() and path_info() to get configuration information. The only extra requirement is to modify the script's <IMG> tag so that the picture directory is appended to the script's URL, for example:

```
<IMG SRC="/cgi-bin/random_pict2.pl/pictures" ALT="[Random Picture]">
```

**Listing 2.6 Selecting a random picture portably.**

```
#!/usr/bin/perl
# script: random_pict2.pl
use CGI qw/:standard/;
$PICTURE_PATH = path_translated();
$PICTURE_URL = path_info();
chdir $PICTURE_PATH
  or die "Couldn't chdir to pictures directory: $!";
@pictures = <*.{jpg,gif}>;
$lucky_one = $pictures[rand(@pictures)];
die "Failed to pick a picture" unless $lucky_one;
print redirect("$PICTURE_URL/$lucky_one");
```

# Adding Trademarks to Product Names

Another use of the additional path information is to preprocess documents before returning them to the browser. You can highlight search terms, change fonts to conform to some site-wide design policy, or replace certain HTML comments with boilerplate text.

The next example shows one way to automatically add the registered trademark symbol to protected product names. Many (if not most) product names are protected by trademarks. To protect a trademark, a company must place the registered trademark symbol (e.g., Coca Cola®) after every use of the name in printed form, and must warn (and possibly prosecute) anyone who uses the name without acknowledgment. However, the need for trademark symbols can very easily be overlooked.

Tm.pl allows you to write HTML without regard to which product names are protected and which aren't. Before returning the document to the browser, the script searches through a long list of protected names and adds the ® symbol to any names that are not already marked. The script finds the document to modify from the additional path information. Instead of referring to a document like this:

```
<a href="/products/info.html">Product information</a>
```

you refer to it like this:

```
<a href="/cgi-bin/tm.pl/products/info.html">Product information</a>
```

Figure 2.20 shows a sample page processed through the sample script. As long as all the HTML documents served this way refer to each other using relative URLs, all links will be automatically filtered through tm.pl. This is because, to the browser, the additional path information looks just like any other URL path, so relative pathnames such as . and .. work automatically.

Listing 2.7 shows the code for tm.pl.

**Figure 2.20 Tm.pl adds the registered trademark symbol on the fly.**

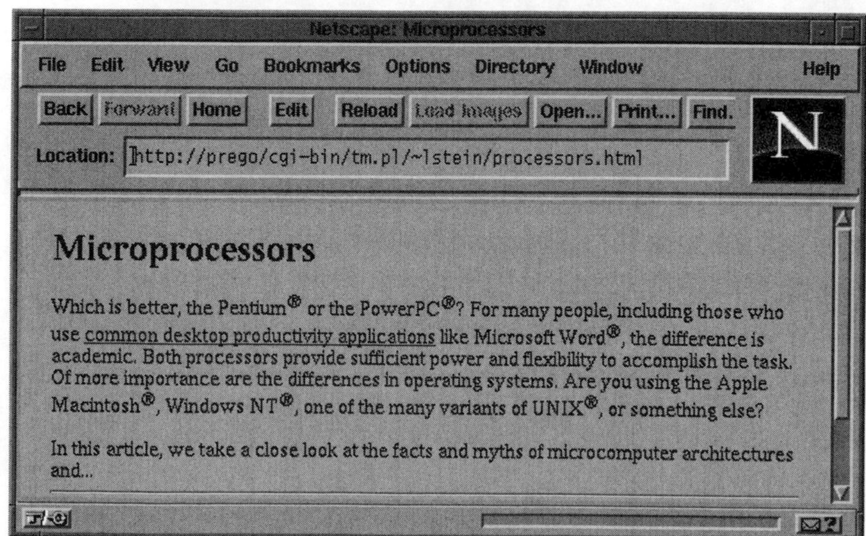

**Listing 2.7 Adding registered trademark symbols on the fly.**

```
#!/usr/bin/perl
# script: tm.pl
use CGI qw/:standard :html3/;

@PROTECTED = ('Windows NT','Windows 95',
        'Macintosh','UNIX','VMS',
        'Microsoft Excel', 'Microsoft Word','Microsoft Office',
        'Pentium','PowerPC');
$pattern = join('|',@PROTECTED);
$pattern =~ s/\s+/\\s+/g; #spaces into whitespace pattern matches
$document = path_translated();
die "Not an HTML document" unless $document=~/\.html$/;
open (DOC,$document) or die "Couldn't open $document: $!";

print header;
while (<DOC>) {
      s/($pattern)(?!&reg;|<sup>)/$1<sup>&reg;<\/sup>/oig;
} continue {
     print $_;
}
```

The script begins by defining a series of words and phrases that are protected by trademarks, then turns them into a pattern match expression by joining them with the | symbol. This sample script is short; in a real-life application the list would contain all the trademarked names that HTML authors were using at your site.

The script then fetches the document to process by calling path_translated(), checks that it is likely to be an HTML document, and attempts to open it.

If successful, the script prints out the HTTP header, then enters a loop in which it examines every line of the file for every occurrence of protected names. Line 16 is a string substitution in which protected names are replaced with the sequence *name*<sup>®</sup>, which is the HTML code for a superscripted registered trademark symbol. The pattern matching operation is crafted so that the substitution only occurs if there is not already a trademark symbol present.

After the substitution, the modified line is printed out.

---

**TIP**

**This script lacks some features that would make it useable in real life. In addition to having a very inadequate list of protected trademarks, the script does little error checking. For instance, it dies if there is no additional path information instead of printing out an explanatory warning.**

---

# Shielding Private Information from Outside Sites

As another example of a script that uses additional path information, consider a script to suppress the display of confidential information when documents are accessed from hosts outside your own organization. For this system, we will invent a new HTML tag called <CONFIDENTIAL>. Any text located between the <CONFIDENTIAL> and </CONFIDENTIAL> tags will be suppressed unless the remote user is connecting from a trusted host machine. An example document might look like this:

```
<H2>New Features</H2>
New features of the Mark I Coffee Grinder include a wake-up timer,
automatic grind selection logic, and an audible alarm when blades need
sharpening. <CONFIDENTIAL>An attachment for grinding spices will be
introduced in the fourth quarter of 1998 </CONFIDENTIAL>.
<P>
```

```
Nobody will be more pleased to receive this elegant new grinder than your
spouse. <CONFIDENTIAL>That is, until she gets her <strong>sleeve</strong>
caught in the thing. Jim, can't we fix this?</CONFIDENTIAL>
```

The script, confidential.pl, is similar to the one introduced in the last section. It scans for sections of the document spanned by <CONFIDENTIAL> tags and removes them. The main difference is that, in this case, the documents will now be kept completely outside the document tree in a place inaccessible to the Web server. This avoids the possibility that the document can be retrieved by bypassing the script. Listing 2.8 shows the code to selectively reveal the text within <CONFIDENTIAL> sections.

**Listing 2.8 Shielding confidential information from untrusted hosts.**

```
#!/usr/bin/perl
# script: confidential.pl
use CGI qw/:standard :html3/;

$TRUSTED = 'friendly.com';
$DOCUMENTS = '/local/documents';

$document = $DOCUMENTS . path_info();
die "Not an HTML document" unless $document=~/\.html$/;
open (DOC,$document) or die "Couldn't open $document: $!";
undef $/;
$text = <DOC>;  # file slurp
close DOC;

$text =~ s!<CONFIDENTIAL>.*?</CONFIDENTIAL>!!sig
         if remote_host() !~ /$TRUSTED$/o;
print header,$text;
```

The script begins by defining the "friendly" domain for trusted hosts that can read the confidential information; in this case friendly.com, and the directory in which the HTML files can be found. Next it turns the path information returned by path_info() into a physical path by combining this with the HTML directory.

The script nows attempts to open and read the document. Because the <CONFIDENTIAL> tag can span several lines, it is most convenient to read the entire file into memory, process it all at once, then write out the modified version. We can safely do this because most HTML documents are relatively short. To perform a file slurp, we undefine the Perl line delimiter variable `$/` and read the file into the variable `$text`.

We check whether the request has come from a browser in the trusted domain or from somewhere else by pattern matching on the string returned by remote_host(). This CGI.pm function call, which we have not encountered before, returns the domain name of the machine that the remote browser is running on, or its IP address if no domain name is known. If the remote host does not match the trusted domain, we perform a pattern substitution to remove text contained between <CONFIDENTIAL></CONFIDENTIAL> pairs, using a case-insensitive, global pattern match. The pattern match is designed to minimize the number of characters between the starting and ending tags (if we failed to do this, we might remove more than was intended). We now print out the header and the modified text.

In addition to remote_host(), there is a variety of other CGI.pm function calls that return information about the session. In addition to the remote hostname, you can retrieve the software name and version number of the browser, information about the operating system the remote user is running, and information about what document types the user's browser can display. You can put this information to good use in customizing the display to the user's capabilities. For example, you can determine if the remote user is running a browser that can handle frames, and produce a frames-enabled document; or a simpler document if not. Chapter 5, *Reference Guide*, lists all the information-retrieval functions.

The next chapter continues the tutorial with more advanced uses of CGI.pm, including server push, cookies, frames, cascading stylesheets, and JavaScript.

## Chapter Three

# Advanced Tricks

CGI.pm's basic functions, HTML shortcuts, CGI parameter recovery, and sticky forms, should meet 90 percent of your server-side scripting requirements. However, the CGI module provides a number of advanced functions for programming large, sophisticated applications.

This chapter begins with techniques for debugging CGI scripts from the command line. Then we will cover topics such as saving script state in files and cookies, accepting file uploads, creating multiframe pages, using cascading stylesheets, and creating "server push" animations.

## Debugging

One of the annoyances of CGI scripting is that the scripts only work correctly when run in the context of a Web server. Because CGI scripts require the environment to be set up in a very specific way, running the script from the command line or within the Perl debugger often does not work well.

CGI.pm provides a partial solution to this problem. When run from the command line, it mocks up a CGI environment, using arguments that you provide to set CGI parameters. This allows you to step through your script inside the Perl debugger, see what your script is doing, and make fixes immediately, all without going through the process of installing the script on a Web site.

The main factor is passing CGI parameters to the script. When you launch a script that uses CGI.pm from the command line (or within the Perl debugger), the module will look for CGI parameters first on the command line, and then on standard input. You can give the script any combination of CGI parameters, have the script read the parameters from a file, or just leave the parameter list blank to simulate what happens when the script is called without any parameters.

The simplest way to pass parameters is using command-line arguments. Consider this invocation of a script:

```
lstein> my_script.pl first_name=Harry last_name=Ward age=33
```

This will run my_script.pl from the command line, passing it CGI parameters named first_name, last_name, and age with the indicated values. From the script's point of view, the effect is exactly as if it had been called from a fill-out form containing similarly named fields. If you want to step through the script in the Perl debugger, you can invoke it like this:

```
lstein> perl -d my_script.pl first_name=Harry last_name=Ward age=33
```

To simulate a multivalued CGI parameter, such as the selected entries of a scrolling listbox, just repeat the parameter name as many times as needed, for example:

```
lstein> my_script.pl vegetable=okra vegetable=celery vegetable=kale
```

You can use this technique to pass scripts and even very complicated parameters containing spaces and other unusual characters. However, you must be careful to protect spaces and unusual characters against interpretation by the UNIX or NT shells either by backslashing the character or enclosing the whole argument in quotes. For example, to pass a value containing a space, you could launch the script in either of the following two ways:

```
lstein> my_script.pl 'name=Harry Ward' age=33
lstein> my_script.pl name=Harry\ Ward age=33
```

The = and & symbols are special in CGI parameter lists. To incorporate one of these characters into a parameter list, you must backslash it:

```
lstein> my_script.pl 'name=John Wiley \& Sons'
```

Without the quotes around the argument, you will have to backslash = and & characters twice—once to protect them from the shell, and once to protect them against misinterpretation by CGI.pm:

```
lstein> my_script.pl name=John\ Wiley\ \\&\ Sons
```

You are also free to use CGI query string format, but in this case you will need to follow the rules for URL escaping (in other words, replacing unusual characters with hexadecimal codes), or you won't get the results you expect. Here is an example of using a correctly-formatted CGI query string:

```
lstein> my_script.pl name=John%20Wiley%20%26%20Sons&month=January
```

If you want your script to behave as if there are no CGI parameters at all, just pass it an empty string, as shown here:

```
lstein> my_script.pl ''
```

If you invoke a CGI.pm using script from the command line without giving it any CGI parameters (not even an empty string), it will try to read its parameters from standard input. The script will print out the message "(offline mode: enter name=value pairs on standard input)" and then wait for input. Type in some parameter pairs, separated by carriage returns, and then press the End-of-File key to indicate you are finished. On UNIX systems, end-of-file is control-D (^D). On DOS/NT systems, end-of-file is control-Z (^Z). The script will process the name/value pairs as if they were provided by a Web server. Here is an example of how you might use this (bold characters are what you type):

```
lstein> my_script.pl
(offline mode: enter name=value pairs on standard input)
first_name=Harry
last_name=Ward
age=33
^D
```

You can use backslashes and quotes to protect spaces and other unusual characters just as with command-line parameter passing, or, if you prefer, use URL-style hexadecimal escape codes. This form of parameter passing is most useful when storing a frequently-used combination of CGI parameters in a file, and reloading them each time. For example, you could create a file named params.txt that contained this text:

```
first_name=Harry
last_name=Ward
favorite\ drink=Popsi\ Cola
age=33
```

To load this list of CGI parameters into your script, just redirect its standard input to read from the file:

```
lstein> my_script.pl <params.txt
```

If you are using the Perl debugger you can reopen STDIN from the file that contains the parameters you wish to use (open STDIN,'params.txt';) Do this right at the beginning of the debug session.

On UNIX systems, another way to pass an empty CGI parameter list to CGI.pm is to redirect standard input from the "empty device" /dev/null. For systems that do not provide /dev/null, the same effect is achieved by redirecting standard input from a zero-length file.

---

**TIP**

**If you plan to run a script from the command line and you do not want it prompted for CGI parameters, you can disable the debugging feature entirely by importing the symbol *-noDebug* when you use it:**

```
use CGI qw/:standard -noDebug/;
```

**This feature is only available in versions 2.38 and higher.**

---

The same method that CGI.pm uses to read parameters from files during debugging can be used internally by your own scripts to save CGI parameter lists to files, and restore them at a later date. This results in a Web page that remembers each visitor, and restores the page's appearance to its original state when the user exits. A later section shows how this is done.

# Graceful Error Messages

Having come this far, you have undoubtedly seen the screenshot shown in Figure 3.1, the dreaded "An internal error has occurred" message. This is the page the server displays whenever a CGI script misbehaves—by crashing, by producing an invalid HTTP header, or by producing a syntax error during the compilation phase.

When scripts go wrong they often produce helpful error messages. For example, if a script has a syntax error, Perl will print an error message giving the line number of the offending statement. It is clear where this information goes when you are running a script from the command line; it goes to standard error and appears in the console window. What happens to this information when the script is running under the Web server?

Figure 3.1 The dreaded "An internal error has occurred" page.

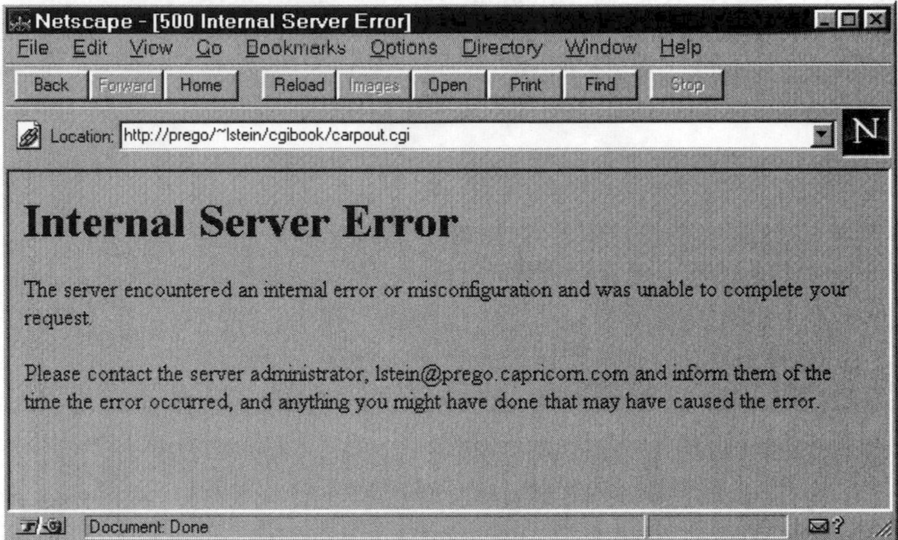


Most Web servers redirect CGI scripts' standard error to a log file before executing them. Any warnings, diagnostic messages, or errors will show up in the log. To see the diagnostic output, open this file up in a text editor. Unfortunately, a few servers, Microsoft IIS included, do not maintain an error log. One of the limitations of the error log is that it intermixes the output of many CGI scripts along with diagnostic output from the Web server itself. On a busy server, it can be difficult to locate the error message produced by your script or to identify a script that is filling the log file with messages.

The CGI::Carp package, part of the standard CGI.pm distribution, helps solve the problem of intermixed output. CGI::Carp redefines the Perl die, warn, carp, confess, and croak functions so that they send named and time-stamped entries to the log file. (The latter three functions are variants of warn and die that produce stack trace information to help you identify what your program was doing when it encountered the error.) You can set the CGI::Carp to redirect error messages to a private error log, and have error messages appear in the browser window rather than the unhelpful "internal error" message.

To understand the advantage of using CGI::Carp, consider the following code fragment:

```
#!/usr/bin/perl
use CGI;
open (CONFIG,"config.txt") || die "couldn't open config: $!\n";
```

If the file config.txt could not be opened, the script would write something like the following into the server error log.

```
couldn't open config: No such file or directory"
```

If there were a lot of error messages above and below this line, it would be hard to identify it. In contrast, if the script were modified to use the CGI::Carp package as shown below, the error message suddenly becomes more easily identifiable. CGI::Carp appends the current time, date, and the script's name to the message.

```
#!/usr/bin/perl
use CGI;
use CGI::Carp;
open (CONFIG,"config.txt") || die "couldn't open config: $!\n";
```

Now the line that appears in the server error log is much more specific:

```
[Tue Oct 28 18:29:28 1997] search.pl: couldn't open config:
    No such file or directory
```

If you want to redirect error messages to your script's own private log file, import the CGI::Carp carpout() function. Open the file you wish to log to, and pass its file handle to carpout(). All error messages will now be redirected to this file. The next bit of code illustrates how to do this.

```
#!/usr/bin/perl
use CGI;
use CGI::Carp ('carpout');
open (LOG,">>/home/fred/logs/search_errors.log") ||
     die "couldn't open log file: $!";
carpout(LOG);
```

It is important to open the log file for appending using the ">>" symbols, otherwise, you will delete its current contents when you open it for writing.

To echo fatal errors to the browser window, import the symbol fatalsTo-Browser. All errors, including ones that occur during the compilation phase, will be displayed in the browser window (see Figure 3.2 for an example). You can use fatalsToBrowser alone, or in combination with carpout(), for example:

```
#!/usr/bin/perl
use CGI;
use CGI::Carp qw(fatalsToBrowser carpout);
open (LOG,">>/home/fred/logs/search_errors.log") ||
     die "couldn't open log file: $!";
carpout(LOG);
```

The effect of these statements will be to log warnings and other nonfatal error messages to a file. Fatal errors, in addition to being sent to the file, will appear in the browser window.

# Fancy HTML Formatting

If you want as much control over the appearance of your Web pages as possible, and don't mind making them incompatible with older browsers, such as NCSA Mosaic or versions of Netscape Navigator prior to 3.0, CGI.pm offers a number of features that are compatible with advanced HTML features such as cascading stylesheets and JavaScript.

The simplest and most portable formatting features are background and font attributes of the <BODY> tag. You can control these attributes by passing

Figure 3.2 CGI::Carp can be used to redirect error messages to the browser window.

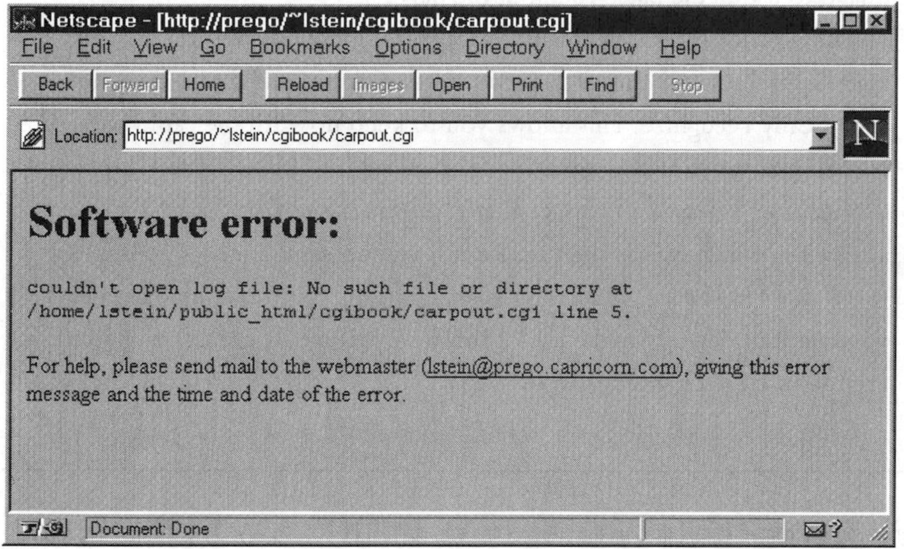


optional arguments to start_html() using a named argument form of the function that we have not yet covered. You can set the browser window's background color, size and color of its font, and the colors of visited and unvisited links. Each argument has the same name as the corresponding HTML attribute. To set the color of visited links to green and the background color to yellow—something you would do in straight HTML with attributes named VLINK and BGCOLOR, respectively—use the -vlink and -bgcolor arguments as follows:

```
print start_html(-title=>'Verditas',
                 -vlink=>'green'
                 -bgcolor=>'yellow');
```

As this example shows, when you use the named argument form of start_html(), you set the title of the page using the -title argument rather than with the bare string used in the simpler form of this function. Other named arguments include -link to adjust the color of unvisited links, -alink to change the color of active links visited during the current session, -text to change the color of plain text, -background to give the URL of a wallpaper image to use in the background of the page.

Like other HTML shortcuts, start_html() defaults to creating an HTML attribute whenever it encounters an argument that it does not specifically recognize. This allows you to keep up with the rapid pace of HTML innovation without waiting for new releases of CGI.pm. For example, if Microsoft releases a browser that recognizes a new LIGHTNING attribute (which causes the user's computer to send a jolt of electricity through its keyboard, making Web surfing a very stimulating experience), you can immediately make use of this new feature by passing a -lightning argument to start_html().

**TIP**

**Newer browsers recognize named fonts, based on the colors of the original IBM PC VGA display: *aqua, black, blue, fuschia, gray, green, lime, maroon, navy, olive, purple, red, silver, teal, white, yellow.* Older browsers (for example, the Netscape Navigator 1.X series) only recognize hexadecimal colors, such as #FF0000 for red. In addition to the 16 "universal" colors, Netscape browsers support several hundred additional named colors. See *HTML, The Definitive Guide*, by Chuck Musciano and Bill Kennedy (O'Reilly & Associates, 1996), or *HTML 4.0 Sourcebook,* by Ian Graham (John Wiley & Sons, 1998) for a complete listing.**

Other useful arguments to start_html() are listed in Chapter Five, *Reference Guide*.

If you import the :html3 group of functions, browser fonts can be adjusted in a number of ways. To globally set the size of the browser font, call the basefont() shortcut somewhere near the top of the document. Like its <BASEFONT> HTML equivalent, the function recognizes a -size argument, which sets the relative size of the font to an integer between 1 and 7. (The default size is 3.) You can then use font() to adjust the size and color of the font with -size and -color arguments, for example:

```
print "Something old, something new, something borrowed,",
      "something ",
      font({-size=>"+2",-color=>"blue"},"blue.");
```

Font sizes can be absolute, like 3, or relative to the base font. In the preceding example, we call for a font two steps larger than the base.

The alignment of paragraphs and headers can be adjusted with the -align argument. In the following example, the header is centered, and the paragraph beneath it is ragged right:

```
print h2({-align=>'CENTER'},The Ballad of the Apple Jack),
      p({-align=>'RIGHT},
         "Sleep not, wake not,",br(),
         "Turn restlessly behind closed eyes.",br(),
         "The apple orchard calls to you,",br(),
         "With destiny and lies."
```

You can apply alignment instructions to arbitrary sections of text using div(). It also takes an -align argument, but you can place larger sections of text inside of it, including multiple paragraphs:

```
print div({-align=>CENTER},
              p("It is not generally known whether the myths and",
              "legends of the Bermuda triangle are true.  Many",
              "people classify them with the legend of the Loch",
              "Ness Monster and UFO's.  Others take official",
              "denials as",i("de facto"),"proof of the veracity",
              "of the tales."),
              p(font({-fontcolor=>'red'},
              "It is clear however, that on that \"fateful day\",
              "the hapless crew of the",i(" Minnow"),
              "may well have sailed into its ineffable grip."))
            );
```

These features allow you to send simple formatting instructions to any browser that is HTML 3.2 compliant. However, you can get access to much more powerful formatting features by using cascading stylesheets, a proposed World Wide Web Consortium (W3C) standard. Stylesheets are supported by recent browsers, including Internet Explorer versions 3.0 and higher, and Netscape Navigator 4.0 and higher. Stylesheets allow you to define document formatting specifications, such as the font, font size, font style, font color, indentation, and many other aspects of the page format. Style definitions can be applied to the whole page, to individual elements within the page, or you can change the style from section to section. Stylesheets can be applied to every document on the site, or to individual documents.

Cascading stylesheets are a rich programming language in their own right. In the following paragraphs, I will give you an idea of how stylesheets are used. For full details, you should read the specification at the W3C's Web site (www.w3.org/pub/WWW/Style/). There you will find the complete text of the specification, a tutorial, and pointers to other sources of information on-line. Among the books that deal with stylesheets is the *HTML Stylesheet Sourcebook*, by Ian Graham (John Wiley & Sons, 1997). Be warned, however, that the stylesheet specification is changing rapidly; you should always check the online sources for definitive information.

A stylesheet consists of a series of named sections that describe how the browser should format the text contained within certain HTML tag. Valid tags are all those that control paragraph formatting, such as <H1> to <H6>, <P>, <BLOCKQUOTE>, <OL>, <UL>, and <DL>. Within each section are directives to set the font size, color, indentation, and so on. Here is a short cascading stylesheet that defines styles for level 1 and 2 headers, paragraphs, and blockquotes. There are many other formatting directives in addition to the ones shown here.

```
H1 {
      font-size: 50pt;
      alignment: center;
      color: blue;
}
H2 {
      font-size: 30pt;
      font-style: italic;
}
```

```
P {
      font-size: 12pt;
      font-family: serif;
      alignment: left;
      indent: 20pt;
}
Blockquote {
      font-size: 12pt;
      font-style: italic;
      margin-right: 50pt;
      margin-left: 50pt;
}
P.Alert {
      font-size: 30pt;
      font-family: sans-serif;
      margin-right: 50pt;
      margin-left: 50pt;
      color: red;
}
```

The stylesheet format is pretty straightforward. There are a series of blocks bracketed by curly braces, each one labeled with the name of an HTML element. Within the block are a series of formatting directives, separated by semicolons. In this example the level-1 header <H1> is defined to use 50 point blue type and be aligned on the center of the page. The level two header <H2> uses a 30 point italic typeface. Paragraphs use a 12 point serif font, and are aligned to the left. The first line of each paragraph is indented 10 points. Blockquotes are offset 50 points inward from the left and right page margins and use a 12 point italic font. Stylesheet-savvy browsers will honor these instructions, overriding the user's preferences and rendering the page with the requested styles. Figure 3.3 shows a screenshot of this stylesheet example.

Figure 3.3 Cascading stylesheets can be used to create stylishly formatted pages.

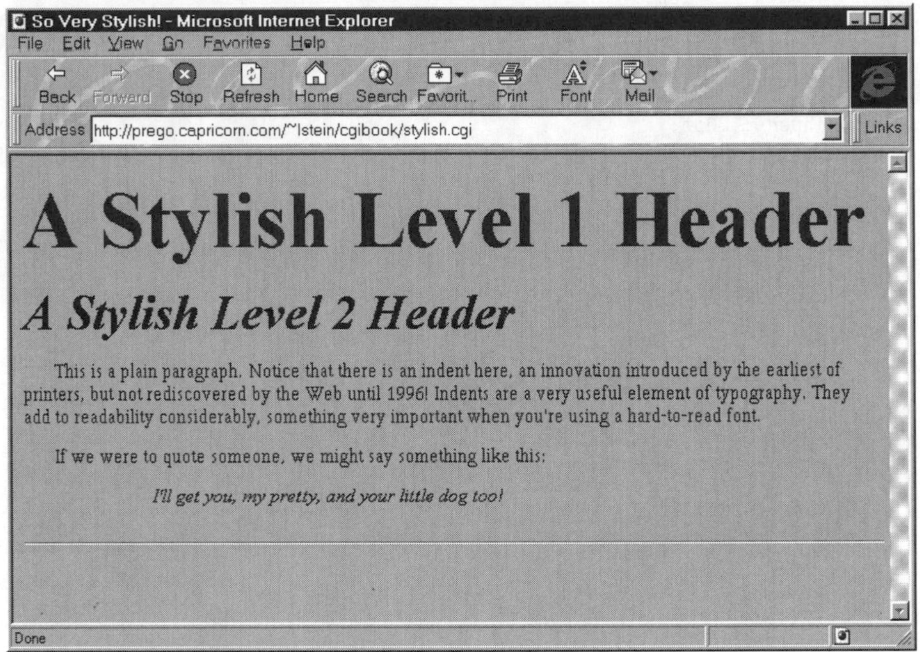


The section labeled P.Alert creates a subclass of <P> that has special formatting. This subclass, intended for important warnings (such as "Improper use of this product will void your warranty") renders its text in a large red sans serif typeface, and indents the text on the right and left sides to make it stand out better. We will see in a moment how to refer to subclasses within CGI.pm scripts.

To incorporate a stylesheet into a dynamically generated page, you can either store the stylesheet as a static file on your site, or incorporate it directly into each script that needs it. Usually you will want to do the former so that other documents (including static HTML pages) can use it as a standard site-wide formatting definition. Save the stylesheet file somewhere within your site's document tree with a .css extension, such as /usr/local/web/htdocs/css/defaults.css. To apply the stylesheet to a CGI-generated document, pass the stylesheet's URL to start_html() using the -style argument:

```
print start_html(-title=>"A Stylish Document",
               -style=>{-src=>'/css/defaults.css'}
               );
```

The syntax is a bit confusing so let's look at it carefully. The -style argument points to an associative array that contains a single key named -src, which in turn, points to the URL of the static stylesheet.

To incorporate the stylesheet directly into the script's code, you would create a variablc containing the stylesheet code, then pass this variable to -style with a key named -code, for example:

```
$LOCAL_STYLE = make_stylesheet();
print start_html(-title=>"A Stylish Document",
              -style=>{-src=>'/css/defaults.css',
                     -code=>$LOCAL_STYLE}
               );
```

As shown in this example, you can use -src and -code together in the same -style section. The defaults defined in the static stylesheet will be overidden by any new definitions in the local stylesheet. When you incorporate stylesheets directly into your own pages, however, you have to be careful. Older browsers that do not support stylesheets will not recognize the definitions and will probably display them in some garbled manner. Since version 2.38, CGI.pm prevents this from happening by putting HTML comments (<!- ->) around the stylesheet. However, if you are using an earlier version of CGI.pm, you will have to enclose the stylesheet between a pair of HTML comments. Here is a general example:

```
$LOCAL_STLE=<<END;
<!-
P.Tip {
margin-right: 50pt;
margin-left: 50pt;
```

```
color: blue;
   }
P.Alert {
font-size: 30pt;
font-family: sans-serif;
color: red;
   }
->
END
print start_html(-title=>'Tres chic',
                 -style=>{-code=>$LOCAL_STYLE});
```

If you call -style with a scalar string value, CGI.pm will treat it as a locally defined stylesheet. Knowing this, you can rewrite the preceding code more simply as:

```
print start_html(-title=>'Tres chic', -style=>$LOCAL_STYLE);
```

After incorporating a stylesheet into a page, the formatting instructions are applied automatically to all the standard HTML tags. However, stylesheets also allow you to define tag subclasses that have special-case formatting. The P.Alert and P.Tip sections given in the preceding examples show how to make the definitions. To use them, add a -class attribute to the appropriate HTML tag. For example, the following code fragment creates a <P> tag using the Alert format:

```
print p({-class=>'Alert'},
        "Warning.  Using this software can be addictive.");
```

It is also possible to temporarily override style definitions within a paragraph, header, block quote, list, or a region defined by a span(). Provide the shortcut with a -style argument of its own, for example:

```
print span({-style=>'color: magenta; font-family: serif'}
           p("Unbound by society's conventions, this",
             "region of text follows its own drummer."
             "It defines its own style, giving it a certain",
             i("je ne sais quoi.")
             ),
            p({-style=>'font-size: 50pt'},
              "Let's increase the font size to make sure",
              "you're paying attention!"
              )
          );
```

As this example shows, you can nest -style arguments. The inner styles override the more general settings defined in outer tags. This is why stylesheets cascade. You do not currently need to import any special symbols to use cascading stylesheets; however, a future version of CGI.pm may include additional shortcut functions that simplify working with stylesheets. Check this book's companion Web site for updates.

# Clickable Image Maps

You can create and process clickable image maps from within CGI.pm. Unlike conventional image maps, which require you to create a file of static associations between image coordinates and URLs to load, a CGI-generated image map allows you to dynamically process the click coordinates. This opens up a number of interesting possibilities, such as navigating a map or graph that the script generates on the fly.

There are two steps to creating a clickable image map. In the first step, your script should create a fill-out form containing an image button. The second step occurs after the user clicks the image button. The browser submits the form, and passes the coordinates of the click to your script as CGI parameters. Your script should then appropriately process the CGI parameters. Like other fill-out form elements, the name of the clickable image button is used as the basis for the name of the CGI parameter returned to your script. In this case, however, two parameters are created: button_name.x, and button_name.y, where button_name is the name you chose for the image button. The two parameters hold the numeric x and y coordinates of the click, where x=0,y=0 is the upper left-hand corner of the image.

This example displays a square image 200×200 pixels in size (it doesn't matter what the image is, in this case). When the user clicks on the image, we calculate what quadrant she clicked in, and print out "top-left," "top-right," "bottom-left," or "bottom-right" as appropriate.

```
#!/usr/bin/perl
use CGI qw/:standard/;
print header,
      start_html('QuadraPhobia'),
      h1('QuadraPhobia'),
      start_form(),
      image_button(-name=>'square',
                   -src=>'/images/red_square.gif',
                   -width=>200,
                   -height=>200,
                   -align=>MIDDLE),
     end_form();
if (param()) {
   ($x,$y) = (param('square.x'),param('square.y'));
   $pos = 'top-left' if $x < 100 && $y < 100;
   $pos = 'top-right' if $x >= 100 && $y < 100;
   $pos = 'bottom-left' if $x < 100 && $y >= 100;
   $pos = 'bottom-right' if $x >= 100 && $y >= 100;
   print b("You clicked on the $pos part of the square.");
}
print end_html();
```

Image buttons act like submit buttons. When the user clicks the image, the contents of other elements in the same form are submitted to script in addition to the click coordinates. This lets you associate magnification menus, zoom options, and other controls with the clickable graphic.

If you regularly work with Web images, you might be interested in GD.pm, a Perl interface to Thomas Boutell's gd image library. GD.pm allows you to create complex GIF images directly within Perl and display them as the output of CGI scripts. GD.pm can be downloaded from any CPAN archive. Check www.perl.com/CPAN/ for the archive nearest you. Precompiled versions of GD.pm are part of the "standard" Windows NT port of Perl and of MacPerl, both of which are available in the CPAN ports/ subdirectory.

## Saving State to Files

As we saw in Chapter Two, *CGI.pm Basics*, the biggest challenge in CGI scripting is keeping track of state. Each time the remote user invokes the script, you have to arrange for the script to remember its previous state in order to preserve the illusion of continuity. Within a single session, the trick of keeping state information inside fill-out forms works quite well. However, how do you maintain this information after the user quits and restarts the browser hours or even days later?

One good technique is to store the state information in a file on the server side of the connection. Each time the user accesses the script, it writes its entire list of CGI parameters out to a file. When the user returns, it restores its state from the file.

This technique involves using two functions we have not seen before, save_parameters() and restore_parameters(). Both are included by default when you import the standard CGI function names. Save_parameters() takes a single argument; a filehandle to write the CGI parameters to. Restore_parameters() also takes a filehandle argument, but in this case it points to a file to read the state from. Here is an example of saving and restoring the state in a single block of code:

```
use CGI qw/:standard/;
open(OUT,">test.txt") || die;
save_parameters(OUT);
close OUT;

open(IN,"test.txt") || die;
restore_parameters(IN);
close IN;
```

The script first opens the file test.txt for writing, calls save_parameters() to write the current CGI parameter list into it, then closes the file. This creates a file in which the CGI name/value pairs are separated by = signs and newlines in the same format that CGI.pm expects from standard input when running from the command line. In the next section of the script, we reopen test.txt for reading and assign it to the filehandle IN. We now call restore_parameters(IN) in order to reinitialize the CGI parameter list from the contents of the file. Saving and restoring the state in immediate succession is not a particularly useful thing to do, however, it is interesting to realize that you can call restore_parameters() hours, days, or even years after the parameters were first saved, and the page will be restored to exactly the state in which the user left it.

The save_parameters() and restore_parameters() functions recognize most of the various ways that Perl programmers pass filehandles around. You can refer to filehandles as simple strings (as previously shown), use glob-references, or even use filehandle objects returned by the IO::File module, for example:

```
use CGI qw/:standard/;
open(OUT,">test.txt") || die;
save_parameters(\*OUT);  # glob ref method
close OUT;

use IO::File; # IO::Filemethod
```

```
$fh = new IO::File("test.txt");
restore_parameters($fh);
close IN;
```

**TIP**

**In addition to saving and restoring state from plain files, you can use any type of resource that can be associated with a Perl filehandle. For example, you can pass the save_parameters() function a filehandle that has been opened up on a pipe to a program that parses name=value pairs and stores them in a relational database.**

The main problem when using files to save the state of a CGI session is to correctly associate the file with the remote user. You must create a unique session key for each user, then use this session key to identify which file belongs to that user. This is not a simple task because there is no standard that automatically identifies a particular user—not his or her browser's IP address, domain name, operating system, nor brand of browser. One trick is to use access control to limit who has permission to run the script. If the user has to provide a username and password in order to access the script (or the site as a whole), then you can recover the username and use it as the basis for deriving a unique file name. Chapter Five, *Reference Guide* lists the function calls that give you the user's login name and other access control information. Another alternative is to keep the session key in a long-lived cookie, a technique discussed in the next section.

An easy way to remember the session key is to trick the remote browser into keeping track of it by hiding it in the URL. For example, consider this URL:

```
http://your.site.com/cgi-bin/graffiti.pl/726331
```

The number at the end of the script, 726331, is a randomly generated session key that has been appended to the end of the script's URL as additional path information. The script uses this key to find the right file to save and restore state from. Because the browser will use this additional path information every time it refers to the script's URL, the state will be maintained within a single browsing session—there is no need to hide the complete set of CGI parameters within fill-out forms. If you need to save state for longer, encourage the user to remember this session key, either by calling it a "user ID" and having her type it into a welcome screen, or by having her bookmark the URL.

Listing 3.1 shows a simple "graffiti" page script. It prompts the user to type a short phrase or sentence into a text field and press the button labeled "Add" as shown in Figure 3.4. The phrase is appended to a growing list and saved to a file. When the user comes back to the page (provided she has bookmarked the session key along with the URL), her list is exactly the way she left it. If the user presses "Clear," the entire list will be emptied.

**Listing 3.1 A script that saves session information in files.**

```
#!/usr/bin/perl
# script: graffiti.pl
# Keep a growing list of phrases from the user.
# CONSTANTS
$STATE_DIR = "./STATES";  # must be writable by 'nobody'
use CGI qw/:standard/;
$session_key = path_info();
$session_key =~ s|^/||;            # get rid of the initial slash
# If no valid session key has been provided, then we
# generate one, tack it on to the end of our URL as
# additional path information, and redirect the user
# to this new location.
```

```
unless (valid($session_key)) {
    $session_key = generate_session_key();
    print redirect(url() . "/$session_key");
    exit 0;
}

# pull out our current CGI state variables to prevent them from being
# overwritten when we restore our previous state.
@new_items = param('item');
$action = param('action');

fetch_old_state($session_key);

# Add the new item(s) to the old list of items
if ($action eq 'ADD') {
    @old_items = param('item');
    param('item',@old_items,@new_items);
} elsif ($action eq 'CLEAR') {
    Delete('item');
}

# Save the new list to disk
save_state($session_key);

# Now, at last, generate something for the use to look at.
print header,
      start_html("The growing list"),
      <<END;
<h1>The Growing List</h1>
Type a short phrase into the text field below.  Press <i>ADD</i>,
to append it to the history of the phrases that you've typed.  The
list is maintained on disk at the server end, so it won't get out of
```

*Continued*

**Listing 3.1 A script that saves session information in files.** ***(Continued)***

```
order if you press the "back" button.  Press <i>CLEAR</i> to clear the
list and start fresh.  Bookmark this page to come back to the list later.
END
    ;

print start_form,
      textfield(-name=>'item',-default=>'',-size=>50,-override=>1),p(),
      submit(-name=>'action',-value=>'CLEAR'),
      submit(-name=>'action',-value=>'ADD'),
      end_form,
      hr,
      h2('Current list');

if (param('item')) {
    my @items = param('item');
    print ol(li(\@items));
} else {
    print em('Empty');
}
print <<END;
<hr>
<a href="/">Home Page</a></address>
END
print end_html;

# Silly technique: we generate a session key from a random number
# generator, and keep calling until we find a unique one.
sub generate_session_key {
    my $key;
```

```
    do {
      $key = int(rand(1000000));
    } until (! -e "$STATE_DIR/$key");
    return $key;
}

# make sure the session ID passed to us is a valid one by
# looking for a numeric-only string
sub valid {
    my $key = shift;
    return $key=~/^\d+$/;
}

# Open the existing file, if any, and read the current state from it.
# We use the CGI object here, because it's straightforward to do.
# We don't check for success of the open() call, because if there is
# no file yet, the new CGI(FILEHANDLE) call will return an empty
# parameter list, which is exactly what we want.
sub fetch_old_state {
    my $session_key = shift;
    open(SAVEDSTATE,"$STATE_DIR/$session_key") || return;
    restore_parameters(SAVEDSTATE);
    close SAVEDSTATE;
}

sub save_state {
    my($session_key) = @_;
    open(SAVEDSTATE,">$STATE_DIR/$session_key") ||
          die "Failed opening session state file: $!";
    save_parameters(SAVEDSTATE);
    close SAVEDSTATE;
}
```

Figure 3.4 The graffiti page allows a user to append a series of messages to a growing disk file.

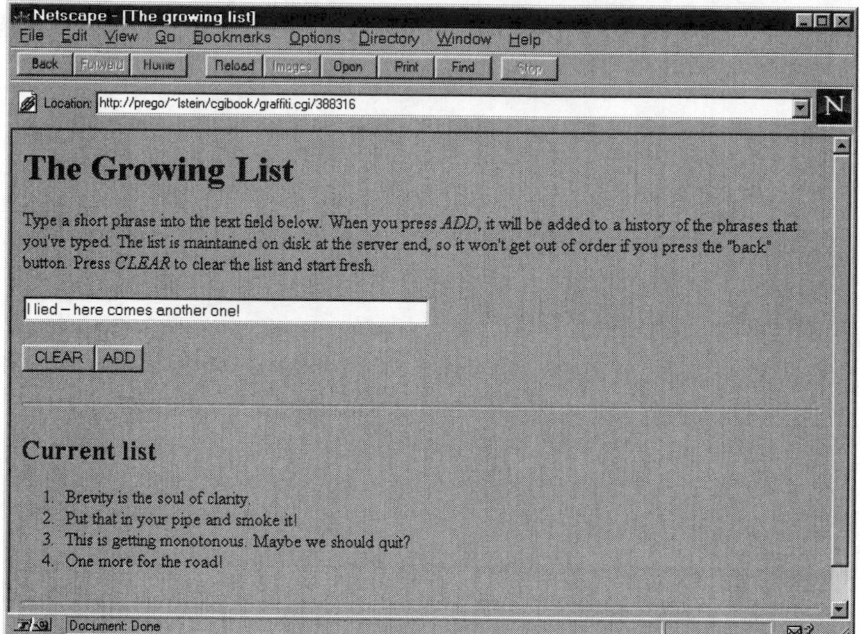


Let's walk through the script line by line to see how it works.

Line 7 defines a single constant, $STATE_DIR, which determines the directory in which to create the saved session files. In this example, we save everything to a relative directory named STATES. Most servers set the current directory to the one the CGI script is located in before executing it—if you write scripts like this one, you will want to check your server to be sure where the current directory is set. A more reliable (but less portable) solution is to refer to the directory using an absolute pathname. In either case, the STATES directory must be created before the script starts. It also must be made writable by the Web server user; otherwise, the script will be unable to create new session files. You can do this either by making the directory world writable, or by changing its ownership to match the Web server account that you are using (nobody, guest, or IUSR_*machinename*).

Lines 11 to 22 generate the unique session key. First we retrieve the additional path information, if any, and strip off the initial slash character. Now we attempt to validate the session key by calling a subroutine named valid() (defined later). Valid() will return false if the session key is either missing (which happens the first time someone tries to fetch the script) or is invalid (which might happen if someone is trying to tamper with the script.) If the session key fails to check out, we generate a new key by calling generate_session_key(), and use the returned key to send a redirect message to the browser.

If the user calls our script without the session key, as in www.yoursite.com/cgi-bin/graffiti.pl, the redirect message will cause the browser to reload the script with the session key attached, for example, www.yoursite.com/cgi-bin/graffiti.pl/726331. We fetch the script's current URL by making a call to CGI.pm's url() function, and append it, along with a slash character, to the newly generated session key (line 20). The whole thing is then passed to redirect(), which sends the correct redirect message to the browser.

Before we look at the rest of the script, let's review how the valid() and generate_session_key() subroutines work (lines 75 through 90). Valid() is extremely simple. Valid() pattern matches the session key against a string of digits. If the key contains unauthorized text (such as a relative pathname that a remote tamperer might add), it returns false.

Generate_session_key() uses Perl's rand() function to generate a series of random numbers between one and a million. For each one, it checks to see whether a file with that name already exists. If one does, it generates a new random number and tries again; otherwise, it remembers this session key and returns it.

This implementation of the generate_session_key() function may not, however, be the best way to return a session number. For one thing, the script will loop endlessly if there are already a million session files in the directory. (Performance will slow to a crawl long before a million sessions are logged because of file system limitations.) For another, there is a small chance that between the time the script chooses a session key and the time it gets around to using it, another copy of the script will have chosen the same key, causing the two to interfere with each other. There are a number of ways around these problems, including the file locking scheme discussed in the Chapter Two, *CGI.pm Basics*. The best solution will depend on the number of simultaneous users you expect, how long you expect their sessions to last, and how many old sessions you're willing to store in the file system.

Lines 24 to 28 of our script recover the current CGI parameters. There are only two fields of importance. The first is the message that the user wishes to add to the bottom of the list. This comes from a text field named item. The second is the action to take on the message list; whether to append the new item to it, or to clear it entirely. The action comes from a pair of submit buttons, both named "action," and having the values "Add" and "Delete." We recover the two fields by calling the CGI param() function and storing them into Perl variables named @new_items and $action, respectively. Although the current form only contains one field for entering new messages, we allow for multiple items in case we later decide to replace the single text field with multiple fields, or with a scrolling listbox.

Using the value of the session key, we retrieve the old state by making a call to a subroutine named fetch_old_state() (line 29). When we discuss the definition of fetch_old_state(), you will see that it has the effect of overwriting the current CGI parameters with the values of the saved parameter set. If this is a new session (that is, the state has not been saved before), this subroutine call will have no effect.

Now we need to modify the old state according to the user's instructions (lines 31 to 37). If the "Add" button was pressed, we append the new value(s) of item to the old list (line 34) and update the item parameter by calling param(). If, on the other hand, we discover that the "Clear" button was pressed, we delete the item parameter entirely from the parameter list by calling the CGI.pm Delete() function.

Line 40 writes the new state to disk by calling a subroutine named save_state().

Let's digress again from the main flow of the script by looking at the definitions for fetch_old_state() and save_state() (lines 92 through 110). Both are straightforward. In fetch_old_state() we retrieve the session key and use it to construct a file path by appending it to the directory of state files. The session key 726331 becomes a file named ./STATES/726331. We then attempt to open the file for reading. If unsuccessful (which happens if the session key is new and the file doesn't already exist), we immediately return. Otherwise, we use the filehandle to restore the CGI parameters using CGI.pm's restore_parameters() function.

Save_state() works similarly to fetch_old_state() , except that we attempt to open the file for writing. If unsuccessful (which can happen when the STATES directory doesn't exist or isn't writable by the Web server account), the script exits with an error message. Otherwise, we pass the returned filehandle to CGI.pm's save_parameters() function, which writes the current CGI parameter list to disk.

The rest is a matter of generating the fill-out form and other visible parts of the page. Lines 42 to 54 print the HTTP header and some instructions to the user. We then create the fill-out form with its text field and submit buttons (lines 55 to 59).

Next, we retrieve the current value of the CGI item parameter and turn it into an ordered list with appropriately placed calls to ol() and li(). If the parameter is empty (which happens in new sessions and after the user presses the "Clear" button), we print the message "Empty".

Last, we print footer material and close the HTML page with end_html().

The save_parameters() and restore_parameters() functions appeared in CGI.pm version 2.38. If you are having trouble calling them, you probably are running an older version. You can either upgrade by downloading a more recent version from CPAN or www.wiley.com/compbooks/stein, or use the object-oriented interface described in the next section.

# Object-Oriented Programming with CGI.pm

In all of the previous examples in this chapter and the last, we have used CGI.pm's function call interface. With this interface, you first import from CGI.pm, the set of functions you need with the Perl use operator, then call them as if they were built-in subroutines. In addition to this function-oriented interface, CGI.pm provides an object-oriented mode of operation that has several advantages over the simpler interface. The object-oriented mode allows you to use all of CGI.pm's function calls without remembering which symbol set to import. Its function calls do not contaminate your own namespace, avoiding problems that crop up when one of CGI.pm's functions conflicts with one of yours. The object-oriented interface is handy in certain complex applications that need to keep track of state over an extended period of time. Most importantly, when you use the object-oriented mode, you can extend the module's abilities by creating your own object classes derived from CGI.pm.

When you use CGI.pm in object-oriented mode, everything is done through a CGI object. The CGI object contains all the CGI parameters passed to your script, and provides methods (CGI function calls) that you use to view and manipulate the parameters.

Here is a simple example of the OO interface. The script allows the user to change the background color of the page by selecting among several radio buttons.

```
#!/usr/bin/perl
# script: customizable.pl
use CGI;
$q = new CGI;
$color = $q->param('color') || 'white';
print $q->header,
      $q->start_html({-bgcolor=>$color},'Customizable Page'),
      $q->h1('Customizable Page'),
      "Set this page's background color to:",$q->br,
      $q->start_form,
      $q->radio_group(-name=>'color',
                           -value=>['white','red','green','black',
                                'blue','silver','cyan'],
                           -cols=>2);
```

```
    $q->submit(-name=>'Set Background'),
    $q->end_form,$q->hr,
    $q->end_html;
```

This script starts by using the CGI module. In contrast to the examples we have seen before, we do not specify any function names or function sets to import. Next we create a CGI object by calling new CGI, and assign it to variable $q. All interaction with the CGI functions will now be through this object.

Using Perl's method invocation syntax, we call the param() method to recover the value of the CGI parameter color. We then create the page, using $q to call CGI.pm's header(), start_html(), h1(), start_form(), radio_group(), and other methods. The only tricky part of the script is the call to start_html(), which uses the -bgcolor attribute to set the page's background to the color of the user's choice. This attribute is only recognized by recent Netscape and Microsoft browsers—other browsers will ignore the color request.

The use of $q in all of the method calls seems repetitious and hard to read, but it does offer an advantage. You can create multiple CGI objects, and read and set their states independently. To see how you might use $q, consider the graffiti.pl script of the previous section. Because restore_parameters() overwrites the current CGI parameter list with a saved list, we had to be careful to save the current parameters in variables before invoking this function. This step is awkward and error prone. The OO interface offers a clear solution. When you create a new CGI object, you can set its state by passing it initialization information. To initialize the CGI object from a filehandle, just give it the file handle as an argument like this:

```
$q = new CGI(FILEHANDLE);
```

Using this method, the logic of the graffiti.pl script can be made much clearer. Listing 3.2 shows the modified script.

**Listing 3.2 The graffiti script using CGI.pm's object-oriented interface.**

```
#!/usr/bin/perl

# script: graffiti2.pl

# Keep a growing list of phrases from the user.

# CONSTANTS
$STATE_DIR = "./STATES";  # must be writable by 'nobody'

use CGI;
$q = new CGI;
$session_key = $q->path_info();
$session_key =~ s|^/||;             # get rid of the initial slash

# If no valid session key has been provided, then we
# generate one, tack it on to the end of our URL as
# additional path information, and redirect the user
# to this new location.
unless (valid($session_key)) {
    $session_key = generate_session_key();
    print $q->redirect($q->url() . "/$session_key");
    exit 0;
}

$old = fetch_old_state($session_key);

# Add the new item(s) to the old list of items
if ($q->param('action') eq 'ADD') {
    $q->param(-name=>'item',
              -value=>[$old->param('item'),$q->param('item')]);
```

```
} elsif ($action eq 'CLEAR') {
    $q->Delete('item');
}

# Save the new list to disk
save_state($session_key,$q);

# Now, at last, generate something for the use to look at.
print $q->header,
      $q->start_html("The growing list"),
      <<END;
<h1>The Growing List</h1>
END
print $q->start_form,
      $q->textfield(-name=>'item',-default=>'',
                    -size=>50,-override=>1),$q->p,
      $q->submit(-name=>'action',-value=>'CLEAR'),
      $q->submit(-name=>'action',-value=>'ADD'),
      $q->end_form,
      $q->hr,
      $q->h2('Current list');

if ($q->param('item')) {
    my @items = $q->param('item');
    print $q->ol($q->li(\@items));
} else {
    print em('Empty');
}
print <<END;
<hr>
<a href="/">Home Page</a></address>
```

*Continued*

**Listing 3.2 The graffiti script using CGI.pm's object-oriented interface.** ***(Continued)***

```
END
print $q->end_html;

# Silly technique: we generate a session key from a random number
# generator, and keep calling until we find a unique one.
sub generate_session_key {
    my $key;
    do {
      $key = int(rand(1000000));
    } until (! -e "$STATE_DIR/$key");
    return $key;
}

# make sure the session ID passed to us is a valid one by
# looking for a numeric-only string
sub valid {
    my $key = shift;
    return $key=~/^\d+$/;
}

# Open the existing file, if any, and read the current state from it.
# We use the CGI object here, because it's straightforward to do.
# We don't check for success of the open() call, because if there is
# no file yet, the new CGI(FILEHANDLE) call will return an empty
# parameter list, which is exactly what we want.
sub fetch_old_state {
    my $session_key = shift;
    open(SAVEDSTATE,"$STATE_DIR/$session_key") || return;
    my $cgi = new CGI(SAVEDSTATE);
```

```
90       close SAVEDSTATE;
91       return $cgi;
92 }
93
94 sub save_state {
95       my($session_key,$q) = @_;
96       open(SAVEDSTATE,">$STATE_DIR/$session_key") ||
97            die "Failed opening session state file: $!";
98       $q->save(SAVEDSTATE);
99       close SAVEDSTATE;
100 }
```

The main thing to notice about the modified script is that instead of calling save_parameters() and restore_parameters(), we create two CGI objects. The first object is created towards the top of the script, at line 10. Because it is called without any arguments, it initializes itself from the current CGI parameters passed to the script from the browser. This object is assigned to the variable `$q`. The second object is created within the subroutine fetch_old_state() (lines 86 to 92) where we initialize a CGI object from a filehandle opened on the user's previously created session file. This object is assigned to variable `$old`. We can now manipulate `$q` and `$old` independently, using the value of the item parameter stored in `$old` to modify the current parameter of the same name (line 28). Later, we write out the contents of the modified parameter list to the user's session file by calling the CGI.pm save() method (line 98). Notice that when using the OO interface you can use the shorter (and easier to remember) save() function rather than save_parameters(). The reason for this is historical.

While we're on the topic of CGI object initialization, it's worth pointing out the alternate ways of creating a CGI object that is preinitialized to the state you want for testing or to establish defaults. You can pass the CGI object a URL-style initialization string like this one:

```
$q = new CGI("first_name=Harriet&last_name=Vane");
```

Alternatively, you can initialize a CGI object from a reference to an associative array like this:

```
$q = new CGI({first_name=>'Harriet',last_name=>'Vane'});
```

If you want to initialize a CGI object to have a multivalued parameter, just use a list reference as done elsewhere in the module, for example:

```
$q = new CGI({first_name=>'Harriet',last_name=>'Vane',
            talents=>['sleuthing','writing','dancing']});
```

There is currently no way to initialize (clone) one CGI object from another, but perhaps this feature will appear in a future version of the CGI library.

The save() and new() methods were designed so that you could save a whole series of CGI objects to a file, then restore them later. Consider this bit of code:

```
$a = new CGI({first_name=>'Harriet',last_name=>'Vane'});
$b = new CGI({first_name=>'Peter',last_name=>'Whimsey'});
$c = new CGI({first_name=>'Hercule',last_name=>'Poirot'});
open (OUT,">./detectives.out");
$a->save(OUT);
$b->save(OUT);
$c->save(OUT);
close OUT;
```

In this example, we first create three CGI objects, then save them, one after the other, to a file. At a later date, we can retrieve them all with the following bit of code:

```
open (IN,"./detectives.out");
while (!eof(IN)) {
```

```
        push(@detectives,new CGI(IN));
}
close IN;
```

At the end of this snippet, the array @detectives will contain three CGI objects, each corresponding to one of the objects that was saved previously.

It is possible to mix the function and object-oriented styles in a single script. The key to doing this successfully is to realize that internally, CGI.pm creates a global CGI object called $CGI::Q the first time you access one of its functions in a function-oriented manner. For example:

```
use CGI qw/:standard/;
if (param('save') eq 'TRUE') {
      open(OUT,'./output.txt') || die $!;
      $CGI::Q->save(OUT);
}
```

You have to be careful with this, because the $CGI::Q object only springs into existence when it is needed. Certain functions, such as those that generate HTML shortcuts, do not create $CGI::Q. Other functions, including any that need access to the parameter list, such as functions that generate fill-out form elements, do cause $CGI::Q to be created. To be safe, call param() at least once before trying to access the global CGI object.

As a parting note, there's no reason not to use the object-oriented and function-oriented styles in the same script. You can call HTML shortcuts as functions, but use CGI objects to fetch and manipulate the CGI parameters.

## Importing All Parameters into a Namespace

If you find it annoying to have to call param() or $q->param() every time you want to get access to one of the CGI parameters, CGI.pm gives you a way to turn all the named parameters into Perl variables in a single step. This trick uses the import_names() function. Call import_names() with the name of a namespace to import to; in turn, CGI.pm will run through the list of CGI parameters and create a Perl variable for each one using a name that is similar to the parameter name. The following code fragment gives the general idea of how to use this:

```
#!/usr/bin/perl
use CGI qw/:standard/;
import_names('IN');
print header('text/plain');
print "First name = $IN::first_name\n";
print "Last name = $IN::last_name\n";
print "\nTalents include:\n";
foreach $talent (@IN::talents) {
      print "\t$talent\n";
}
```

This code fragment assumes that the CGI parameters will include single-valued fields named first_name and last_name, and a multivalued field named talents. The example starts by importing the standard set of functions from CGI.pm in the usual way. It then calls import_names() to import the parameter list into the Perl namespace named IN (this namespace need not be previously defined). The script is now free to use the fields as variables. The single-valued fields become scalar variables named $IN::first_name and $IN::last_name. The multivalued field is turned into an array named @IN::talents. These variables can now be used just like any other Perl variable.

Why is it necessary to provide a namespace to import to? Although it would seem natural to have import_names() create variables directly in the main namespace, this has several undesirable side effects. The most serious is the possibility that a remote user could define CGI parameters named INC, PERLLIB, ARGV, or one of the other globals that have special significance to Perl. This might cause the Perl script to crash or behave unpredictably. In order to avoid this possibility, CGI.pm forces you to import parameter names into a separate, safe namespace. If you try to import into the main namespace, CGI.pm will exit with an error.

---

**TIP**

**CGI parameter names can contain spaces and other characters that are not legal in Perl variable names. In such cases, the unusual characters are converted into underscores. For example, a CGI parameter named "last name" is converted into Perl variable $IN::last_name. Be careful not to be caught unaware by this conversion. If you have two CGI parameters, one called "last name" and the other called "last-name" they will both be converted into $IN::last_name, probably not what you expect.**

---

# Using Cookies to Maintain State

The graffiti script that we covered in previous sections shows how you can store information on the server side of the connection to maintain the state of a CGI script over an extended period of time. The main problem with this technique, however, is that it has to play tricks with the URL in order to associate a particular user with a particular CGI session. Unless the user bookmarks the URL with its session key attached, the script will forget the user's identity the next time she connects. This section shows how you can use HTTP cookies to solve this problem.

What is a cookie? A cookie is an idea that Netscape devised for the Navigator 1.1 release. A cookie is a name=value pair much like the named parameters used in the CGI parameter list. When a Web server or CGI script wants to save some state information, it creates a cookie or two and sends them to the browser within the HTTP header. The browser tracks all of the cookies sent to it by a particular server and stores them in an on-disk database so that the cookies persist even when the browser is closed and reopened later. The next time the browser connects to a Web site, it searches its database for all cookies that belong to that server and transmits them back to the server within the HTTP header.

Cookies can be transient, meaning they disappear as soon as the user quits the browser, or they can be persistent, in that they are stored in a small database on the user's machine for a period of time ranging from hours to years. A cookie can be made to be site-wide so that it is transmitted to every URL on your site, or it can be restricted to a site subdirectory. You can also set a flag in the cookie, transmitting it over the Internet only when the browser and server are communicating by a secure protocol such as Secure Sockets Layer (SSL). You can also create promiscuous cookies that are sent to every server in a particular Internet domain.

The idea is simple but powerful. If a CGI script needs to save a small amount of state information, such as the user's preferred background color, then it can store it directly in a cookie. Larger quantities of state information can be stored as a record in a database on the server side, and the cookie used to record a session key or user ID that identifies the record. Although the idea originated with Netscape, other browser vendors have implemented cookies, which are now on their way to becoming a part of the HTTP standard.

The CGI.pm library makes it simple to create a cookie. Consider this short example:

```
#!/usr/bin/perl
use CGI qw(:standard);
$cookie1=cookie(-name=>'regular',
                -value=>'chocolate chip');
$cookie2=cookie(-name=>'high fiber',
                -value=>'cinnamon oatmeal raisin');
print header(-cookie=>[$cookie1,$cookie2]);
```

The first line of this code loads the CGI library and imports the standard set of function calls. The next lines create two new cookies using the CGI cookie() function. The required parameters for this method call are -name, for the cookie's name, and -value for its value. The last step is to incorporate the cookies into the document's HTTP header. We do this by printing out the results of the header() method, passing it a -cookie argument and an array reference containing the two cookies.

When we run this script from the command line, the result is an HTTP header that looks like this:

```
Set-cookie: regular=chocolate%20chip
Set-cookie: high%20fiber=cinnamon%20oatmeal%20raisin
Content-type: text/html
```

CGI.pm performs some character escaping on the contents of the cookie. The Netscape cookie specification disallows whitespace and certain other characters, such as the semicolon. (It also places an upper limit of a few kilobytes on the size of a cookie, so do not try to store large amounts of information in one.) When the browser sees these two cookies it ferrets them and then returns them the next time the script needs a document from your server.

To retrieve the value of a cookie sent to you by the browser, use cookie() without providing a -value argument, for example:

```
#!/usr/local/bin/perl
use CGI qw(:standard);
$regular=cookie('regular');
$high_fiber=cookie('high fiber');
print header(-type=>'text/plain'),
      "The regular cookie is $regular.\n",
      "The high fiber cookie is $high_fiber.";
```

In this example, the third and fourth lines retrieve the two cookies by name. We then print out an HTTP header (containing no cookie this time) and two lines of text giving the cookie values. The output of this script, when viewed in a browser, would be

```
The regular cookie is chocolate chip.
The high fiber cookie is cinnamon oatmeal raisin.
```

The cookie() function is fairly flexible. You can save whole Perl arrays as cookies by giving the -value parameter an array reference, for example:

```
$c = cookie(-name=>'specials',
            -value=>['oatmeal','chocolate chip','alfalfa']);
```

Or you can save and restore entire associative arrays by providing cookie() with an associative array reference like:

```
$c = cookie(-name=>'prices',
            -value=>{'oatmeal'=>'$0.50',
                     'chocolate_chip'=>'$1.25',
                     'alfalfa'=>'free'});
```

Later, your script can recover the cookies returned to the script by the browser by asking for them by name with the cookie() function:

```
@specials = cookie('specials');
%prices   = cookie('prices');
```

Like param(), calling cookie() without any arguments returns the names of all the cookies available to your script, irrespective of whether they were originally generated by this script or by another CGI script at your site.

By default, browsers will remember the cookies that you pass to them only until they exit, and will only send the cookie out to scripts with a URL path that is similar to the script that generated it. If you want browsers to remember the cookie for an extended period of time, give cookie() an -expires argument. To adjust the URL path over which the browser returns the cookie to scripts at your site, use the -path argument:

```
$c = cookie(-name=>'regular',
            -value=>'chocolate chip',
            -path=>'/cgi-bin/bakery',
            -expires=>'+3d');
```

This cookie will expire in three days (+3d). You could use +3M to expire the cookie in three months, +3y to expire in three years, or +3h to expire in three hours. The -path parameter tells the browser to send the cookie to every script located in the /cgi-bin/bakery directory. Other cookie() parameters allow you to adjust the domain names and URL paths that trigger the browser to send a cookie, and to turn on cookie secure mode (see Chapter Five, *Reference Guide*, for details).

---

**TIP**

**Although giving cookie() a negative expiration time, as in "-3d", would seem to be nonsensical, it actually serves a useful purpose. It tells the browser to immediately delete any stored cookies by that name.**

---

Listing 3.3 gives the full code for a CGI script called configure.pl. When you call this script's URL you are presented with the fill-out form shown in Figure 3.5. You can change the page's background color, the text size and color, and even customize it with your name. The next time you visit this page (even if you have closed the browser and return to the page weeks later), it will remember all of these values and build a page based on them.

This script recognizes four CGI parameters used to change the current configuration:

| | |
|---|---|
| *background* | Set the background color to the indicated value |
| *text* | Set the text color to the indicated value |
| *size* | Set the size to the indicated value (1 to 7) |
| *name* | Set the username to the indicated value |

Usually these parameters are sent to the script by submitting the fill-out form that it generates, but you could set them from within a URL this way:

```
/cgi-bin/configure.pl?background=silver&text=blue&name=Lincoln
```

Figure 3.5 The configure.pl script uses cookies to customize pages over a long period of time.

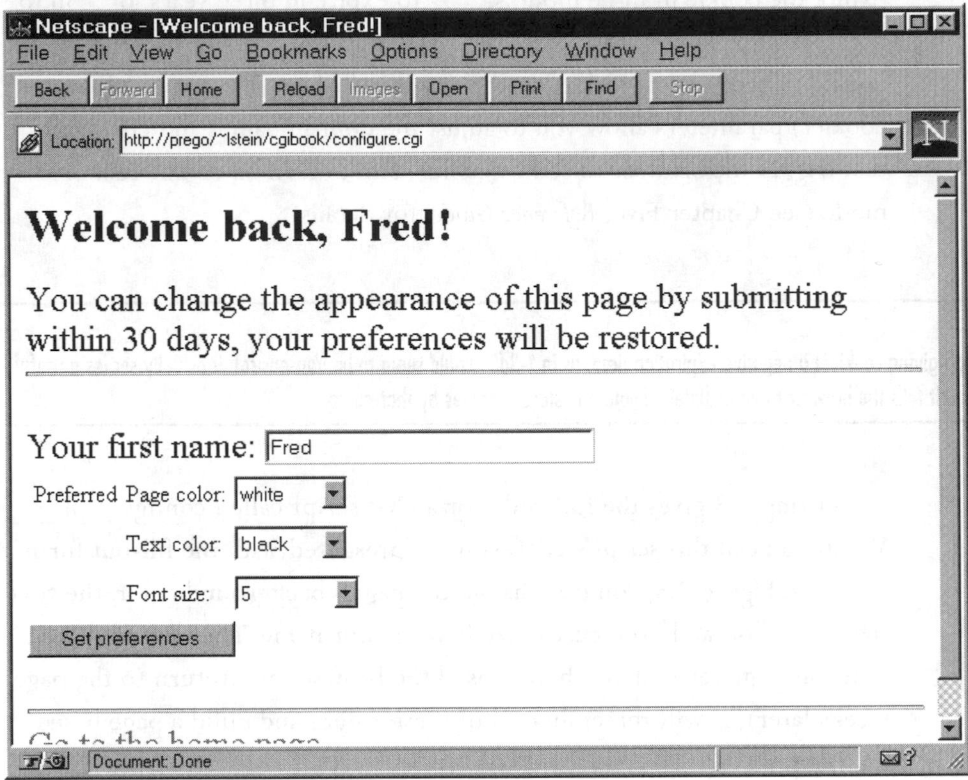


Listing 3.3 Saving user preferences with cookies.

```
#!/usr/bin/perl

use CGI qw(:standard :html3);

# Some constants to use in our form.
@colors=qw/aqua black blue fuschia gray green lime maroon navy olive
    purple red silver teal white yellow/;
@sizes=("<default>",1..7);

# recover the "preferences" cookie.
```

```
%preferences = cookie('preferences');

# If the user wants to change the background color or her
# name, they will appear among our CGI parameters.
foreach ('text','background','name','size') {
    $preferences{$_} = param($_) || $preferences{$_};
}

# Set some defaults
$preferences{'background'} = $preferences{'background'} || 'silver';
$preferences{'text'} = $preferences{'text'} || 'black';

# Refresh the cookie so that it doesn't expire.
$the_cookie = cookie(-name=>'preferences',
                    -value=>\%preferences,
                    -path=>'/',
                    -expires=>'+30d');
print header(-cookie=>$the_cookie);

# Adjust the title to incorporate the user's name, if provided.
$title = $preferences{'name'} ?
    "Welcome back, $preferences{name}!" : "Customizable Page";

# Create the HTML page.  We use several of the HTML 3.2
# extended tags to control the background color and the
# font size.  It's safe to use these features because
# cookies don't work anywhere else anyway.
print start_html(-title=>$title,
                -bgcolor=>$preferences{'background'},
                -text=>$preferences{'text'}
        );

```

*Continued*

**Listing 3.3 Saving user preferences with cookies.** ***(Continued)***

```
print basefont({-size=>$preferences{size}}) if $preferences{'size'} > 0;

print h1($title),<<END;
You can change the appearance of this page by submitting
the fill-out form below.  If you return to this page any time
within 30 days, your preferences will be restored.
END
    ;

# Create the form
print hr,
    start_form,

    "Your first name: ",
    textfield(-name=>'name',
              -default=>$preferences{'name'},
              -size=>30),br,

    table(
    TR(
       td("Preferred"),
       td("Page color:"),
       td(popup_menu(-name=>'background',
                     -values=>\@colors,
                     -default=>$preferences{'background'})
                     ),
           ),
    TR(
       td(''),
       td("Text color:"),
```

```
72          td(popup_menu(-name=>'text',
73                        -values=>\@colors,
74                        -default=>$preferences{'text'})
75          )
76       ),
77       TR(
78          td(''),
79          td("Font size:"),
80          td(popup_menu(-name=>'size',
81                        -values=>\@sizes,
82                        -default=>$preferences{'size'})
83             )
84          )
85       ),
86
87       submit(-label=>'Set preferences'),
88       end_form,
89       hr;
90
91  print a({HREF=>"/"},'Go to the home page');
```

Let's walk through the code. Line 2 imports the CGI library, bringing in both the standard method calls and a number of methods that generate HTML3-specific tags. Next we define a set of background colors and sizes.

Line 10 is where we recover the user's previous preferences, if any. We use the cookie() method to fetch a cookie named preferences, and store its value into a like-named associative array.

In lines 14 to 16, we fetch the CGI parameters named text, background, name, and size. If any of them are set, it indicates that the user wants to change the corresponding value saved in her browser's cookie. We stuff the changed parameters into the %preferences associative array, overwriting the original values, if any.

Lines 19 and 20 set the text and background colors to reasonable defaults if they can not be found in either the cookie or the CGI script parameters.

Lines 23 to 27 generate the page's HTTP header. First we create the cookie containing the user's preferences using the cookie() method. We set the expiration date for the cookie for 30 days in the future so that the cookie will be removed from the browser's database if the user does not return to this page within that length of time. We also set the optional -path argument to /. This makes the cookie valid over our entire site so that it is transmitted to every URL the browser fetches. Although we do not take advantage of this yet, it is useful later if we decide that these preferences are going to have a site-wide effect. Lastly, we emit the HTTP header with the -cookie parameter set.

In lines 33 through 42, we start the HTML page. True to the intent of making this a personalizable page, we base the page title on the user's name. If it is set, the title and level-1 header are made to read "Welcome back name!" Otherwise, the title is an impersonal "Customizable page." Line 37 calls the start_html() method to create the top part of the HTML page. It sets the title, the background color, and the text color based on the values in the %preferences array. Line 42 sets the text size by calling the basefont() function. This generates a <BASEFONT> HTML tag, used by HTML 3.2 and higher to set the default size of the page font.

Lines 44 through the end of the listing generate the content of the page. There is a brief introduction to the page, followed by the fill-out form used to change the settings. As in previous examples, we use table() to embed the form elements in an HTML table, forcing them to line up nicely.

On a real site you would want the user's preferences to affect all pages, not just a single one. Fortunately, this is not a major undertaking. Many modern Web servers now allow you to designate a script that will preprocess all files of a certain type. You can create a variation on the script shown here that takes an HTML document and inserts the appropriate <BASEFONT> and <BODY> tags based on the cookie preferences. Now you configure the server to pass all HTML documents through this script to affect all pages. You can use the tm.pl script from the previous chapter (which added the registered trademark symbol to static HTML pages) as the starting point for this script.

# File Uploads

Netscape Navigator (versions 2.0 and up) and Microsoft Internet Explorer (version 4.0, or 3.X versions with a patch installed) have the ability to upload files from the user's local disk to your CGI script. You can read the contents of the uploaded file, save a copy of it to the server's disk, or process the file in some way.

In order to use file uploads, you must do three things:

1. Use start_multipart_form() to create a fill-out form.
2. Include a filefield() input element in the form.
3. Read the contents of the uploaded file from a filehandle provided by the param() function.

For obscure reasons relating to the evolution of the MIME and HTTP specifications, there are two formats that a browser can use to send the contents of a fill-out field to a Web server. It can use the original application/x-www-form-urlencoded format, or the newer multipart/form-data format. The familiar start_form() function produces an HTML tag that tells the browser to submit form contents with the original format. The start_multipart_form() function causes the browser to use the newer format. In most circumstances there is no functional difference between the two, and all things being equal, it is best to use the older format because it guarantees compatibility with even ancient browsers. However, file uploads are only supported by the multipart/form-data format, so if you are going to use file uploads, you must remember to call start_multipart_form() instead of start_form().

After starting the form, you must create a field to capture the name and path of the uploaded file. You do this with filefield(). This fragment of code produces the page shown in Figure 3.6. On Windows95/NT systems, upload fields appear as a short text input area where the user can type the path of the file she wishes to upload. There is also a button that brings up a file browser for the user's convenience. Upload fields look slightly different on other operating systems.

```
print start_multipart_form,
      filefield(-name=>'upload',-size=>60),br,
      submit(-label=>'Upload File'),
 end_form;
```

The filefield() function takes all the arguments of the more familiar textfield() function, including -name to set the CGI parameter's name, and -size to set its width. Unlike text fields, however, it is impossible to set a default value for a file upload field. This is because of concerns that malicious Webmasters could fool unsuspecting users into uploading private or security-sensitive files to a remote system. For this reason, file fields are not sticky in the way that other form elements are.

A single fill-out form can contain one or several file upload fields, allowing users to send multiple files at the same time. The main restriction is that each upload field must have a unique name.

Once the file is uploaded, your script can access it in various ways using param(). Param(), called with the name of the file upload field, will return the contents of the upload field. If you treat the returned value as a string, it will contain the name of the uploaded field (which might be a simple filename, or the complete path of the file on the user's computer, depending on the browser implementation). If you treat the returned value as a filehandle,

Figure 3.6 This fill-out form contains a single file upload field.

you can read the contents of the file. You can also use this value to return other information about the file, such as its MIME type.

Listing 3.4 shows a simple but complete example that illustrates how this uploading works. Figure 3.7 displays the screenshot for this example.

This script starts out by bringing in the CGI library and printing HTTP and HTML headers. It then examines the current CGI parameters by calling param(). If no parameters are present, it calls print_form() to prompt the user to upload a file. This subroutine (defined in lines 10 through 15) uses start_multipart_form() and filefield() to produce the same fill-out form we discussed earlier.

If CGI parameters are available, then this script is invoked when the user submits the form, so we call the subroutine print_results() (lines 17 to 31). This subroutine attempts to retrieve the contents of the upload field by calling param() with the field's name. If there is nothing there, param() will return an undefined value and exit with an error message; otherwise, we print out some information on the file. First we print its name by treating the field contents like an ordinary string (line 24). Next we retrieve its MIME type by calling the function uploadInfo() with the filename. This function returns an associative array containing certain information that the browser transmits along with the file (in a format similar to e-mail headers). Currently, the only information that browsers send is the file's MIME type, in the field Content-Type. In the future, you may be able to learn the document's language by looking for a field named Content-Language.

Lastly, we read the file's contents (lines 27 to 29). By treating the value returned by param() as a filehandle, we can read it line by line using the Perl angle brackets operator <>. For each line we retrieve, we calculate its length using strlen() and increment a variable. When we reach the end of the file, we print out the total calculated length and exit. We can confirm that the entire file was transferred successfully by comparing the length calculated by the script with the true length of the file on the local disk.

**Listing 3.4 A CGI script to calculate the length of an uploaded file.**

```
#!/usr/bin/perl
use CGI qw/:standard/;
print header,
    start_html('file upload'),
    h1('file upload');
print_form()     unless param;
print_results() if param;
print end_html;

sub print_form {
    print start_multipart_form(),
        filefield(-name=>'upload',-size=>60),br,
        submit(-label=>'Upload File'),
        end_form;
}

sub print_results {
    my $length;
    my $file = param('upload');
    if (!$file) {
        print "No file uploaded.";
        return;
    }
    print h2('File name'),$file;
    print h2('File MIME type'),
    uploadInfo($file)->{'Content-Type'};
    while (<$file>) {
        $length += length($_);
   }
    print h2('File length'),$length;
}
```

Figure 3.7 This script calculates the length of uploaded files.

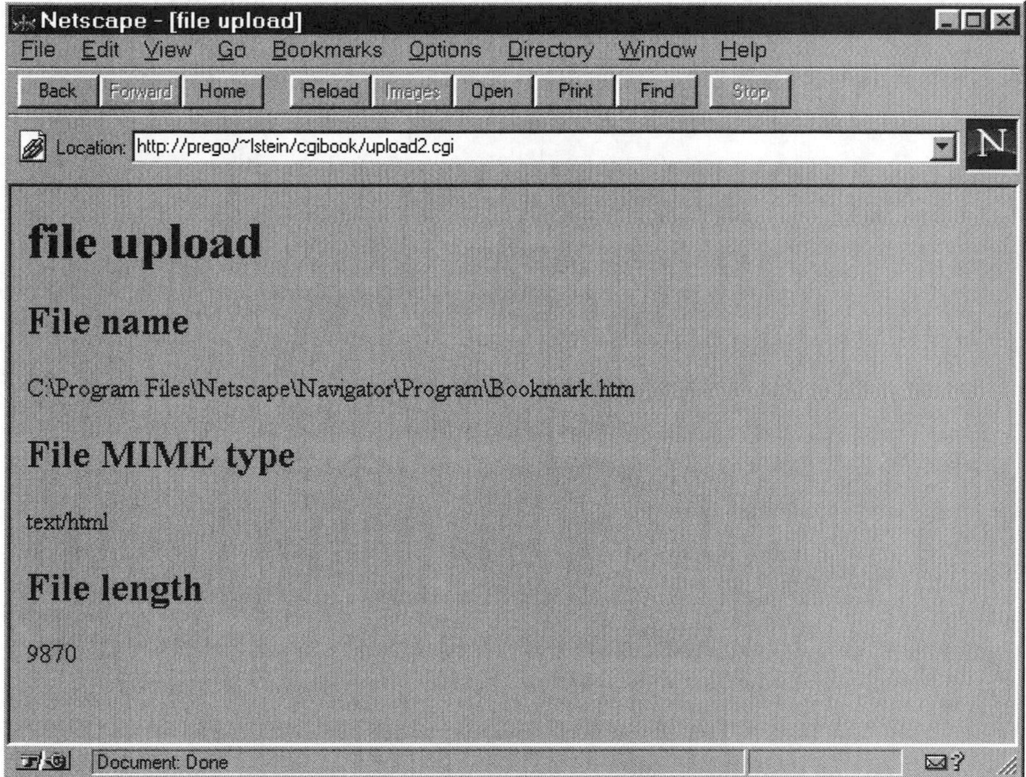


This script does not do anything with the file besides determine its size. In a real script, you would probably want to save it for safekeeping. To save this script, follow the model of the following code fragment:

```
$file = param('upload');
open (SAVE,">./saved_file_23.out") || die $!;
while (<$file>) {
   print SAVE $_;
}
close SAVE;
```

There is, however, a problem with this code fragment. Because angle brackets read files in a line-oriented fashion, they will not work well for nontext files such as images and executables. For this type of file, you should use the lower-level read() function. This code fragment will read the uploaded file in 1024 byte chunks and copy them to another file. It is guaranteed to work with all types of files, binary and text alike:

```
$file = param('upload');
open (SAVE,">./saved_file.out") || die $!;
while (read($file,$data,1024)) {
     print SAVE $data;
}
close SAVE;
```

In some cases, you may depend on a file being of a certain type. In this case, it is a good idea to check the uploaded file's MIME type before trying to process it. This code fragment will check that the file is one of the text types, such as text/plain or text/HTML:

```
$file = param('upload');
$type = uploadInfo($file)->{'Content-Type'};
unless ($type=~m|^text/|) {
   print "Uploaded file not a text file!";
   return;
}
```

Internally, CGI.pm spools each uploaded file to a temporary directory on the Web server machine, and returns to your script a filehandle opened on the temporary file. After your script exits, this temporary file is automatically deleted. It is possible to directly access this file in order to rename it or move it to a new location entirely, in order to prevent it from being deleted automatically. To get the name of the temporary file, call tmpFileName() with the contents of the file upload field, for example:

```
$file = param('upload');
$tmpfile = tmpFileName($file);
rename $tmpfile,"./saved_file.out";
```

**TIP**

**Try to avoid accessing the uploaded temporary file directly. This can interfere with some of CGI.pm's security features, and is not guaranteed to be compatible with future versions of the library.**

## FILE UPLOADS AND SERVER SECURITY

File uploads present certain security issues for a Web server because they allow remote users to create files on the server host machine. One potential problem is that a malicious user can use the file upload feature to force a script to accept an uploaded file hundreds of megabytes in length, causing the server's disk to fill up. (The large file will be deleted automatically when the script exits, but there may be problems until that happens.) Your script does not have to create a fill-out form with an upload field in order to be taken advantage of, because the remote user can invoke your script from a form she created herself.

Another potential problem is that the temporary files created by different CGI scripts are visible to each other. If a Web server supports multiple CGI script authors who don't trust each other, it is possible for one author to access the temporary files created by another author's CGI scripts.

CGI.pm has several configuration variables that allow you to protect against this kind of abuse. Because they restrict and/or disable certain features, they are not activated by default. To activate these features, you will need to open up the CGI.pm source code file with a text editor, and make the indicated changes. You will find all the relevant variables towards the top of the file in a subroutine named initialize_globals():

- $DISABLE_UPLOADS = 0;
  Change this to a true value in order to disable file uploads entirely.

- $POST_MAX = -1;
  This controls how many bytes a user is allowed to upload. Leave it at a negative value to allow unlimited uploads, or set it to a positive value to limit uploads to a certain number of bytes. The byte total applies to the total size of all uploaded files, plus the size of all other form fields. This prevents a malicious user from attacking your script by pasting the collected works of William Shakespeare into a text field.

- $PRIVATE_TEMPFILES = 0;
  If this variable is set to a true value, all temporary files created by a script are private. Other CGI scripts will be unable to access them. CGI.pm does this by creating the file, opening a file handle on it, then immediately deleting the file. This makes the file inaccessible to other processes, while allowing your script to continue to access it. Unfortunately, because of the differences between Windows and UNIX file systems, this technique does not currently work correctly on Windows95 and NT hosts. If you enable this feature, you will be unable to use tmpFileName() to access the temporary file directly.

If you enable these restrictions, you can always disable them selectively for those scripts that really need access to the features. For example, if you have disabled file uploads globally, you can turn them on temporarily by resetting the variable within your script, for example:

```
#!/usr/bin/perl
use CGI qw/:standard/;

# reactivate file uploads
$CGI::DISABLE_UPLOADS = 0;
```

This script will now be able to process uploaded files. Other scripts at the site will not be able to accept uploads unless they too explicitly reset the $DISABLE_UPLOADS variable.

If you are at all security conscious, there are several other precautions you should take to avoid inadvertently introducing security holes in your CGI scripts. A good discussion can be found in the "perlsec" manual page that comes with the Perl 5.003 and 5.004 distributions. For an extensive treatment of the subject, see *Web Security: A Step-by-Step Reference Guide*, by Lincoln Stein (Addison-Wesley, 1998).

# Fancy HTTP Headers

The HTTP header is used to send information about the document to the browser. It is usually not very interesting; it contains the document's MIME type and little else. However, if you are familiar with the HTTP protocol, you can manipulate the header in various ways to achieve interesting effects.

## THE STATUS CODE

One of the more useful features of the HTTP header is the status code, a numeric value that tells the browser what the status of its request is. The usual status code is 200, indicating that everything is OK and that the browser should expect a document to follow. Other status codes include: 301 (Moved), used to redirect the browser to a different URL (this status code is used internally by CGI.pm for the redirect() method); 403 (Forbidden), used to tell the browser that it is not allowed to view the requested URL; 401 (Unauthorized), used to tell the browser that it must provide password information to obtain the URL; and 502 (Service Overloaded), generated by servers when they are processing too many requests and can not service a new one.

By default, the CGI.pm header() function produces a status code of 200. If you wish, you can change the status code by providing a -status argument.

The value of this argument should be a numeric code, optionally followed by a human-readable content. For example, here is how to emit a "Service Overloaded" code:

```
print header(-status=>'502 Service Overloaded',
             -type=>'text/plain'),
      "Sorry, but no one can come to the phone right now. ",
      "Please try again later.";
```

To see how you might use this in real life, consider a site that does routine system maintenance between the hours of 2 and 3 o'clock on Sunday afternoons. This site might want to make the Web server unavailable to anyone outside its local domain during this period of time. Rather than shutting down the server completely, which will make it unavailable locally, the administrators funnel all page requests through a single CGI script named "gate". During the system maintenance period, gate returns a 403 (Forbidden) error, with a message explaining the problem. At all other times, gate returns the requested document. Listing 3.5 gives the source code for gate. See Figure 3.8 for a screenshot of this script at work.

Gate starts by fetching the local time in an array context, returning the time broken out into bite-sized units (line 5). Next it checks to see if access is currently forbidden. If the weekday is zero (Sunday), the hour is between 2 and 3 P.M. (using 24 hour military time), and the remote host is not in the local domain oursite.com, then access is forbidden. In this case, we print out a header with the 403 status and an explanatory message; otherwise, we use the URL's additional path information to determine the file to fetch. We then open the file and send it.

In order for gate to work correctly, all access to the site must be through URLs that look like this:

```
http://www.oursite.com/cgi-bin/gate/docs/document.html
```

**Listing 3.5 The gate script.**

```
#!/usr/bin/perl
use CGI qw/:standard/;
use CGI::Carp 'fatalsToBrowser';
# script: gate
($sec,$min,$hour,$mday,$mon,$year,$wday) = localtime;
$forbidden = $wday == 0 &&
              $hour >= 14 && $hour <= 15 &&
              remote_host()!~/\.oursite\.com$/;

if ($forbidden) {
   print header(-status=>'403 Forbidden'),
          start_html('Down for System Maintenance'),
          h1('Down for System Maintenance'),
         "The system is down between the hours of 2 and ",
         "3 PM on Sundays.  Please try back later.",
         end_html;
  exit 0;
}

open(FILE,path_translated()) ||
           die "Couldn't open ",path_info(),": $!\n";
print header;
while (<FILE>) {
   print $_;
}
close FILE;
```

To prevent the user from bypassing the script entirely and going directly to the document, you will have to put the site's HTML documents under access control. A simpler solution is offered by Web servers like Apache, which allow you to configure the server to perform string substitutions on

Figure 3.8 The gate script prevents access to files at certain times of the week.

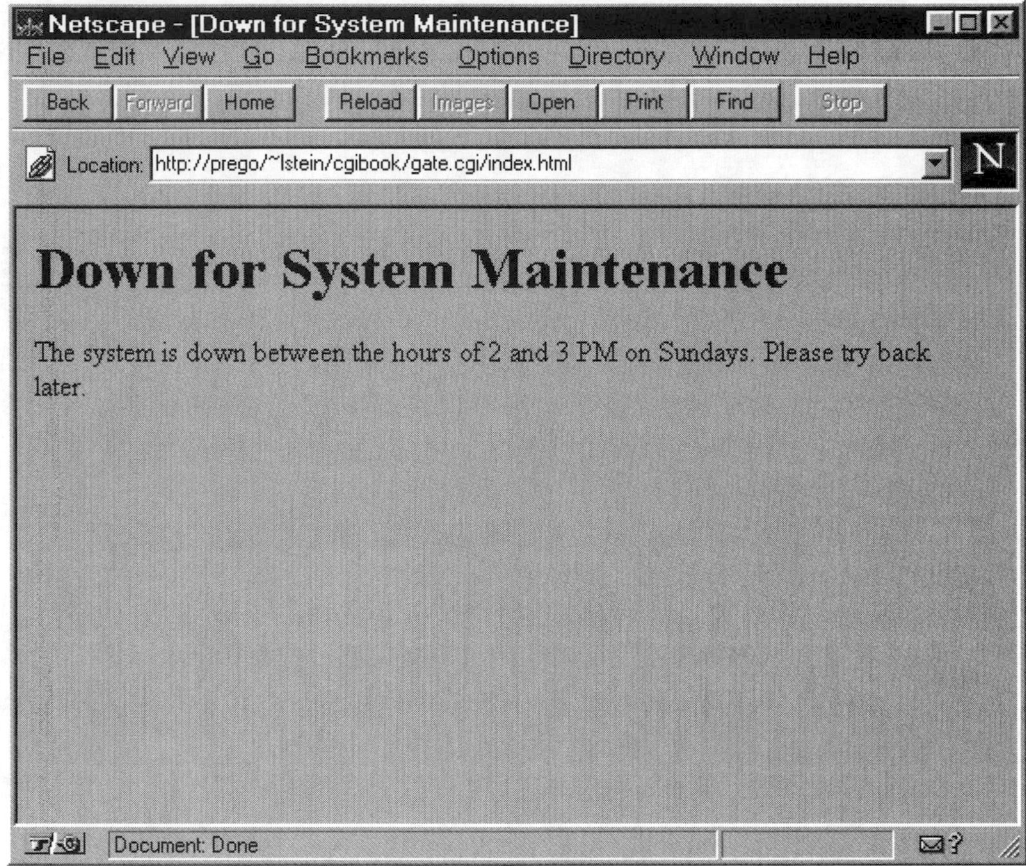


URLs on the fly. If you have such a server, you can use this facility to automatically change requests for /docs/document.html into requests for /cgi-bin/gate/docs/document.html, completely shielding the existence of the script from the remote user's eyes.

## CONTROLLING CACHING

Part of a modern Web browser's job is to speed up the user's Web surfing by caching frequently requested documents locally. When a user returns to a page she previously visited, the browser will return a copy from the local cache, provided that there is a recent copy of the document to be found there.

Pages generated by CGI scripts are usually not cached because they are expected to change dynamically. In most cases, this is what you want to happen, but occasionally, you would like different behavior. A case in point is the gate script presented in Listing 3.5. Even though the script is only serving static HTML files, the browser will refuse to cache the documents because they appear to be originating within a script. In other cases, some browsers may not realize that they are communicating with a script, and will cache the script's output inappropriately.

You can control browser caching behavior by using the -expires and -pragma arguments. The -expires argument sets an expiration date for documents, and can be used to make a browser cache a script's output when it ordinarily would not. The -pragma argument is used to send a variety of miscellaneous information to the browser, and can be used to turn off caching when the browser is mistakenly caching a script's output.

-Expires accepts a relative time value in the same format as the like-named argument in the cookie() function. The browser will cache the returned file for the indicated time, after which it will fetch a new copy. In the gate script, it might make sense to set the expiration time for seven days, since site maintenance is done at weekly intervals. We can do this by modifying the call to header() in line 22 very slightly:

```
print header(-expires=>'+3d');
```

You can also set an absolute expiration date if you are careful to use the official HTTP time/date format. This requires dates to be expressed in Greenwich Mean Time (GMT), and to follow the format *day, dd-Mmm-yyyy hh:mm:ss GMT*. Here is a way to make a document expire on April Fool's Day:

```
print header(-expires=>'Thu, 01-Apr-1999 00:00:00 GMT');
```

The -pragma argument has the opposite effect when given the argument no-cache. Use it this way:

```
print header(-pragma=>'no-cache');
```

The HTTP 1.1 specification defines several more pragmas for controlling how documents are cached in intermediate proxy servers. You can find a complete, if somewhat dense, description on-line at www.w3.org.

## REFRESHING A PAGE AFTER A DELAY

One of the more overused effects on the Web is displaying a page for a few seconds, then reloading a different page. You can use this as a splash screen, or to display a warning notice. In static HTML pages, this effect is created using a <META> tag to simulate the effect of the HTTP Refresh header. If you are CGI scripting, however, you do not need to use <META> tags because you can control the contents of the HTTP header yourself.

To tell the browser to refresh the page after a certain time has elapsed, follow this template:

```
print header(-refresh=>'10; URL=http://your.site/new/doc.html');
```

The -refresh argument generates the appropriate field. Its value has two parts. The number before the semicolon indicates the time the browser should wait before reloading the page (in this case, 10 seconds). Following the semicolon is a space and the text URL=*URL*. The URL is the page that the browser should load after the period of time has elapsed. If you do not provide a URL, the browser will reload the current page. This might be what you want if the script produces random messages or a series of images. In fact, this technique is used to produce the crude form of animation known as *browser pull*.

Not all browsers support the Refresh option. Netscape browsers 2.0 and higher support it, as does Internet Explorer 3.0 and higher.

# Frames

I'm not much of a frame fan. Many sites overuse frames, making navigation harder for the user rather than easier. Nevertheless, CGI.pm provides support for frames in several different ways:

1. You can create a frame design using frameset() and frame() HTML shortcuts.
2. You can direct the output of the script to a particular frame by passing a -target argument to header().
3. You can redirect the destinations of all a page's hypertext links and forms to a different frame by passing a -target argument to start_html().
4. You can redirect the destination of a fill-out form's results by passing a -target argument to start_form() or start_multipart_form().

The simplest way to use forms is to create windows that popup when needed. If you refer to a frame that does not already exist, the browser will create a new window to display it in. Listing 3.6 is a simple script that illustrates this principle.

This script is similar to other question/response scripts we have seen. When called without parameters, it generates a fill-out form; otherwise, it prints out a response (in this case, echoing back the parameter fields to the user). The main innovation here is the argument pair -target=>answer in the call to start_form(). When the user presses the submit button, the presence of this argument causes the browser to create a new standalone window containing a single frame named answer. (The user never sees this frame name, but it is accessible to CGI scripts and JavaScript programs.) The script is now reinvoked, and its output (the results page) is placed into the new window. If the user goes back to the window containing the fill-out form, changes the

**Listing 3.6 Using frames to pop up a new window.**

```
#!/usr/bin/perl

use CGI qw/:standard/;
print header,
start_html('Popup Window');

if (!param) {
   print h1("Ask your Question"),
   start_form(-target=>'answer'),
   "What's your name? ",textfield('name'),
   p(),
   "What's the combination?",
   checkbox_group(-name=>'words',
                  -values=>['eenie','meenie','minie','moe'],
                  -defaults=>['eenie','moe']),
   p(),
   "What's your favorite color? ",
   popup_menu(-name=>'color',
              -values=>['red','green','blue','chartreuse']),
   p(),
   submit,
   end_form;
} else {
   print h1("And the Answer is..."),
   "Your name is ",em(param(name),
   p(),
   "The keywords are: ",
   em(join(", ",param('words'))),
   p(),
   "Your favorite color is ",em(param('color'));
}
print end_html;
```

form settings, and presses the submit button again, the script's output replaces the contents of the answer window.

---

**TIP**

**Certain frame names are special. The name _blank creates a new nameless pop-up window. The name _parent loads the page into its parent's frame, destroying one level of nesting. The name _top destroys all existing framesets and loads the page into the whole window. The name _self loads the page into the current frame.**

---

To do anything more complicated with frames, you will need to understand <FRAMESET> declarations. You can find this information in any recent book on HTML; for example, *HTML 4.0 Sourcebook* by Ian Graham (John Wiley & Sons, 1998). With the following HTML code example, you can create a simple side-by-side frame arrangement:

```
<TITLE>A Frameset</TITLE>
<FRAMESET COLS="50%,50%">
     <FRAME NAME="left" SRC="/cgi-bin/do_frame/left">
     <FRAME NAME="right" SRC="/cgi-bin/do_frame/right">
</FRAMESET>
```

This creates two vertical frames of equal size named left and right, and fills them with the output from a CGI script named do_frame. Since the same script is being used to fill both frames, it is important to tell the script which frame it is filling (otherwise, both frames will contain identical contents). We do this by passing do_frame the appropriate frame name in the additional path information.

If you want to generate the frameset definition from within the CGI script itself, use the frameset() and frame() functions. Because frames were originally a Netscape innovation, you will need to import the :netscape set in order to access to these functions. Here's the same pair of vertical columns generated by a CGI script:

```
#!/usr/bin/perl
use CGI qw/:standard :netscape/;
print header,
   title('A Frameset'),
   frameset({-cols=>'50%,50%'},
      frame({-name=>'left',-src=>'/cgi-bin/do_frame/left'}),
      frame({-name=>'right',-src=>'/cgi-bin/do_frame/right'})
   );
```

Notice that there are no calls to start_html() or end_html() in this script. CGI.pm produces HTML <HEAD> and <BODY> tags when you call start_html(), but these are not permitted in a document that defines a frameset. Once the frames have been set up, the script is free to use the two frame names to control where its output goes. For example, the script can create a fill-out form that uses -target to direct its output to the right-hand frame, creating an arrangement in which the question and response are displayed side by side.

Of course, it would be really convenient if everything was generated by a single script: the frameset and the contents of each of the frames themselves. This is not too hard to do. The trick is to divide your script into multiple functional units, one responsible for creating the frameset, and the others responsible for filling out the frames. Listing 3.7 shows one way of doing this.

**Listing 3.7 Side-by-side frames in a single script.**

```
#!/usr/bin/perl
# file side_by_side.pl

use CGI qw/:standard :netscape/;
print header;

```

```
$frame_name = path_info();
$frame_name =~ s!^/!!;

# If no path information is provided, then we create
# a side-by-side frame set
if (!$frame_name) {
   print_frameset();
   exit 0;
}

# If we get here, then we either create the query form
# or we create the response.
print start_html();
print_query()     if $frame_name eq 'left';
print_response() if $frame_name eq 'right';
print end_html();

# Create the frameset
sub print_frameset {
   my $script = url();
   print title('Side by Side'),
       frameset({-cols=>'50%,50%'},
         frame({-name=>'left',-src=>"$script/left"}),
         frame({-name=>'right',-src=>"$script/right"})
       );
   exit 0;
}

sub print_query {
   my $script = url();
```

*Continued*

**Listing 3.7 Side-by-side frames in a single script. *(Continued)***

```
36     print h1("Frameset Query"),
37             start_form(-action=>"$script/right",
38                         -target=>"right"),
39             "What's your name? ",textfield('name'),p(),
40             "What's the combination?",p(),
41             checkbox_group(-name=>'words',
42                   -values=>['eenie','meenie','minie','moe']),p(),
43             "What's your favorite color? ",
44             popup_menu(-name=>'color',
45                  -values=>['red','green','blue','chartreuse']),
46             p(),submit,
47             end_form;
48 }
49
50 sub print_response {
51     print h1("Frameset Result");
52     unless (param) {
53          print b("No query submitted yet.");
54          return;
55     }
56     print "Your name is ",em(param(name)),p(),
57     "The keywords are: ",em(join(", ",param('words'))),p(),
58     "Your favorite color is ",em(param('color'));
59 }
```

Side_by_side.pl starts by fetching the additional path information and stripping off the leading slash that the URL naming rules attach (lines 6 and 7) and assigning it to the variable $frame_name. The script now examines the path information. If it is empty, then we know the script is being called for the first time, probably from a hypertext link. The script prints out the frameset definition by calling the subroutine print_frameset() and exits.

Otherwise, we print out the HTML header used for both the left and right frames. We examine $frame_name to determine which frame we are in (lines 19 and 20). If it is equal to the string "left" we execute the subroutine print_query(). If it is equal to "right," we execute print_response() instead. We call end_html() to close the page, and exit.

Lines 24 to 32 contain the definition for print_frameset(), which is similar to what we have seen before. The only interesting detail here is our use of the CGI.pm url() function to retrieve the script's URL, avoiding the necessity of hard-coding its name.

Lines 34 to 48 create the fill-out form that populates the left side of the window. Again we use url() to fetch the script's name and pass it to start_form's -action argument, appending the string "/right" to the end so that the script will know what frame it is responsible for. The remainder of the subroutine creates a useless but otherwise conventional fill-out form.

Lines 50 to 59 create the response that appears in the right-hand frame. Its job is simple; call param() to see if there are any CGI parameters to process. If not, it prints out the message "No query submitted yet" and exits. Otherwise, it echoes the parameters back to the user. The resulting page is shown in Figure 3.9.

This script uses the start_form() -target argument to direct the output of the script to the appropriate frame, putting the browser in charge of directing the script's output to the correct frame when the submit button is pressed. Another way to accomplish the same thing is to put the script itself in charge of selecting its frame. To do this, omit the -target argument from start_form() and pass an appropriate -target to header() instead. With these modifications, the top of side_by_side.pl now looks something like this:

```
3   use CGI qw/:standard :netscape/;
4
5   $frame_name = path_info();
6   $frame_name =~ s!^/!!;
7   $frame_name = '_top' unless $frame_name;
8
9   print header(-target=>$frame_name);
10
```

```
if ($frame_name eq '_top') {
    print_frameset();
    exit 0;
}
...
```

We recover the frame name from path_info() and pass it as the target frame to header(). If no frame name is specified, we set it to _top, which is a special name that causes the browser to destroy any current frameset and load the page into the entire window. We then proceed as before.

---

**TIP**

**Although it would be nice for a single script to generate the contents of several frames in a single pass (for example, by printing several headers with different -target arguments), the HTTP protocol doesn't currently allow this. Each execution of a script can only fill a single frame.**

---

-Target can be used within a hypertext link to load the new document into a named frame. The following snippet creates a link that loads info/specs.html into a frame named right. If the frame does not already exist, a new window will be created to hold it.

```
print a({-href=>'info/specs.html' -target=>'right'},
      "Read the product specs.");
```

If you want every link in a particular page to get loaded into a particular frame, you can pass -target to the start_html() function, for example:

```
print start_html(-title=>'Table of Contents',
                 -target=>'DocBody');
```

Now, by default every link and fill-out form submission will be loaded into a frame named "DocBody." You can override this on a case-by-case basis

Figure 3.9 The side_by_side.pl script shows the response in the right-hand frame.

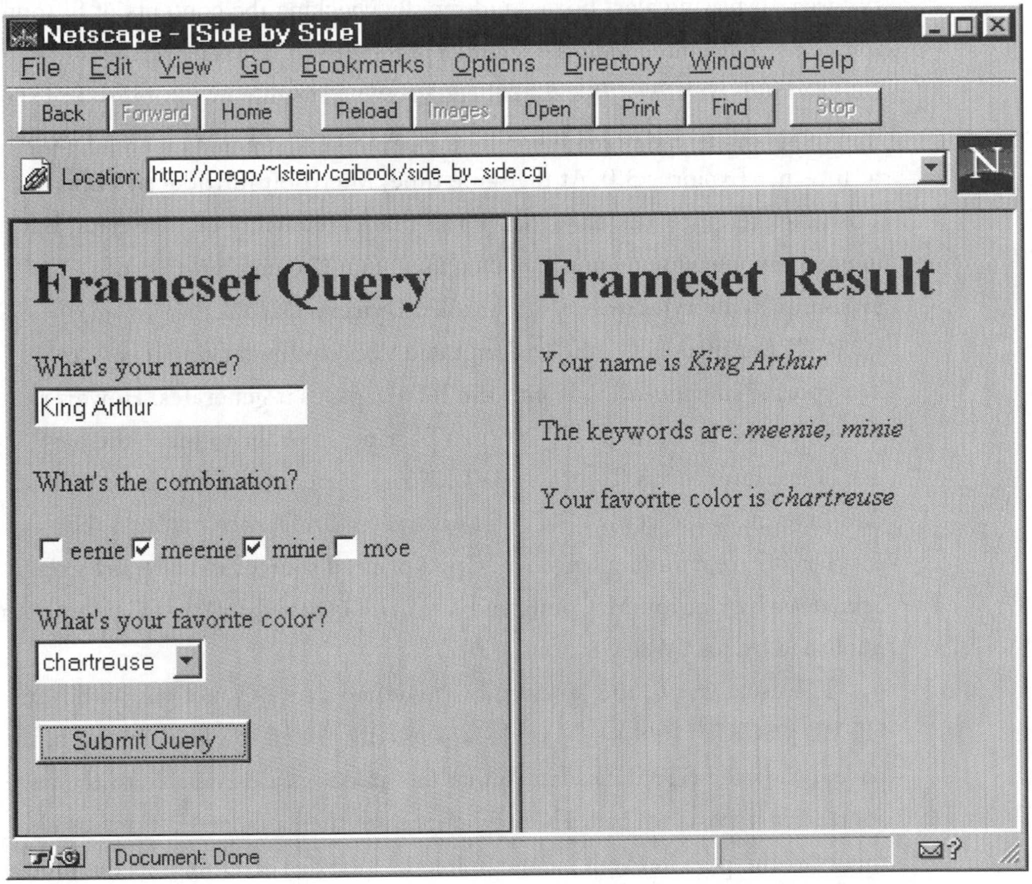

by specifying a -target to the a() or start_form() tag. Frame names explicitly provided to header() will also override this default.

## JavaScript-Enhanced Pages

JavaScript is a browser scripting language developed by Netscape for use in its line of Navigator products. Not to be confused with the Java programming language, JavaScript-enhanced pages can do a lot of things that are awkward or impossible to accomplish with straight CGI scripting, such as opening and closing windows, manipulating the contents of the browser status area, displaying alert boxes, and rapidly checking the contents of fill-out forms *before* the information is submitted to the script. JavaScript was first released in Navigator 2.0 and has been growing steadily in capability and stability ever since. Microsoft introduced a JavaScript look-alike called JScript to Internet Explorer 3.0. At the same time, Microsoft introduced VBScript, a browser scripting language that has all the functionality of JavaScript, but uses a syntax similar to BASIC rather than Java. The combination of JavaScript with stylesheets is often called Dynamic HTML.

CGI.pm supports both JavaScript and VBScript by making it easy to incorporate snippets of code into the HTML pages it generates. However, you will need to know JavaScript (or VBScript) in order to make the best use of these functions. The *Netscape JavaScript Manual* (which you can find at developer.netscape.com/) is a good tutorial and reference guide to the JavaScript programming language. Good printed sources include *JavaScript Sourcebook* by Gordon McComb, and *JavaScript Cookbook* by Yosef Cohen (both published by John Wiley & Sons, 1997).

The usual way to use JavaScript is to define a set of functions within an HTML <SCRIPT> block. This block is usually placed towards the top of the page, inside the HTML header, so that the functions are available to the page soon after it starts to load. These functions are then attached to various elements of the page as event handlers. Events include such things as the mouse passing over a form element, a button being clicked, the contents of a text field changing, or a form being submitted. When an event occurs that involves an element that has registered an event handler, its associated JavaScript function gets called.

The elements that can register event handlers include the <BODY> of an HTML document, hypertext links, all the various elements of a fill-out form, and the form itself. There are a large number of events, and each applies only to the elements for which it is relevant:

- ***onLoad, onUnload*** The browser is loading or leaving the current document. Valid in:

  The HTML <BODY> section only.

- ***OnSubmit*** The user has pressed the submit button of a form. This event happens just before the form is submitted, and your function can return a value of *false* in order to abort the submission. Valid for:

  Forms only.

- ***onClick*** The mouse has clicked on an item in a fill-out form. Valid for:

  Buttons (including submit and reset buttons)
  Checkboxes
  Radio buttons

- ***onChange*** The user has changed the contents of a field. Valid for:

  Text fields
  Text areas
  Password fields
  File fields
  Popup menus
  Scrolling lists

- ***onFocus*** The user has selected a field to work with. Valid for:

  Text fields
  Text areas
  Password fields
  File fields
  Popup menus
  Scrolling lists

- ***onBlur*** The user has deselected a field (gone to type somewhere else). Valid for:

  Text fields
  Text areas
  Password fields
  File fields
  Popup menus
  Scrolling lists

- *onSelect* The user has changed the part of a text field that is selected. Valid for:
  Text fields
  Text areas
  Password fields
  File fields

To register a JavaScript event handler with an HTML element, use the event name as a parameter when you call the corresponding CGI method. For example, if you have defined a JavaScript function named validateAge(), you can arrange for this function to be executed every time the user finishes filling out a textfield named "age," by generating the field this way:

```
print textfield(-name=>'age', -onBlur=>"validateAge(this)");
```

By calling validateAge() with an argument named "this," we are able to pass the function a reference to the text field object. "This" is an automatic JavaScript variable that refers to the current form element. This allows the function to recover information about the field, including its current contents.

Similarly, you can create a form that checks itself for consistency and aborts the submission if some essential value is missing, by generating the field this way:

```
print $q->startform(-onSubmit=>"validateMe(this)");
```

In addition to the standard form elements, JavaScript-enhanced pages recognize an additional type of button that calls a fragment of JavaScript when pressed. The CGI.pm function for generating this button is button(), and it recognizes -name, -value, and -onClick arguments, for example:

```
print button(-name=>'surprise', -value=>"Don't Press Me",
         -onClick=>'alert("Don't press this button!")'
         );
```

These examples assume that you have already declared the validateAge() and validateMe() functions by incorporating them into a <SCRIPT> block. The CGI.pm start_html() method provides a convenient way to create this section. In a manner entirely analogous to cascading stylesheets, you can add a block of JavaScript code into a page either by incorporating it directly into the HTML, or by placing the JavaScript in a file on the Web site and referring to its URL. Here is an example that shows the simplest way of doing this:

```
use CGI;
print header;
$JSCRIPT=<<END;
  // Ask a silly question
  function riddle_me_this() {
     var r = prompt("What walks on four legs in the morning, " +
                    "two legs in the afternoon, " +
                    "and three legs in the evening?");
     response(r);
  }
  // Get a silly answer
  function response(answer) {
     if (answer == "man") || (answer == "human")
         alert("Right you are!");
     else
         alert("Wrong!  Guess again.");
  }
END

print start_html(-title=>'The Riddle of the Sphinx',
                 -script=>$JSCRIPT,
                 -onLoad=>'riddle_me_this()');
```

This code fragment defines a small JavaScript block containing just two functions: one called riddle_me_this(), which asks a classical riddle, and another called response(), which checks the answer for correctness. The script is incorporated directly into the HTML page with the start_html() -script argument. At the same time, we arrange for the riddle_me_this() function to be called when the page first loads, by referring to it with an -onLoad argument.

If you want to share the definitions of riddle_me_this() and response() among several different pages, you can save the definitions to a text file somewhere on your site and refer to it using a variant of the same notation you use to incorporate cascading stylesheets into pages. The -script argument, instead of pointing directly to a JavaScript string, points to an associative array that contains -src and, optionally, -code keys. -Src points to the URL of the script text, while -code contains any additional JavaScript statements you want appended to the imported code library. For instance, if the JavaScript definitions were stored at the URL /javascripts/sphinx.js and you wanted to display a message after the definitions had loaded, you could write something like the following:

```
print start_html(-title=>'The Riddle of the Sphinx',
                 -script=>{-src=>'/javascripts/sphinx.js',
                           -code=>'alert("Loaded...")'}
                 );
```

An optional -language key allows you to use other scripting languages, such as VBScript or PerlScript (the latter is a component of the free ActiveWare port of Perl to Windows NT). The syntax is simple:

```
print start_html(-title=>'The Riddle of the Sphinx',
                 -script=>{-src=>'/basic/sphinx.bas',
                           -language=>'VBScript'}
                 );
```

**TIP**

**The JavaScript language is changing rapidly. If you make heavy use of it, make sure you are not using new features that leave out users with older browsers.**

Listing 3.8 shows the code for javascript.pl, an example taken directly out of the CGI.pm distribution. This page asks you to answer a variety of personal questions and then comments on them. Its main feature is that it shows how to use JavaScript event handlers to check the contents of the fill-out form for validity before submitting them to the CGI script. Figure 3.10 shows what this script does when the user tries to submit a birthdate that is not within the acceptable range.

**Listing 3.8 This script validates fill-out forms with JavaScript.**

```
#!/usr/bin/perl
# Script: javascript.pl

use CGI qw(:standard);

# Here's the javascript code.
$JSCRIPT=<<EOF;
// validate that the user is the right age.  Return
// false to prevent the form from being submitted.
function validateForm() {
    var today = new Date();
    var birthday = validateDate(document.form1.birthdate);
    if (birthday == 0) {
        document.form1.birthdate.focus()
        document.form1.birthdate.select();
        return false;
    }
```

*Continued*

**Listing 3.8 This script validates fill-out forms with JavaScript. *(Continued)***

```
    var milliseconds = today.getTime()-birthday;
    var years = milliseconds/(1000 * 60 * 60 * 24 * 365.25);
    if ((years > 20) || (years < 5)) {
        alert("You must be between the ages of 5 and 20 " +
                "to submit this form");
        document.form1.birthdate.focus();
        document.form1.birthdate.select();
        return false;
    }
    // Since we've calculated the age in years already,
    // we might as well send it up to our CGI script.
    document.form1.age.value=Math.floor(years);
    return true;
}

// make sure that the contents of the supplied
// field contain a valid date.
function validateDate(element) {
    var date = Date.parse(element.value);
    if (0 == date) {
        alert("Please enter date in format MMM DD, YY");
        element.focus();
        element.select();
    }
    return date;
}

// Compliments, compliments
function doPraise(element) {
    if (element.checked) {
```

```
      self.status=element.value +
                  " is an excellent choice!";
      return true;
   } else {
      return false;
   }
}

function checkColor(element) {
   var color = element.options[element.selectedIndex].text;
   if (color == "blonde") {
      if (confirm(
          "Is it true that blondes have more fun?"))
            alert("Darn.  That leaves me out.");
      } else
      alert(color + " is a fine choice!");
   }
EOF
;

# here's where the execution begins
print header;
print start_html(-title=>'Personal Profile',
                 -script=>$JSCRIPT);
print h1("Big Brother Wants to Know All About You");
print_prompt(),hr;
print_response() if param;
print end_html;

sub print_prompt {
   print start_form(-name=>'form1',
                    -onSubmit=>"return validateForm()"),
```

Continued

**Listing 3.8 This script validates fill-out forms with JavaScript. *(Continued)***

```
 80           "Birthdate (e.g. Jan 3, 1972): ",
 81           textfield(-name=>'birthdate',
 82                     -onBlur=>"validateDate(this)"),p(),
 83           "Sex: ",
 84           radio_group(-name=>'gender',
 85                       -value=>[qw/male female/],
 86                       -onClick=>"doPraise(this)"),p(),
 87           "Hair color: ",
 88           popup_menu(-name=>'color',
 89                      -value=>[qw/brunette blonde red gray/],
 90                      -default=>'red',
 91                      -onChange=>"checkColor(this)"),p(),
 92           hidden(-name=>'age',-value=>0),
 93           submit(),
 94           end_form;
 95 }
 96
 97 sub print_response {
 98     import_names('Q');
 99     print h2("Your profile"),
100           "You claim to be a ",b($Q::age),
101           " year old ",b($Q::color,$Q::gender),".",
102           "You should be ashamed of yourself for lying so ",
103           "blatantly to big brother!",
104         hr;
105 }
```

Most of the action in this script takes place between lines 6 and 66, where a number of JavaScript functions are defined and placed in a string variable named $JSCRIPT. The validateForm() function is the most interesting. It

Figure 3.10 The javascript.pl script uses JavaScript to validate the contents of a fill-out form before it is submitted.

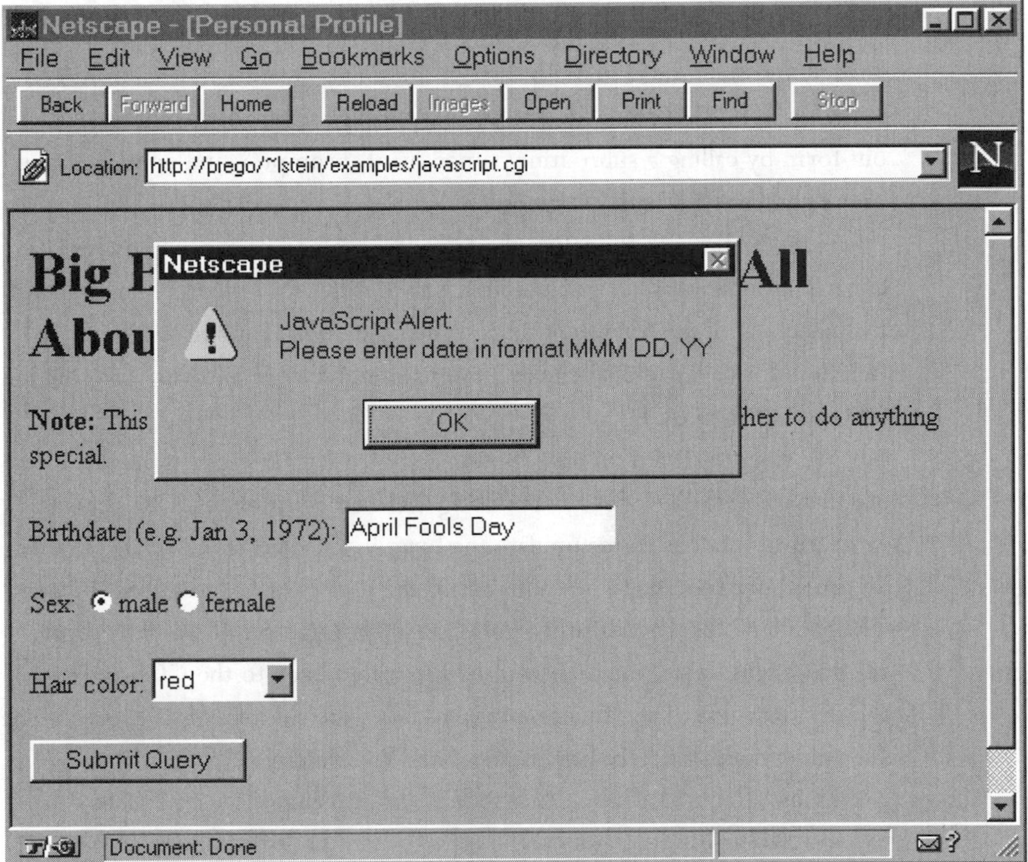


retrieves the contents of the fill-out questionnaire and checks each of its fields for validity. The main check is for a text field where the user enters his or her birth date. The code calls a subsidiary function, validateDate(), to make sure that what is entered into the field can be converted into a date. Then, just for fun, the function does range checking on the user's age, and complains if the user is not between the ages of 5 and 20 (this range was chosen so that most people trying the script would see the error message). Other functions make live comments on the user's input. For example, when a male user enters his gender, the doPraise() function displays the string "Male is an excellent choice!" in the browser status area (of course, women get praised, too). The checkColor() function does something similar with the hair color field, but treats blondes specially (see if you can figure out what it does from the code).

The Perl part of the script begins on line 68. We print out the HTTP header, and start the page with start_html(). The JavaScript definitions contained in $JSCRIPT are added to the page using -script. We create the fill-out form by calling a subroutine named print_prompt(), and echo back the user's choices with print_response().

Lines 77 through 95 define the fill-out form and its special JavaScript-enhanced behaviors. The general idea is that each of the form elements does live checking of the forms contents. When the form is submitted, a single function does a last global check for consistency before allowing the contents to be submitted.

We start the form on line 78 with a start_form(). The new features here are that we give the form a name using the -name argument. This allows JavaScript functions to manipulate the form in various ways. We also define an -onSubmit handler to be called when the user presses the submit button. The handler calls the validateForm() JavaScript function. If validateForm() returns a true value, the form will be submitted back to the CGI script in the ordinary way. If the function returns false, the submission is aborted. The user must make the necessary changes and try again.

Lines 81 and 82 define the text field for entering the user's birth date. It has an -onBlur handler that will be called when the user finishes entering a value in the field and moves on to another part of the form. The handler calls validateDate() with an argument of "this", which has the effect of passing a reference to the text field of the JavaScript function.

Next we define a radio cluster for selecting the user's gender (lines 84 through 86). This uses the -onClick handler to call the doPraise() function whenever a member of the cluster is pressed. Similarly, a popup menu for selecting the user's hair color calls checkColor() via its -onChange handler. Whenever the menu selection is changed, the JavaScript handler is invoked.

The print_response() subroutine, defined in lines 97 through 105, is very conventional, the only twist is that it uses the import_names() function to import the CGI parameters into Perl variables in the Q:: namespace.

# Incremental Updates: NPH Mode

Sometimes you will want to display part of a page, wait awhile, then display some more. For instance, you may be displaying a series of stock quotes that comes in at short intervals. Every few seconds you receive a new quotation and print out a line for display on the user's browser.

Conventional CGI scripting won't handle this requirement because the server buffers script output, waiting until a sufficiently large chunk of text has been produced before forwarding it to the browser. To get around this problem, you can activate something called NPH mode. In NPH mode, short for "No Parsed Headers," the server attaches the script's output directly to the browser's input. The advantage of this is that the script controls exactly what gets sent to the browser and when it is sent. The disadvantage is that the script is responsible for producing many of the HTTP headers that the server ordinarily adds as a courtesy.

CGI.pm makes it as easy to create NPH scripts as to create normal ones. When running in NPH mode, the library adds all the appropriate headers. All you have to do is to signal the library that you want to run as an NPH script. While there are several ways of doing this, the easiest is in the use statement. Just import the symbol -nph along with any other function sets you require like this:

```
use CGI qw/:standard -nph/;
```

You can now call header(), redirect(), start_html(), and so forth in the usual way, and CGI.pm will make whatever alterations are necessary. If you wish to have text displayed as you output it, you will have to turn off Perl's own buffering somewhere towards the top of your script. This is done by setting the magic variable `$|` to a true value.

Unfortunately, it is not quite as simple as this, because you also have to inform the server that the script will be running in NPH mode. On some servers, this is a matter of giving the script a name that starts with the prefix nph-. On other servers, the Microsoft IIS server in particular, this is not necessary; the server figures out that a script requires NPH handling by looking at the first few lines of its output.

Listing 3.9 gives the code for nph-quote.pl, a simulated stock quoting script. As Figure 3.11 shows, it prints out a continuous list of imaginary quotes, printing out a new quote every few seconds. New quotes are appended to the growing list; the page continues to grow until the user presses the "Stop" button or goes to a new page.

**Listing 3.9 The code for the nph-quote.pl script.**

```
#!/usr/bin/perl
# script: nph-quote.pl

use CGI qw/:standard :html3 -nph/;
$| = 1;
@STOCKS = qw/IBM Microsoft Intel Apple HP
             Adobe Netscape 3Com Adaptec/;
$INTERVAL = 4; #seconds
$INCREMENT = 4; #maximum number of points up or down
initialize_stocks();

print header,
    start_html('Stock Ticker'),
    h1('Stock Ticker'),
    "Quotes when you want them, the way you want them.",p(),
    table(TR({-align=>LEFT},
            th({-width=>100},'Stock'),
            th({-width=>50},'Current'),
            th({-width=>50},'Change'))
    );

while (1) {
    my($stock,$current,$change) = get_next_quote();
    print table(TR({-align=>LEFT},
                    th({-width=>100},$stock),
                    td({-width=>50},to_eighths($current)),
```

```
                    td({-width=>50,-align=>RIGHT},
                        to_eighths($change,1)))
    ),"\n";
    sleep(rand($INTERVAL));
}

sub initialize_stocks {
    foreach (@STOCKS) {
        $CURRENT{$_} = $STARTING{$_} = rand(1000)/10;
    }
}

sub get_next_quote {
    my $stock = $STOCKS[rand(@STOCKS)];
    my $increment = $INCREMENT - rand(2*$INCREMENT);
    $CURRENT{$stock} += $increment;
    $CURRENT{$stock} = 0 if $CURRENT{$stock} < 0;
    return ($stock,$CURRENT{$stock},
                        $CURRENT{$stock}-$STARTING{$stock});
}

sub to_eighths {
    my($number,$add_sign) = @_;
    my $sign = ($number>0) ? "+" :
               ($number<0) ? "-" : ''
            if $add_sign;
    my $quotient = int(abs($number));
    my $remainder = ((abs($number)-$quotient) * 8) % 8;
    my $string = "$sign$quotient " . sup("$remainder/8");
    return font({-color=>red},$string) if $number < 0;
    return $string;
}
```

This script begins by importing the CGI module, along with the standard functions, the HTML3 functions, and the NPH mode symbol. It sets `$|` to 1 in

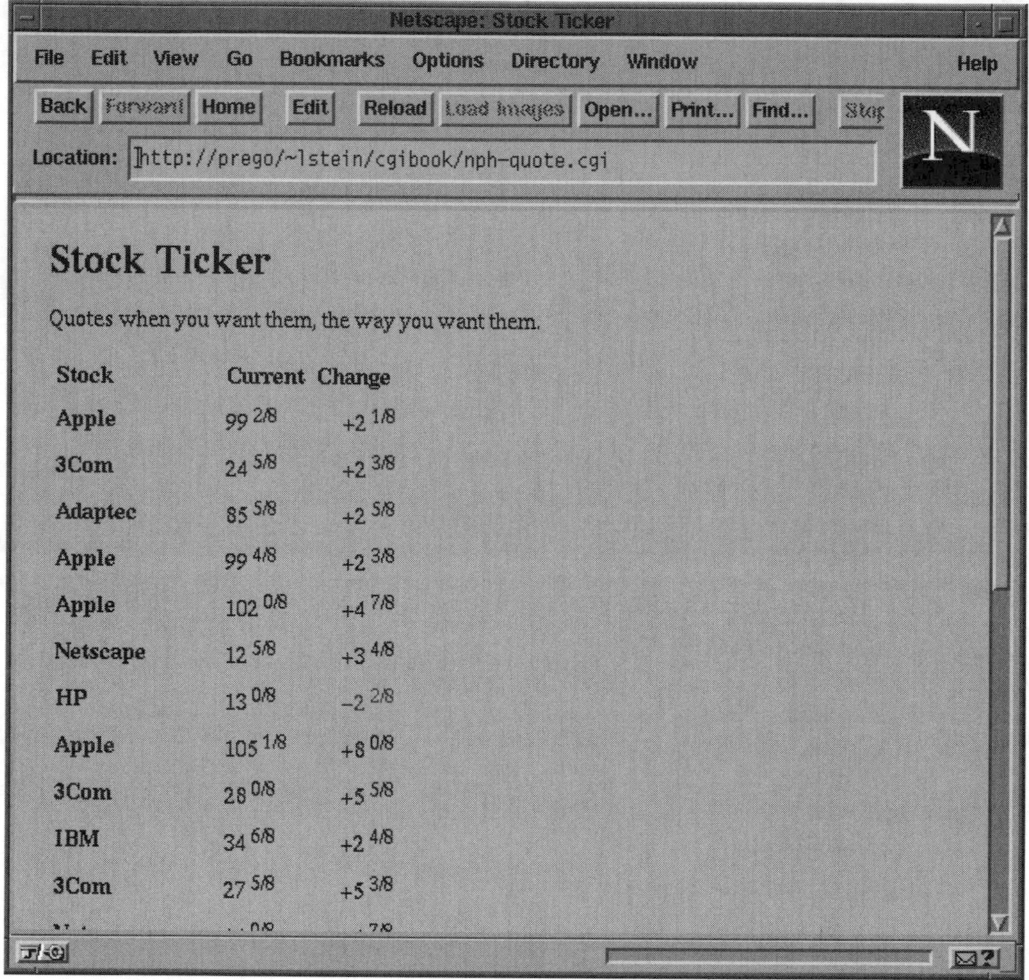


**Figure 3.11 Nph-quote.pl uses NPH mode to create a continuously growing page.**

order to turn off Perl's output buffering. Next it defines some globals, including a list of stocks, the interval at which to report changes in prices, and the maximum amount that a stock is allowed to change in a single step. The script calls initialize_stocks() to create starting prices for each of the stocks.

In lines 12 to 20, the script creates the boilerplate material at the top of the page, including the HTTP header, the HTML title, a logo, and a table of column headings for the stock quotes. Notice that we use the -width attribute extensively in the table headings. This is to prevent the browser's automatic formatting from misaligning the headers with the columns that will be produced in the next section.

Lines 22 to 31 are an infinite loop. In each step through the loop, we call the internal subroutine get_next_quote() to return the stock's name, its current price, and its change from the opening price. We format the returned values and place them in a one-row table, being careful to use the same width values as the table headers produced earlier. The script sleeps from a random interval, then continues looping.

Lines 33 to 37 define initialize_stocks(), where a random number generator is used to set the stock's initial value. This is probably done differently on Wall Street, but the effect is much the same.

Lines 39 to 46 are where get_next_quote() is defined. It calls the random number generator to pick a stock, then calls rand() again to determine a suitable amount to change its value by.

Lines 48 to 58 define to_eighths(), where the decimal fractions returned by get_next_quote() are turned into the fractions of 1/8 used by the NY Stock Exchange (Apparently this system is derived from the famed "pieces of eight" that pirate captains were so keen to capture. Its use by the "captains of industry" must be pure coincidence.) The interesting thing about this function is that it uses the sup() function to make the fraction into a superscript, and the font() function to make negative changes red.

## SERVER PUSH

It is also possible to create a page that updates itself continuously, not by adding text at the bottom, but by replacing the entire contents of the page. You can do this with HTML documents or with an image, and is one way of creating animated images. The technique is called *server push* and uses a special MIME type called multipart/x-mixed-replace. If you understand the format of this MIME type, you can use CGI.pm's NPH mode to implement server push. But it is even easier than that, because a special module called CGI::Push will take care of all the details for you.

CGI::Push is part of the standard CGI distribution. CGI::Push inherits from CGI, and adds one new function to the standard CGI suite, do_push(). When you call this function, you pass it a reference to a subroutine that is responsible for drawing each new page. Here is a fragment of code that shows how it works:

```
use CGI::Push qw/:standard/;
do_push(-next_page=>\&draw_a_page);

sub draw_a_page {
   my($q,$counter) = @_;
   return undef if $counter > 100;
   my $burst = $counter / 10;
   my $time = localtime();
   return start_html('testing'),
          img({-src=>"/images/starburst$burst.gif",-align=>RIGHT}),
          h1('testing'),
          "This page called $counter times",
          hr,
          $time,
          end_html();
}
```

In this example, we use CGI::Push rather than CGI, importing the standard set of functions in the ordinary way. Now we make a single call to do_push(), using the -next_page argument to pass it a reference to the subroutine that will do the actual drawing; in this case, a function called draw_a_page(). Do_push() contains a loop that calls the drawing subroutine repeatedly, formatting it in the manner needed by multipart/x-mixed-replace, and returning the new contents to the browser. Every time do_loop() calls the -next_page function, it passes it two parameters, the CGI object and a counter giving the number of times the function has been called. The function is expected to return (not print) the contents of the page as a string or a list of strings. It can return an undefined value in order to signal do_push() to quit. This example prints out a simple page that reads "This page called N times," where N is the number of times the page has been redisplayed. It uses the counter to create an <IMG> tag that points to a set of files named starburst0.gif, starburst1.gif, and so forth. It also returns the current local time, using the Perl localtime function. The end result is that every second, the page is redisplayed with an updated count, clock, and starburst image.

Optional arguments to do_push() include: -delay, the number of seconds to wait between redisplaying the page (fractional values are allowed; the default is one second); -type, the MIME type of the pages that the draw subroutine will produce; and -last_page, a reference to a subroutine to call at the very end after the draw subroutine has returned undef. You can use this to display a goodbye page or something similar. Also allowed in do_push() are any other arguments that header() accepts, including -cookie, -expires, and the like. You can create animated GIF images using a series of inline images in the manner shown in the previous example, or more simply by setting -type argument to image/gif, then reading and returning the contents of a series of GIF images from within the draw subroutine.

Although you will most often create multiple pages that share a common MIME type, it is possible to return a different type of document each time the draw routine is called. To do this, pass do_push() a -type of "heterogeneous" (or "dynamic" if you have spelling bee trauma). Then modify the draw routine to return the HTTP header along with the document itself, for example:

```
sub my_draw_routine {
   my($q,$counter) = @_;
   return header('text/html'),
          start_html('testing'),
          h1('testing'),
          "This page called $counter times";
}
```

You can add any header fields that you like, but some (cookies and status fields included) may not be interpreted by the browser. One interesting effect is to display a series of pages, then, after the last page, to redirect the browser to a new URL. Because redirect() will not work in this context (the HTTP header has already been sent), you can do this by passing a -refresh argument to the header() function called by the last-page draw routine, for example:

```
do_push(-next_page=>\&my_draw_routine,
         -last_page=>\&my_last_page);

sub my_draw_routine {
    my($q,$counter) = @_;
    return undef if $counter > 10;
    return header('text/html'),
              start_html('testing'),
              h1('testing'),
              "This page called $counter times";
}
sub my_last_page {
    return
        header(-refresh=>'5; URL=/docs/finished.html',
                -type=>'text/html'),
        start_html('Moved'),
        h1('This is the last page'),
        'Goodbye!'
        hr,
        end_html;
}
```

If you need to change the delay between pages, call the CGI::Push function page_delay() from within the draw routine, and pass it the number of seconds to delay between the current page and the next one. As in the -delay argument to do_push(), the value may be fractional.

If you have come this far, you have learned all of the essential features of CGI.pm and much of the esoterica as well. The next chapter takes you deep into the module, showing you how to extend CGI.pm with your own subclasses in order to expand its capabilities and customize its behavior for your own needs.

# Chapter Four

# Extending CGI.pm

CGI.pm was designed with an "everything but the kitchen sink" philosophy. If it currently doesn't do something you want, chances are that the next version will. Nevertheless, there may be times when you need to extend CGI.pm's functionality with your own custom code. This chapter explains how to do this.

This chapter also gives information on using CGI.pm with FastCGI and mod_perl, two packages that markedly improve the performance of CGI scripts under certain Web servers. We will end the chapter with advice for updating older scripts that were written to use Perl 4's cgi-lib.pl library.

## Extending CGI.pm's Object-Oriented Interface

If you use CGI.pm's object-oriented calling style exclusively, the Perl object inheritance mechanism can be used to customize CGI.pm's behavior and extend its abilities. To do this, create a new .pm module that "uses" CGI.pm, then add "CGI" to the module's @ISA array.

Here is a concrete example. CGI.pm's param() function allows you to add a single named CGI parameter to the CGI parameter list. If you want to add several CGI parameters, you will have to call param() repeatedly. A convenient interface would be a function named add_multiple(), which takes a hash list and turns each key into a CGI parameter, as follows:

```
$q = new CGI::Multiple;
$q->add_multiple('vegetables'=>['okra','cabbage','anise'],
                 'fruit'=>['bananas','mangos'],
                 'diet'=>'vegetarian'
                 );
```

As another enhancement, we can create a new hidden_multiple() function that returns a <HIDDEN> tag for every parameter named on the new functions list of arguments. For example:

```
print $q->hidden_multiple('vegetables','fruit','diet');
```

This allows you to turn the *entire* CGI parameter list into a set of hidden fields by calling:

```
print $q->hidden_multiple($q->param);
```

A complete module to accomplish these tasks, which we will call CGI::Multiple, is given in Listing 4.1.

**TIP**

**If you have trouble following this section, I recommend reading about the Perl object-oriented system. The *perlbot* manual page, and *Programming Perl* by Larry Wall, Tom Christiansen and Randal Schwartz, are both excellent references.**

**Listing 4.1 The CGI::Multiple Module.**

```
package CGI::Multiple;
$VERSION = '1.0';
use CGI;
@ISA = qw/CGI/;

sub add_multiple {
    my ($self,%params) = @_;
    my $p;
    foreach $p (keys %params) {
        $self->param(-name=>$p,-value=>$params{$p});
    }
}

sub hidden_multiple {
    my ($self,@params) = @_;
    my($p,@results);
    foreach $p (@params) {
        push(@results,$self->hidden(-name=>$p));
    }
    return @results;
}
1; # have to return TRUE from all modules
```

The code is very straightforward. We declare the package name and define a $VERSION variable (recent versions of Perl recommend that all packages contain this variable; it should be all uppercase as shown here and set to a floating point number). Next we load CGI and add its name to the @ISA array in order to tell Perl that we intend to inherit functions from it.

Lines 6 to 12 define the add_multiple() function. We simply call the inherited param() method once for each key in the passed associative array, setting the value of the CGI parameter. Because param() already knows how to deal with multivalued parameters, we don't have to do anything special to accommodate values that are list array references.

Lines 14 to 21 define hidden_multiple(). Like the previous function, it works by calling the inherited hidden() function once for each parameter on the argument list. The returned <HIDDEN> tags are appended to a list named @result, and returned to the caller at the end of the loop.

Do not forget to return a true value (usually 1) at the end of the module. Modules that neglect to do this may fail unexpectedly.

---

**TIP**

**Prior to CGI.pm version 2.37, all inheriting modules were expected to live in the CGI:: namespace. This restriction has since been lifted.**

---

To install and start using this module, name it Multiple.pm and place it in the CGI subdirectory of your Perl5 library directory. On many UNIX installations, this will be /usr/local/lib/perl5/site_perl/CGI. On Windows NT machines, the Perl5 library is often C:\perl5\lib\site_perl\CGI.

## EXTENDING THE FUNCTION-ORIENTED INTERFACE

If you try to use CGI.pm's function-oriented interface with CGI::Multiple, you will find that while you can access all of CGI.pm's functions, the new add_multiple() and hidden_multiple() functions are unavailable. For example, a script that looks like this:

```
use CGI::Multiple qw/:standard/;
print header();
add_multiple('veggies'=>['kale','carrots','broccoli']);
```

will fail with the error *Unknown function &main::add_multiple() at line 3.*

Internally, CGI.pm plays a variety of tricks with the Perl inheritance mechanism and autoloader facility. This gives it the ability to handle both object-oriented and functional interfaces with the same code, and speeds up load time considerably. However, it makes extending the function call interface a bit tricky. If you wish to extend CGI.pm in such a way that new subroutines can be exported as function calls, you must adjust the following three package globals somewhere towards the top of the new module.

1. ***Define the $CGI::DefaultClass global to be the name of the current package.*** This variable tells certain CGI internal routines what package to use when creating the default CGI object ($CGI::Q) that responds to function-oriented calls.
2. ***Create a package global named $AutoloadClass to be the name "CGI".*** This tells CGI.pm's autoloading routine to look for undefined subroutine names in the CGI package if it doesn't find them in the current package.
3. ***Add the functions you wish to export to the %CGI::EXPORT_TAGS array.*** This makes the functions available for exportation to the caller's namespace.

Lastly, you must call the CGI internal function self_or_default() at the beginning of each function you want to export.

Listing 4.2, a revised CGI::Multiple class, illustrates these steps.

Most of the changes are in lines 5 to 11. We set the $CGI::DefaultClass global to the name of the current package, CGI::Multiple, and conversely set the value of our own package's $AutoloadClass global to CGI.

Next we define a new symbol export tag named :multiple. When a caller imports the :multiple symbol, the add_multiple() and hidden_multiple() functions will be exported to its namespace. The %CGI::EXPORT_TAGS global is an associative array in which the names of symbol sets are mapped to lists of function names to import. Because we are creating a new symbol set, rather than adding to an old one, we can get away with doing a straight assignment. If we want to modify an existing symbol set, say by adding the

**Listing 4.2 The CGI::Multiple module revised to handle function-oriented calling.**

```
package CGI::Multiple;
$VERSION = '1.0';
use CGI;
@ISA = qw/CGI/;
$CGI::DefaultClass = 'CGI::Multiple';
$AutoloadClass = 'CGI';

# Export add_multiple() and hidden_multiple() when caller
# imports a new ":multiple" set
$CGI::EXPORT_TAGS{':multiple'} =
                      ['add_multiple','hidden_multiple'];

sub add_multiple {
    my ($self,%params) = CGI::self_or_default(@_);
    my $p;
    foreach $p (keys %params) {
        $self->param(-name=>$p,-value=>$params{$p});
    }
}

sub hidden_multiple {
     my ($self,@params) = CGI::self_or_default(@_);
     my($p,@results);
     foreach $p (@params) {
         push(@results,$self->hidden(-name=>$p));
     }
     return @results;
}
1; # have to return TRUE from all modules
```

two multiple functions to the standard set, we would have to append them to the end of the existing list like this:

```
push(@{$CGI::EXPORT_TAGS{':standard'}},
       'add_multiple','hidden_multiple');
```

Another example would be to define the new :multiple symbol set, and then add :multiple to the standard set like this:

```
$CGI::EXPORT_TAGS{':multiple'} =
                  ['add_multiple','hidden_multiple'];
push(@{$CGI::EXPORT_TAGS{':standard'}},':multiple');
```

The last thing to do to make CGI::Multiple compatible with the function call interface is to call CGI::self_or_default() in all exportable functions. This internal function checks its first argument. If the argument is a CGI object or one of its descendents, self_or_default() returns it; otherwise, the function creates a new default object and returns it. This allows object-oriented and function-oriented functionality to live side by side.

## INTERNAL FUNCTIONS

In addition to self_or_default(), several internal CGI.pm functions may be helpful for module writers.

### Rearrange()

The most useful of these is CGI::rearrange(). Rearrange() is used to process named argument lists and to assign their values to Perl variables. You typically use it this way:

```
sub some_function {
   my $self = shift;
```

```
    my ($fee,$fie,$foe,$fum,@rest) =
        $self->rearrange(['FEE','FIE','FOE',['FUM','FUMS']],@_);
}
```

This example defines a function that expects the arguments -fee, -fie, -foe, and -fum, as in:

```
$q->some_function(-fee=>'Englishman',-foe=>'Russian');
```

The values of the named arguments, if present, are assigned to the Perl variables $fee, $fie, and so forth. -Fum and -fums are synonyms for each other and can be used interchangeably in the function's argument list.

Rearrange() expects two or more arguments. The first argument is an array reference containing the names of the expected arguments. Names are case insensitive: the arguments -fee, -FEE, and -Fee are all equivalent. You can pass a list of synonyms (arguments that are to be considered equivalent) by using an array reference as a member of the list. The remaining arguments to rearrange() are a list of argument pairs to be processed. Ordinarily, you will obtain this from the @_ array passed to the function, but be careful to first remove the object reference (i.e., self) that Perl automatically places there when using object-oriented function calls.

Rearrange() returns a list containing the arguments in the order in which they appear in the array reference. If an argument does not appear on the argument list, that element of the list will be undefined. Any arguments from the caller that do not appear on the list of argument names are formatted as if they were HTML attributes and returned at the end of the list. You are free to use these additional arguments or not, as you choose. In the previous example, they are stored in the variable @p. So, if the caller called some_function() with the argument list (-fee=>'Englishman',-giant=>'Fred'), the result from rearrange() would define $fee as Englishman; $fie, $foe, and $fum would all be undefined; and @p would contain the one element list ('GIANT="Fred"').

## Escape(), Unescape()

Two other useful internal functions include escape() and unescape(). As their names imply, these functions escape and unescape strings using standard URL encoding rules (whitespace and funny characters replaced by the percent sign and a hexadecimal code), as in:

```
$escaped = CGI->escape("Now, isn't that a rum kitten!");
```

After execution of this code, the $escaped variable will contain "Now%2C%20isn%27t%20that%20a%20rum%20kitten%21." As you would expect, unescape() reverses this transformation, returning the original string.

## EscapeHTML()

You can call escapeHTML() to perform string substitutions on anything you plan to display in a browser. It will replace < , >, and &, which have special meanings in HTML, with the appropriate character entities, >, <, and &, making them safe to incorporate into a page, as in:

```
$safe = CGI->escapeHTML(">>>>>> Look here! <<<<<<");
```

## expires()

The internal expires() function can be used to calculate a timestamp relative to the present. Call it like this:

```
$timestamp = CGI::expires("+29d");
```

This will return a time stamp for 29 days in the future, in a format suitable for use in an HTTP or MIME header. Be sure to notice that expires()

does not use the object-oriented calling style. Call it directly as shown in the previous snippet.

For unclear reasons, the cookie specification does not use exactly the same format for dates as the HTTP specification (one uses dashes to separate fields; the other, spaces). For this reason, you can pass an optional second argument to expires() with a value of "cookie" in order to return the timestamp in cookie format, for example:

```
$cookie_timestamp = CGI::expires("+29d","cookie");
```

# Using CGI.pm with FastCGI and mod_perl

FastCGI and Apache's mod_perl are two popular solutions for improving the performance of CGI scripts. CGI.pm has been written to be compatible with them. This section gives you the background information needed to use CGI.pm successfully with either of these products.

## FASTCGI

FastCGI is a protocol invented by OpenMarket that markedly speeds up CGI scripts. It works by opening up the script at server startup time and redirecting the script's I/O to a UNIX domain socket. Every time a new CGI request comes in, the script is passed new parameters to work on. This allows the script to perform all its time-consuming operations at initialization (including loading CGI.pm), thereby responding quickly to new requests. Scripts show the most marked improvement when running on heavily loaded servers, or when they need to perform lengthy startup operations, such as opening a connection to a relational database.

FastCGI modules are available for the Apache and NCSA servers as well as for OpenMarket's own server. In order to use FastCGI with Perl, however, you must run a version of the Perl interpreter that has been compiled using Perl's abstract I/O interface. The FastCGI module gives instructions on how to do this.

The standard CGI.pm distribution comes with an inherited module, CGI::Fast, that implements the FastCGI interface. To use CGI::Fast in your scripts, you will need to do two things:

1. Enter "use CGI::Fast" at the top of the script.
2. Put the entire script into a "while(new CGI::Fast)" loop. The script will wait at the top of the loop until a new CGI request comes in, then execute the contents of the loop and wait for the next request.

To further understand the changes you need to make, consider the following code:

**Old Script**

```
#!/usr/bin/perl
use CGI qw(:standard);
print header,
      start_html("CGI Script"),
      h1("CGI Script"),
      "Not much to see here",
      hr,
      address(a({href=>'/'},"home page"),
      end_html;
```

To convert this to work with FastCGI, change the code to read something like this:

**New Script**

```
#!/usr/bin/perl
use CGI::Fast qw(:standard);

# Do time-consuming initialization up here.
# ......
while (new CGI::Fast) {
   print header,
      start_html("CGI Script"),
      h1("CGI Script"),
      "Not much to see here",
      hr,
      address(a({href=>'/'},"home page"),
      end_html;
}
```

The main change is the use of CGI::Fast rather than CGI at the top of the script. You can continue to import whatever function sets you need. Then do any time-consuming initialization, such as opening databases, bringing in other code libraries, or initializing data structures. We then enter a while() loop waiting for a new CGI connection to come in.

If you want to use the object-oriented interface, modify the while() loop to read:

```
while ($q = new CGI::Fast) {
   ....
}
```

Each time through the loop, the call to CGI::Fast's new() function will retrieve a different object.

Beyond this, your scripts should not need any other specific changes. However, you must be cautious about allocating and using global variables. Many CGI programmers are profligate in their use of globals because they know the variables will be deallocated as soon as the script exits. FastCGI scripts, however, remain for a long period of time, and the use of globals left over by previous runs through the loop may have unwanted consequences.

You can get more information about FastCGI along with Perl source code and executables at www.fastcgi.com.

## mod_perl

Mod_perl is a module for the Apache Web server that actually embeds a Perl interpreter within the server itself. As a result, the server reads and compiles the scripts only once. After that, every time the script is needed, the server simply executes its precompiled code. This speeds up the latency of typical CGI scripts enormously, often ten-fold or more. Mod_perl is actively being ported to the Windows NT version of Apache, and has been ready to use on Windows systems since January 1998.

Recent versions of Perl, mod_perl, and CGI.pm are completely interoperable. No source code changes need to be made in CGI scripts to make them run with mod_perl. You will need at least CGI.pm 2.36, mod_perl 1.07, and Perl 5.004. If you are using an earlier version of any of these components, and for some reason cannot upgrade, a module called CGI::Apache is included in the standard CGI distribution. This implements an object-oriented (but not function-oriented) interface that works correctly with mod_perl.

As explained in greater detail in the mod_perl documentation, you should prepare a new directory in the Apache server root to hold mod_perl scripts; for example, /usr/local/etc/httpd/cgi-perl. You must then tell Apache to invoke the embedded Perl interpreter when accessing files in this directory. Here are the configuration directives that you should add to the srm.conf and access.conf configuration files:

```
#srm.conf
Alias /cgi-perl /usr/local/etc/httpd/cgi-perl

#access.conf
<Location /cgi-perl>
  SetHandler  perl-script
  PerlHandler Apache::Registry
  Options ExecCGI
</Location>
```

In srm.conf, the Alias directive adds /cgi-perl to the site's virtual document tree, and associates it with the indicated physical path. In access.conf, the <Location> section sets the properties for this directory. The SetHandler directive tells Apache to associate all files in this directory with the embedded Perl interpreter. PerlHandler, in turn, tells mod_perl to pass scripts in this directory to a module named Apache::Registry. This module is responsible for the simulation of the standard CGI environment. Finally, turn on the ExecCGI option in order to allow executable scripts to run in this directory.

It is important not to enable the mod_perl, PerlSendHeader, or PerlSetupEnv directives in directories that contain CGI.pm-using scripts. These directives are designed to be used in scripts written specifically for the mod_perl environment. When you use CGI.pm, these functions are handled automatically. If you do inadvertently enable these directives, the script may generate an internal server error, or other undesirable output at the beginning of the page.

When using CGI.pm in conjunction with mod_perl, there are certain optimizations that can improve performance. One trick is to create a startup script that loads CGI.pm when Apache first starts up. This avoids the initial penalty of compiling CGI.pm for each script that uses it. To implement a startup script, add a PerlScript directive to Apache's httpd.conf configuration file. This directive should point at the file you wish to load at startup time:

```
PerlScript /usr/local/web/scripts/startup.pl
```

Startup.pl should contain a series of *use* statements that load the modules you want to be available to all scripts. One of these statements should load CGI.pm and call its compile() method:

```
#file: startup.pl
use CGI();
CGI->compile(':all');
1;
```

The compile method tells CGI.pm to precompile all its autoloaded functions. This slows down the Apache startup process slightly, but greatly speeds up the initial loading of all scripts that need CGI.pm. Notice that the startup script does not import any functions or function sets from CGI.pm (the empty parenthesis, although unecessary, makes this more obvious). The individual mod_perl scripts should import just the symbols they need from CGI.pm with their own *use* statements.

Each time a mod_perl script imports a function or function set from CGI.pm, its memory consumption increases slightly. If you have many scripts running, this consumption can become significant. An experimental feature introduced with CGI.pm 2.38 allows you to avoid this overhead by importing the -autoload pragma:

```
use CGI '-autoload';
```

When a mod_perl script loads CGI.pm in this manner, the script's autoload function is overidden in such a way that any time the script calls a function that isn't recognized, Perl defers to CGI.pm to provide it. The script can call any of the functions defined by CGI.pm without explicitly importing it, and without the memory overhead of importing functions. One drawback of this approach is that it prevents you from defining an autoload function in your own script. Another drawback is that you cannot use the so-called "poetry mode" in which one can call predefined functions without the parenthesis (e.g., *hr* rather than *hr()* for a horizontal rule). However, you can selectively restore poetry mode with a "use subs" statement:

```
use subs qw/hr br p/;
```

More information about obtaining and installing mod_perl is available at the Apache Organization's Web site: www.apache.org.

# Migrating from cgi-lib.pl

Cgi-lib.pl is a Perl 4 library written by Steve Brenner. Until Perl 4 was eclipsed by Perl 5, cgi-lib.pl was the standard for CGI scripting. Many sites still use cgi-lib.pl, and in most cases, there is no compelling reason to rewrite scripts to use CGI.pm.

However, if you need to use the fancy features of CGI.pm, including sticky forms, state maintenance, HTML shortcuts, and cookies, you may wish to migrate your older CGI scripts. To facilitate this upgrade, CGI.pm provides a cgi-lib.pl compatability mode. To use it, change your scripts to import a CGI.pm function set named :cgi-lib as follows:

```
use CGI qw/:cgi-lib/;
```

This will import a function named ReadParse() that is compatible with cgi-lib's function of the same name. When you call this function, CGI.pm creates an associative array named %in that contains the named CGI parameters. Multivalued parameters are separated by \0 characters in exactly the same way as cgi-lib. The function returns the number of parameters parsed, allowing you to determine whether the script is being called with or without parameters.

Here is an example of an older script being converted to use CGI.pm:

**Old Script**

```
require "cgi-lib.pl";
ReadParse();
print "The price of your purchase is $in{price}.\n";
```

**New Script**

```
use CGI qw(:cgi-lib);
ReadParse();
print "The price of your purchase is $in{price}.\n";
```

You may pass ReadParse() a variable global (starred variable) to have it parse the CGI parameters into the variable of your choice:

```
ReadParse(*Q);
@partners = split("\0",$Q{'golf_partners'});
```

You can freely intermix the cgi-lib.pl style of scripting with the function-oriented CGI.pm style. If you would like to use object-oriented calls, you will need to recover the CGI object used internally by ReadParse(). You can get to it by reading the special key CGI stored in the %in array:

```
ReadParse();
$q = $in{CGI};
print $q->textfield(-name=>'wow',
                    -value=>'does this really work?');
```

This allows you to add the more interesting features of CGI.pm to your old scripts without rewriting them completely. As an added benefit, the %in variable is actually tied to the CGI object so that changing the CGI object using param() will dynamically change %in, and vice versa. The hash entry, $in{CGI}, is automatically set to the default $CGI::Q object, so you can simply refer to the latter if you prefer.

Less often used cgi-lib.pl functions are also supported, including HtmlTop(), HtmlBot(), SplitParam(), MethGet(), and MethPost(). However the @in and $in variables are *not* supported. In addition, the extended version of ReadParse() that allows you to spool uploaded files to disk is not available; you should use CGI.pm's file upload interface instead.

More information on porting cgi-lib.pl scripts to CGI.pm can be found in the document cgi-lib_porting.html that is included in the CGI.pm distribution.

Chapter Five, *Reference Guide*, is a complete reference to all the variables, functions, and methods defined by CGI.pm.

# Chapter Five

# Reference Guide

This chapter is a comprehensive list of all CGI.pm's functions and features. It starts with a listing of CGI.pm's function sets and pragmas, and continues with a guide to its syntax. The remainder is a glossary of the module's functions, grouped first by topic, then alphabetically within the topic. If you are having trouble locating a particular CGI.pm function, please check this book's index.

## Function Sets and Pragmas

You can import individual or commonly used sets of CGI.pm functions. Function sets are distinguished from individual functions with a leading colon (:) character. The following line of code imports the HTML2 set, the HTML3 set, and the https() function:

```
use CGI qw/:html2 :html3 https/;
```

Because HTML is constantly updated by browser vendors, CGI.pm allows you to import functions that may not yet be known to HTML. These functions will create HTML tags that follow the syntax rules of HTML shortcut functions. For example, the following line will create a function to support the nonstandard Internet Explorer <MARQUEE> tag:

```
use CGI qw/marquee/;
```

In addition to function sets, CGI.pm recognizes several pragmas that change the module's default behavior. As of version 2.38, these pragmas all begin with a leading dash character. In previous versions, the pragmas begin with a colon. This form is still supported for backward compatibility.

## FUNCTION SETS

CGI.pm recognizes the following function sets:

- ***:all*** The union of :html2, :html3, :netscape, :form, and :cgi.
- ***:cgi*** Functions related to retrieving and setting CGI parameter lists, the CGI environment, and cookies. Note that a few functions begin with caps to avoid conflicts with Perl operators.
  accept(), auth_type(), cookie(), Delete(), Delete_all(), dump(), header(), http(), import_names(), param(), path_info(), path_translated(), put(), query_string(), raw_cookie(), redirect(), referer(), remote_host(), remote_addr(), remote_ident(), remote_user(), request_method(), restore_parameters(), save_parameters(), script_name(), self_url(), server_name(), server_port(), server_protocol(), server_software(), url(), url_param(), use_named_parameters(), user_agent(), user_name(), virtual_host()
- ***:cgi-lib*** Compatibility with Steve Brenner's cgi-lib.pl.
  HtmlBot(), HtmlTop(), PrintHeader(), ReadParse(), SplitParam()

- ***:form*** Fill-out form elements.

  autoEscape(), button(), checkbox(), checkbox_group(), defaults(), end_form(), endform(), filefield(), hidden(), image_button(), isindex(), MULTIPART(), password_field(), popup_menu(), radio_group(), reset(), scrolling_list(), start_form(), start_multipart_form(), startform(), submit(), textarea(), textfield(), tmpFileName(), uploadInfo(), URL_ENCODED()
- ***:html*** The union of :html2, :html3, and :netscape.
- ***:html2*** HTML version 2 shortcuts. Most are lowercase versions of the corresponding HTML tags, but a few use initial caps in order to prevent conflicts with built-in Perl operators.

  a(), address(), b(), base(), blockquote(), body(), br(), cite(), code(), comment(), dd(), defn(), dl(), dt(), em(), end_html(), h1(), h2(), h3(), h4(), h5(), h6(), hr(), head(), html(), i(), img(), input(), li(), kbd(), Link(), menu(), meta(), nextid(), ol(), option(), p(), pre(), samp(), Select(), start_html(), ul(), strong(), title(), tt(), var()
- ***:html3*** HTML version 3.2 shortcuts.

  applet(), basefont(), caption(), div(), embed(), layer(), ilayer(), Param(), span(), strike(), style(), sub(), sup(), table(), th(), td(), Tr()
- ***:netscape*** Common Netscape (and Microsoft) specific HTML extensions.

  blink(), big(), center(), font(), fontsize(), frameset(), frame(), script(), small()
- ***:ssl*** SSL (Secure Socket Layer) related functions.

  https()
- ***:standard*** The union of :html2, :cgi, and :form.

## PRAGMAS

CGI.pm recognizes the following pragmas. To use pragmas, import them into the "use" statement just like functions and function sets:

- ***-autoload*** Turns on an experimental mode in which all of CGI.pm's functions are made available without explicitly importing them. This minimizes memory use and is useful in long-running environments such as mod_perl.
- ***-compile*** Precompile all the functions or function sets listed in the *use* line. This slows down the initial loading of the module, but improves performance in long-running scripts, such as when scripts are run under FastCGI or mod_perl.
- ***-no_debug*** Inhibit debugging. When running in this mode, CGI.pm will not prompt for CGI parameters when called from the command line.
- ***-nph*** Turn on NPH (no-parse header) mode.
- ***-private_tempfiles*** Unlink the temporary files used for file upload immediately after creation, keeping them away from prying eyes. This will deactivate the tmpFileName() function.

# CGI.pm Syntax

CGI.pm supports both object-oriented and function-oriented syntaxes. In addition, most calls (whether invoked as object methods or as function calls) can be passed arguments using either a named argument list style, or a simpler ordered list style.

## OBJECT-ORIENTED SYNTAX

When using CGI.pm's object-oriented syntax, you need not import any symbols into the use statement. However, before you use any of CGI.pm's functions, you must first create a CGI object with CGI::new(). You may then use the returned object to call CGI methods, manipulate the state of the CGI parameter list, and save the changes to a disk file or database. For example:

```
use CGI;
$q = new CGI;
print "The current value of NAME is ",$q->param('NAME'),"\n";
$q->param(-name=>'NAME',-value=>'Fred');
print "The new value of NAME is ",$q->param('NAME'),"\n";
```

Most of the examples in this chapter use the object-oriented syntax and assume that the Perl variable $q has already been created with a call to new().

## new(), restore_parameters()

In the object-oriented syntax, you must create a CGI object with CGI::new() in order to gain access to CGI.pm's other functions. The new() call may take no arguments, in which case, the CGI object is initialized with the current Web request's CGI parameters, or with a single argument. The contents of the returned CGI object depend on the type of this argument.

- ***A string*** The string is parsed as a CGI query string using the standard URL escaping rules and parameter list conventions. For example:

  ```
  $q = new CGI('first_name=Fred&last_name=Smith');
  ```
- ***A filehandle*** The CGI object is initialized from name=value pairs read from the indicated filehandle. Each pair must be located on a separate line. Whitespace and other funny characters must be escaped, either using URL hex escapes, or by preceding the character with a backslash. The correct format is automatically created by CGI::save() and save_parameters().
- ***A reference to an associative array*** The CGI object is initialized from the key/value pairs of the associative array. For example:

  ```
  $q = new CGI({'first_name'=>'fred','last_name'=>'Smith'});
  ```

If new() is called without arguments more than once, the second and subsequent CGI objects will be derived from the original CGI parameter list, regardless of changes that you may have made to a previously created CGI object.

In the function-oriented syntax (see the next section), you must use restore_parameters(). This is to avoid a possible collision between new() and your own subroutines that potentially use this common name.

### save(), save_parameters()

Given a filehandle, write the contents of the current CGI object out to the filehandle in a format that can be read in again using new().

If you are using the function-oriented syntax (see the next section), you must use the function save_parameters() instead of save(). This is to avoid collisions between save() and your own subroutines that potentially use this common name.

## FUNCTION-ORIENTED SYNTAX

In the function-oriented style, specific functions or function sets must be imported with the "use" statement. Calls to CGI routines can then be made without creating a CGI object in advance. Internally, a default object named $CGI::Q is created in the CGI namespace. You can access this variable by referring to it explicitly. For example:

```
use CGI qw/:standard/;
print print "The current value of NAME is ",$param('NAME'),"\n";
param(-name=>'NAME',-value=>'Fred');
print "The new value of NAME is ",param('NAME'),"\n";
$q = $CGI::Q;
print $q->strong("This works too.");
```

## NAMED AND POSITIONAL ARGUMENT LISTS

All CGI.pm functions can be called with named argument lists, allowing CGI.pm to support functions with many possible combinations of optional arguments. Frequently used functions often have a simpler calling style that use one or two positional arguments.

Named argument lists are passed to CGI.pm functions as a series of -name=>value pairs, as in:

```
print textfield(-name=>'credit_card_no',-value=>'0000000');
```

Argument names are always proceeded by dashes unless the useNamedParameters() function has been called, as you will see in the following example. In some cases, argument names may conflict with Perl operators, causing warnings to appear in the server error log. For example, the -values argument conflicts with the Perl "values" operator (which retrieves the values of an associative array). You can avoid this warning by enclosing the argument in quotes, or by using a synonym for the argument. For example, CGI.pm functions recognize and treat -value as synonymous with -values. You can also take advantage of the fact that argument names are case insensitive. If -values is generating annoying warnings you can use -Values instead.

Many frequently used functions also accept positional arguments. For example, these two ways of calling the param() function are equivalent:

```
param('NAME');
param(-name=>'NAME');
```

The CGI.pm functions that create simple HTML tags, as opposed to those that create sticky forms or HTTP headers, do not take named arguments. Instead, they take a variable number of string arguments to be placed between the start and ending tags of the HTML element they generate. If the first argument is a hash reference, its key/value pairs will be turned into

HTML attribute pairs and incorporated into the leading tag. If any of the arguments is a list reference, the tag will be *distributed* across it. Here are two typical examples:

| **Source** | **Result** |
|---|---|
| hr(); | <HR> |
| h1('Page','One') | <H1>Page One</H1> |
| img({-src=>'/img/star.gif'}) | <IMG SRC="/img/star.gif"> |
| h1({-align=>CENTER},'Page Two') | <H1 ALIGN="CENTER">Page Two</H1> |
| li([1,2,3]); | <LI>1</LI><LI>2</LI><LI>3</LI> |

Like named arguments, attributes are case insensitive. Unlike named arguments, you can safely omit the initial dash, regardless of the setting of useNamedParameters(). For example:

```
print h1({ALIGN=>CENTER},'Page 2');
```

The distinction between HTML shortcuts that are passed an attribute list as an anonymous hash (using curly braces), and other functions in the CGI.pm module that expect named arguments (without the braces) can be confusing for new users. It may help to know that all the functions in the :html2, :html3, and :netscape function sets expect attribute lists. Aside from a few capitalization differences, these functions are named identically to standard HTML tags. Every other function in CGI.pm expects named arguments.

Because the distinction between attribute lists and named arguments is confusing, CGI.pm versions 2.38 and higher allow you to pass named arguments as a hash reference:

```
print start_html({-title=>'First Page',-author=>'Fred Smith'});
```

You can therefore use the curly brace notation to pass arguments to all CGI.pm functions, without worrying about which ones are the simple HTML shortcuts.

# HTTP Header and Environment

These functions allow you to create the outgoing HTTP header and retrieve information about the current session. These functions are imported when you use the :cgi set.

## accept()

**Retrieve list of recognized MIME types:**

```
@types = $q->accept();
```

**Check whether browser accepts a particular MIME type:**

```
$png_ok = $q->accept("image/png");
```

Called without arguments, accept() returns a list of MIME types that the remote browser accepts. If you give this function a single argument corresponding to a MIME type, as in $q->accept('text/html'), it will return a floating point value corresponding to the browser's preference for this type from 0.0 (don't want) to 1.0. Wild card types (for example, text/*) are handled correctly both in the argument list and when present in the browser's own accept list.

## auth_type()

```
$authenticated++ if $q->auth_type() eq 'Basic';
```

This function returns the authorization type for the current session if user authentication is active for the script's directory. Under HTTP/1.0, this function will either return Basic, when basic authentication is in use, or undef, when no authentication is being used. This function takes no arguments.

## cookie()

### Retrieve all cookie names:

```
@names = cookie();
```

### Retrieving value of one cookie (simple form):

```
@vegetables = cookie('veggies');
```

### Retrieving value of one cookie (named argument form):

```
@vegetables = cookie(-name=>'veggies');
```

### Creating new cookie:

```
$new_cookie = cookie(-name=>'veggies',
                     -values=>['okra','kale','cabbage']);
```

This function creates and retrieves HTTP cookies from the current session. Scripts create cookies and sends them to the browser in the HTTP header. When the browser reconnects, it returns all the cookies (none, one, or several) that the script has previously sent it. Each cookie is named and contains scalar or list data, but the maximum practical size for cookie data is a few kilobytes.

Called with no arguments, cookie() returns the name of all cookies sent by the browser to your script. Called with the name of a single cookie, the function returns the contents of the cookie, or undef if the cookie does not exist. Alternatively, you may use the named argument list form of the function call to retrieve the cookie named with the -name argument.

New cookies can be created by specifying their name and contents with the -name and -value arguments. The complete list of arguments follows:

- ***-domain*** The range of domain names over which the browser will return this cookie. Possible values include complete hostnames, such as www.capricorn.com, and partial domain names, such as .capricorn.com (note the leading dot). It is not possible to specify a top level domain, such as .com or .edu. This argument is optional, and if absent, the browser will return the cookie only to the server that created it.

- ***-expires*** The absolute or relative expiration date for this cookie (optional). The format is described in the next section in the description of header(). Values in the future will cause the browser to store the cookie in a local database and return it to your script until the cookie expires. Negative values cause the browser to delete the cookie from its database immediately. If no -expires argument is given, the browser will maintain the cookie until the user quits the browser application.
- ***-name*** Specifies the name of the cookie. Names may be any combination of ASCII or non-ASCII characters, including whitespace.
- ***-path*** The optional partial path for which this cookie will be valid, as previously described.
- ***-secure*** If set to true, the browser will only return this cookie to the server when SSL is active. It will not prevent your script from sending the cookie over an insecure connection. See the section on https() function for information on determining the status of SSL.
- ***-value, -values*** Specifies the contents of the cookie. The value may be a scalar string containing any combination of ASCII and non-ASCII characters, or may be a reference to a list or associative array. Be sure to assign the contents of the cookie to the appropriate data type when retrieving the value of the returned cookie (that is, do not create a cookie from a list and expect to get it back intact if you assign its contents to a scalar). If you wish to store more complex data types in cookies, you may use the Data::Dumper module (available from CPAN) to serialize the object.

## header()

**Simple form:**

```
print $q->header('image/gif');
```

**Named argument form:**

```
print $q->header(-type=>'image/gif');
```

The simple form of the header() function returns a valid HTTP header that indicates that the document to follow will be of the given MIME type. If no argument is specified, it will default to text/html. Header() is generally the first thing that a CGI script will print.

The named argument version of this method allows you to specify the MIME type with a -type argument, and control various other features as well.

- ***-cookie, -cookies*** The -cookie parameter generates a header that tells Netscape browsers to return a magic cookie during all subsequent transactions with your script. Netscape cookies have a special format that includes interesting attributes such as expiration time. Use the cookie() method to create and retrieve session cookies. The value of this parameter can be either a scalar value or an array reference. You can use the latter to generate multiple cookies. The alias -cookies can be use for readability.
- ***-expires*** Some browsers, such as Internet Explorer, cache the output of CGI scripts; others, such as Netscape Navigator, do not. This leads to annoying and inconsistent behavior when going from one browser to another. You can force the behavior to be consistent by using the -expires parameter. When you specify an absolute or relative expiration interval with this parameter, browsers and proxy servers will cache the script's output until the indicated expiration date. The following forms are all valid for the field:

| | |
|---|---|
| +30s | 30 seconds from now |
| +10m | 10 minutes from now |
| +1h | 1 hour from now |
| -1d | yesterday (i.e., "ASAP!") |
| now | immediately |
| +3M | in 3 months |
| +10y | in 10 years' time |
| Thu, 25-Apr-96 00:40:33 GMT | at the indicated time & date |

When you use -expires, the header() function also generates a correct time stamp for the generated document to ensure that your clock and the browser's clock agree. This allows you to create documents that are reliably cached for short periods of time. CGI::expires() is the static function call used internally that turns relative time intervals into HTTP dates. You can call it directly if you wish.

- ***-nph*** The -nph parameter, if set to a nonzero value, will generate a valid header for use in no-parsed-header scripts. For example:

```
print $query->header(-nph=>1,
                        -status=>'200 OK',
                        -type=>'text/html');
```

You will need to use this if:

1. If you need to create unbuffered output, for example for use in a server push script.
2. To take advantage of HTTP extensions not supported by your server.

Using the -nph argument is equivalent to importing the -nph pragma in the "use" statement.

- ***-status*** Set the numeric status code and human readable message for the HTTP header.
- ***-target*** Name the frame in which the document should be displayed (Netscape-compatible browsers only). Example:

```
print $q->header(-type=>'text/html',-frame=>'responses');
```

- ***-type*** Set the MIME type for the returned document.

### Other Arguments

Any other arguments that you pass to header() will be turned into correctly formatted HTTP header fields, even if they are not part of the current HTTP specification. Use underscores instead of hyphens, if necessary. For example, to roll your own password authentication system using the HTTP WWW-Authenticate header, you could create the header in this way:

```
print $q->header(-status=>'401 Authorization Required',
                 -WWW_Authenticate=>'Basic; realm="Members"');
```

You will need a working knowledge of the HTTP protocol in order to make the best use of this feature.

## https()

```
print "SSL is active" if https()=~/ON/i;
print "Key length is " https('SECRETKEYSIZE');
```

Https() can be used to determine whether SSL is active, and to gather information about the session. Called with no arguments, https() will return undef if SSL is not in use, or the word “on” if SSL is active (it is uppercase in some servers and lowercase in others).

Called with a single argument X, https() returns the value of the corresponding HTTPS_*X* environment variable. There are a large number of such variables, but the ones that are available differ somewhat from server to server. Check your server's documentation for details. In the preceding example (taken from the Stronghold server), we retrieve the secret key length by examining the HTTPS_SECRETKEYSIZE variable.

The https() variables are read only. They cannot modified.

## path_info()

**Retrieve additional path information:**

```
$document_URL = $q->path_info();
```

**Set additional path information:**

```
$q->path_info('/plans/q4/index.html')
```

This function returns additional path information from the script URL. For example, if your script was called with the URL

```
/cgi-bin/your_script/additional/stuff
```

then the function will return /additional/stuff.

In addition to reading the path information, you can set the path by giving path_info() an optional string argument. The argument is expected to begin with a /. If not present, one will be added for you. The new path information will be returned by subsequent calls to path_info(), and will be incorporated into the URL generated by self_url(). *See also* path_translated().

## path_translated()

```
$physical_path = $q->path_translated();
```

As per path_info(), but returns the additional path information translated into a physical file path, for example: /usr/local/etc/httpd/htdocs/additional/stuff. You cannot change this value, either with path_translated() or with path_info(). The reason for this restriction is that the translation of path information into a physical path is ordinarily done by the server in a layer that is inaccessible to CGI scripts.

## query_string()

```
$query = $q->query_string();
```

Returns the raw, unprocessed, query string from the current Web request. Ordinarily, you will want to user the param() high level interface. This function takes no arguments.

## raw_cookie()

```
@dough = $q->raw_cookie();
```

This function returns the list of unprocessed HTTP cookies returned by the browser. You are responsible for parsing out the name/value pairs, and unescaping the data, if necessary. You will probably want to use cookie() instead, which gives you a high-level interface to the cookie functions. This function takes no arguments.

## redirect()

**Simple form:**

```
print $q->redirect('http://somewhere.else/index.html');
```

**Named argument form:**

```
print $q->redirect(-location=>'http://somewhere.else/index.html');
```

This function generates an HTTP header containing a redirection request. When the browser receives this header, it will immediately load the indicated destination URL. Your script should exit soon after printing the header because all other output will be ignored by the browser. The simple form takes a single argument, the URL of the location to jump to. In the named argument form, the following arguments are recognized:

- ***-location, -uri*** These two arguments are interchangeable, and indicate the URL of the destination page to load. You should always use absolute or full URLs in redirection requests. Relative URLs will not work correctly.
- ***-nph*** Create the HTTP header in no-parse-header mode. This is equivalent to importing the -nph pragma.

All named arguments recognized by header() are also recognized by redirect(). However, most HTTP headers, including those generated by -cookie and -target, are ignored by the browser.

## referer()

```
print "You were last reading ",$q->referer();
```

Returns the URL of the page the browser was viewing prior to fetching your script, usually the page that the link to your script appears on. This function takes no arguments.

## remote_addr()

```
die "Unauthorized" unless $q->remote_addr()=~/^18\.157\.0/;
```

Returns the dotted IP address of the remote host. Be aware that this may be the IP address of a proxy server, rather than the user's desktop machine, if the user goes through an ISP or firewall system.

## remote_ident()

```
print "You are logged in as ",$q->remote_ident();
```

For remote hosts that have the identd identity-checking daemon activated, returns the remote user's local login name. This is only available for some UNIX hosts, and is not to be trusted as a source of authentication information. This function takes no arguments.

## remote_host()

```
print "Welcome to our visitor from ", $q->remote_host();
```

Returns the DNS name of the remote host. If no name is available, returns the dotted IP address as in remote_addr(). This function takes no arguments.

## remote_user()

```
die "Unauthorized access" unless $q->remote_user() eq 'Fred';
```

If the script is under password protection (Basic authentication), this function will return the account name used to authenticate. If authentication is not in use, this call will return undef. There is no call for retrieving the password itself, because this is not part of the CGI/HTTP environment. However, if your script has access to the server's password file, you can obtain the encrypted password yourself by looking up the account name. This function takes no arguments.

## request_method()

```
if ($q->request_method() eq 'POST') {
    process_form();
```

```
} else {
   generate_form();
}
```

Returns the HTTP method used to request your script's URL, usually one of GET, POST, or HEAD. Ordinarily, this will be handled automatically for you by param(). This function takes no arguments.

## script_name()

```
$name = script_name();
```

Returns the URL of this script, relative to the top of the Web document tree. To retrieve the physical path name of the script, use $0 instead. *See also* url() and self_url(). This function takes no arguments.

## self_url()

```
$me = $q->self_url();
print $q->a({-href=>$me},"Reload me");
```

This function returns a URL containing the communications protocol, host, port number (if necessary), path to the script, additional path information, and the entire current CGI parameter list. If the user selects a link containing this URL, the script will be reinvoked with as much of its internal state intact as possible. For example:

```
http://your.site:8000/cgi-bin/search/WEBSITE?first=andy&last=smith
```

If the CGI parameter list is long, the URL generated by this function may be sizable. When it is resubmitted to the Web server, it is possible that the end of the URL will be truncated by the server, causing information to be lost. Only use this function for CGI parameter lists of manageable length.

Certain types of parameter information, such as uploaded files, cannot be restored in this way. *See also* url() and script_name() for related functionality. This function takes no arguments.

## server_name()

```
print "Welcome to ",$q->server_name();
```

Returns the name of the Web server. When virtual hosts are in use, this function will return the name of the main site. *See also* virtual_host(). This function takes no arguments.

## server_software()

```
print "Server version ",$q->server_software();
```

Returns the name and version of the server software as a string. You can use this to check whether certain server-specific features are available to your script. This function takes no arguments.

## server_port()

```
die "Not the official SSL port" unless $q->server_port() == 443;
```

Returns the communications port the current session is using. This is usually 80 for HTTP sessions and 443 for encrypted SSL sessions. This function takes no arguments.

## url()

```
$url = $q->url();
print $q->a({-href=>$url},"Reload this script");
```

Url() returns the URL of the current script, minus the additional path information and query string. This is useful for reloading the script with an empty CGI parameter list and no additional path information. The string returned is similar to that returned by script_name(), except that the communications protocol, server hostname, and port number (if necessary) are prepended to the path (in other words, http://your.host/cgi-bin/search.pl rather than /cgi-bin/search.pl). This function takes no arguments.

## user_agent()

```
print "Welcome Explorer user" if $q->user_agent()=~/MSIE/;
```

Returns a string identifying the remote user's browser software. For example, "Mozilla/1.1N (Macintosh; I; 68K)". This function takes no arguments.

## user_name()

```
print "Hello ",$q->user_name();
```

This function attempts to obtain the remote user's name, using a variety of means. It first looks for a username provided during authentication. If this is not available, it checks the From: HTTP header provided by some older browsers. Failing this, the function tries to recover the user's login name using the identd mechanism. *See also* remote_ident(). This function takes no arguments.

## virtual_host()

```
print "Welcome to ",$q->virtual_host();
```

When using the virtual host feature of some servers, returns the name of the virtual host the browser is accessing. See also server_name(). This function takes no arguments.

# CGI Parameters

This set of functions allows you to access and modify the CGI parameter list. These functions are imported as a group when you use the :cgi set.

## delete(), Delete()

**Positional argument form:**

```
$q->delete('veggies');
```

**Named argument form:**

```
$q->delete(-name=>'veggies');
```

**Function-oriented forms:**

```
Delete('veggies');
Delete(-name=>'veggies');
```

This function deletes the named CGI parameter from the parameter list. The parameter will no longer be returned by param(), self_url(), or used to set the value of sticky form elements. Note that when using the function-oriented interface, the name of this function is Delete() with an initial capital. This is to avoid a conflict with the built-in Perl operator of the same name. Takes the following argument:

- ***-name*** Specify the name of the CGI parameter to delete.

## delete_all(), Delete_all()

```
$q->delete_all();
```

Delete_all() deletes all CGI parameters from the parameter list. The CGI object will be empty. This may be useful for forcing all sticky form elements to their defaults. Although there is no conflict with built-in Perl operators, the function-oriented synonym Delete_all() is provided for symmetry with Delete(). This function takes no arguments.

## import_names()

```
$q->import_names('R');     # import and add
print "Your name is $R::name\n"
print "Your favorite colors are @R::colors\n";
$q->import_names('Q',1);  # import and delete
```

Import_names() imports all CGI paramcters into the namespace of your choice. For example, if there were parameters named foo1, foo2 and foo3, after executing $query->import_names('R'), the variables @R::foo1, $R::foo1, @R::foo2, $R::foo2, and so forth would conveniently spring into existence. Since CGI has no way of knowing whether a given CGI parameter is single or multivalued, each parameter becomes two different variables. One is an array that contains all the values for the parameter, and the other is a scalar containing just the first member of the array. Use whichever one is appropriate. For keyword parameter lists created by <ISINDEX> pages, the variable @R::keywords will be created.

CGI parameter names can contain whitespace and control characters, but Perl variables are much more restricted. If a CGI parameter is named something that can not be represented as a Perl variable, the illegal characters will be converted into underscores. In other words, CGI parameter, Full Name, will become Perl variable $R::Full_Name. No check for overlap between translated names is performed, so avoid giving two CGI parameters names that will collide when unusual characters are converted to underscores.

If you do not specify a namespace, this method assumes namespace Q. For security reasons, you are not allowed to import into namespace main. CGI.pm will die with a fatal error if you attempt to do so.

Ordinarily, import_names() will add the CGI parameters to the given namespace without disturbing any variables that are already defined there (unless they are unfortunate enough to have the same name as an imported variable; in which case, they are overwritten). You can change this behavior by providing an optional second argument to import_names(). If this argument is nonzero, CGI.pm will delete the contents of the name space before importing into it. This is mostly used in environments like mod_perl in which the script does not exit after processing each CGI request.

## keywords()

```
@search_terms = $q->keywords()
```

A very few older scripts are called from pages declared searchable using the <ISINDEX> HTML tag. When a page is searchable, the browser will display a single text input field and prompt the user to press Return after typing one or more terms to search for. The keywords are appended to the script's URL using a query string in the format *keyword1+keyword2+keyword3*.

When called in this manner, your script can obtain the list of keywords with the keywords() function. It is also possible to recover the same information by calling param('keywords'). This function takes no arguments.

## param()

**Retrieving the names of all CGI parameters:**

```
@names = $q->param
```

**Retrieving the value of a single parameter (positional form):**

```
@vegetables = $q->param('veggies');
```

**Retrieving the value of a single parameter (named argument form):**

```
@vegetables = $q->param(-name=>'veggies');
```

**Setting the value of a parameter (named argument form):**

```
$q->param(-name=>'veggies',-value=>['okra','cabbage','squash']);
```

Param() provides access to the CGI script's parameter list, the set of name=value pairs returned by the browser when the user submits a fill-out form. Called with no arguments param() returns an array of all the parameter names in the parameter list and will return the parameter names as a list. Called with a single argument, or with the named argument -name, param() returns the value of that CGI parameter, or undef if absent. In a scalar context, param() will return the contents of single-valued parameter, or the first element of a multivalued parameter. In an array context, param() will return a list containing the contents of a multivalued parameter as shown in the preceding examples. (A single-valued parameter will be returned as a list of size 1.)

For backwards compatibility, this method will work even if the script was invoked as an <ISINDEX> script: in this case, there will be a single parameter name returned named keywords.

The following arguments are recognized. Others will be silently ignored:

- ***-name*** This argument selects the CGI parameter to read or modify. There are no restrictions on names: they can include whitespace and control characters.
- ***-value, -values*** This argument specifies a new value for the CGI parameter given by -name. You may provide this argument with either a scalar value or a reference to an array. In the latter case, a multivalued CGI parameter will be created. The argument -values is identical to -value, and is provided to make references to multivalued parameters more readable.

When a CGI parameter refers to an uploaded file submitted with a file upload field, the string returned from param() has some special properties. Used as a string, the parameter contains the name of the file on the user's local computer. Used as a filehandle, the parameter can be used to read the contents of the file. The parameter can also be passed to uploadInfo() and tmpFileName() to retrieve other information about the file. See "File Uploads" in Chapter Three, *Advanced Tricks*, for more information.

## tmpFileName()

```
$uploaded_file = $q->param('file_to_upload');
$tmpFile = $q->tmpFileName($uploaded_file);
```

This function gives access to the name of the temporary file that CGI.pm uses internally to spool uploaded files. The use of this function is deprecated because the implementation of file uploads may change at some point in the future. Also be aware that this file is automatically deleted when your script exits. If you want to save it, you must copy it to a safe location before exiting.

TmpFileName() will return undef if upload file security has been augmented by setting the $PRIVATE_TEMPFILES global in the CGI.pm source file (see Chapter Three, *Advanced Tricks*).

## uploadInfo()

```
$uploaded_file = $q->param('file_to_upload');
$info = $q->uploadInfo($uploaded_file);
$mime_type = $info->{'Content-Type'};
```

UploadInfo() provides additional information about uploaded files by examining the HTTP header provided by the browser. To retrieve the information, pass the name of the uploaded file to the function. It will return a reference to a hash in which the keys correspond to MIME header fields. Browsers that support file uploading currently only provide the MIME type of the uploaded file, in a field named Content-Type. The preceding example shows one way to retrieve this field. See "File Uploads" in Chapter Three, *Advanced Tricks*, for more details.

# Fancy Tags and Fill-Out Forms

These are smart functions that generate from one to several HTML tags. Unlike the simple HTML shortcuts discussed in the next section, they recognize arguments that do not necessarily correspond to HTML tag attributes. You ordinarily pass named arguments to these functions as a simple list, as in function(-arg1=>value1,-arg2=>value2), rather than as a hash reference, as in function({-arg1=>value1,-arg2=>value2}). In version 2.38 and higher of CGI.pm, you can use the curly bracket form for all functions without worrying about the distinction.

Another difference between the fancy tags and the simple ones is that fancy tags do not always automatically generate a closing HTML tag. In some cases, you are responsible for printing the closing tag yourself. The functions that this applies to are start_html(), which must always be paired with end_html(), and start_form(), which must always be paired with end_form(). Because these tags typically bracket large chunks of HTML code, doing it this way avoids an unmanageable degree of function nesting.

These functions are imported as a group when you use the :form set.

## autoEscape()

```
$q->autoEscape(0);
```

By default, all names and values that you pass to HTML-producing functions are run through an HTML escaping function to convert characters that have special meaning to HTML, such as the > and < symbols, into character entities. This prevents you from inadvertently creating pages that do not display correctly because of an HTML syntax error.

However, the autoescaping also interferes with your ability to enter useful HTML character entities, such as umlauts and accents. You may wish to turn the feature off temporarily by calling autoEscape() with a false (0) value. Call it with a nonzero value to reactivate escaping.

## button()

```
print $q->button(-name=>'button1',
                 -value=>'Click Me',
                 -onClick=>'doButton(this)');
```

This function creates a push button that invokes a JavaScript event handler when pressed. The HTML it produces can only be used within a fill-out form and will be silently ignored by browsers that do not include a JavaScript interpreter. Although pressing the button will not automatically submit the form, the JavaScript code that it invokes may do so by calling the form's submit() method. See the JavaScript documentation for details.

The following named arguments are recognized:

- ***-name*** This argument gives the button a name. The button can then be referred to by name within JavaScript.
- ***-onClick*** This argument assigns some JavaScript code to the button to be executed when it is pressed. Usually, it is just a call to a function previously defined somewhere else. *See also* start_html().
- ***-value, -label*** This argument assigns the button a value. The value is used for the human-readable label printed on the top and is interchangeable with -label. *See also* submit(), reset(), defaults(), and image_button().

## checkbox ()

```
print $q->checkbox(-name=>'checkbox_name',
                   -checked=>1,
                   -value=>'ON',
                   -label=>'Turn me on');
```

This function creates a single named checkbox and human-readable label. If the checkbox is selected when the form is submitted, it will be turned into a CGI parameter whose value is the value of the checkbox (on by default). If the checkbox is not selected, its corresponding CGI parameter will be empty. It takes the following arguments:

- ***-checked, -selected, -on*** These arguments, all synonyms for each other, control whether the checkbox is initially checked when the form is displayed. A nonzero value turns the checkbox on. A zero value or empty string turns it off. Note that the presence of a CGI parameter with the same name and value as the checkbox will override the -checked argument due to the sticky nature of fill-out forms.
- ***-label*** Sets the human-readable label printed next to the checkbox. If not provided, it will default to being the same as the -value argument.
- ***-name*** Sets the name of the checkbox. This name will become the CGI parameter name when the form is submitted.
- ***-onClick*** This argument sets a JavaScript event handler to be called when the checkbox is clicked. See "JavaScript-Enhanced Pages" in Chapter Three, *Advanced Tricks*, for more information.
- ***-override, -force*** This argument overrides the sticky behavior of fill-out form elements and forces the checkbox to have the selection state given to it by -checked, regardless of the state of a CGI parameter with the same name. -Force is a synonym provided for your convenience.
- ***-value*** Sets the value that the checkbox returns to the script when selected. If not provided, this will be the string on. The value will also be printed next to the checkbox unless the -label argument is also provided.

## checkbox_group()

```
%labels = ('eenie'=>'hey',
           'meenie'=>'that',
           'minie'=>'tickles');
print $q->checkbox_group(-name=>'pick_some',
                         -values=>['eenie','meenie','minie','moe'],
                         -default=>['eenie','moe'],
                         -linebreak=>1,
                         -labels=>\%labels);
```

The checkbox_group() function creates a set of checkboxes all linked by a common name. In a scalar context, the function returns a string containing the properly formatted HTML tags. In an array context, the function returns a list of checkbox elements. You can manipulate the elements in various ways (such as putting them into a table) in order to achieve fine control over their layout.

The string returned by this function is only valid when placed within a fill-out form.

- ***-columns, -cols*** If this argument is present, the checkboxes will be placed in a neatly formatted HTML 3.2 table with the number of columns indicated. This argument must point to a positive integer. *See also* -rows, -rowheaders, and -colheaders. -Columns is a synonym for -cols, provided for your convenience.
- ***-colheaders*** If you use the -columns or -rows arguments, this argument can be used to create headings for the table columns; otherwise it is ignored. The argument should point to an array reference containing the column headers.
- ***-default, -defaults*** Sets the checkboxes to be checked when the group is first displayed. The value of this argument must be a string that matches one of the checkboxes defined by -values, or an array reference that contains multiple checkbox names. Because of form stickiness, the actual set of checked boxes may be different from the

one you request if a CGI parameter with the same name as the list already exists. The synonym -defaults is provided as a convenience.

- ***-labels*** Sets the human-readable label displayed next to each checkbox. By default, the checkbox values provided in -values is used for this purpose, but you can override this behavior by providing a hash reference in -labels. The hash keys are the checkbox values (from -values) and the values are the labels to be displayed to the user. In the example at the beginning of this entry, the checkboxes will return values of "eenie," "meenie," "minie," or "moe" to your script, but display "hey," "that," and "tickles" next to the first three boxes. Because no label is defined for "moe", that checkbox displays its value as is.
- ***-linebreak*** Ordinarily, the checkboxes will be displayed as a long horizontal row that word-wraps at the end of the line along with other HTML elements. By providing an argument of -linebreak with a nonzero value, you can change this behavior so that the linebreaks are placed between each button, causing them to display as a vertical list down the left margin of the page. You can also surround the list with other HTML elements, such as a centering directive, in order to tweak the formatting further.
- ***-name*** Set the name of the checkbox group. This name will become the CGI parameter name when the form is submitted.
- ***-nolabels*** If set to a nonzero value, -nolabels suppresses the display of labels next to the buttons. You may want to do this if the buttons are being used to select cells in tables or in-line images.
- ***-onClick*** This argument sets a JavaScript event handler to be called when any of the checkboxes in the group are clicked. See "JavaScript-Enhanced Pages" in Chapter Three, *Advanced Tricks*.
- ***-override, -force*** This argument overrides the sticky behavior of fill-out form elements. If set to a nonzero value, -override forces the checkbox to display with the -default items checked, even if a CGI parameter with the same name as the list already exists. -Force is a synonym provided for your convenience.

- ***-rows*** If this argument is present, the checkboxes will be placed in an HTML 3.2 table with the number of rows indicated. This argument must point to a positive integer. *See also* -columns, -rowheaders, and -colheaders.
- ***-rowheaders*** If you use the -columns or -rows arguments, this argument can be used to create headings for the table rows; otherwise, it is ignored. The argument should point to an array reference containing the row headers.
- ***-value, -values*** This argument sets the values of each checkbox in the group (-value and -values are synonymous). The argument should point to an array reference containing a series of strings. Each string becomes a different checkbox. When the form is submitted, the currently checked members are transmitted to your script as a CGI parameter whose name is the name of the group, and whose value is the checked member. If multiple checkboxes are selected, param() will return the selected values as an array. In CGI.pm 2.38 and higher, you may use a hash reference as the value of this argument, in which case, the keys of the hash will be used as the CGI parameter values, and the values are used as the human-readable labels. However, this format does not allow you to specify the order in which the checkboxes appear. If you see warnings from your script about the use of -values being ambiguous, use the alternate -value argument, place the entire argument in quotes, or change the capitalization to -Values.

## defaults()

```
print $q->defaults('Undo Everything');
```

The defaults() function will create a fill-out form button, which, when pressed, submits the form to your script in such a way that it appears as if the script were being called with an empty CGI parameter list. The result is as if your script were being called for the very first time. When your script regenerates the fill-out form, all stickiness will be lost and the various elements will take on the values that you provide with the -default and -value arguments.

Defaults() takes a single argument only, a label to be printed on the top of the button. The HTML it returns is only valid within a fill-out form.

Do not confuse defaults() with reset(), which generates a button that undoes any immediate changes that the user has made to the form but does not wipe the CGI parameter list clean.

## end_form(), endform()

```
print $q->end_form();
```

These functions (the two names are synonymous) produce a </FORM> tag to terminate an HTML fill-out form. You must provide one end_form() for every start_form() and start_multipart_form() in the script.

## end_html()

```
print $q->end_html();
```

This function returns the </BODY> and </HTML> tags necessary for properly ending an HTML document (although many pages will display just fine without them). If you start a page with start_html(), you should balance it with a call to end_html() before your script exits.

## filefield()

**Simple form:**

```
print $q->filefield('file_to_upload');
```

**Named argument form:**

```
print $q->filefield(-name=>'file_to_upload',
                    -size=>50,
                    -maxlength=>80);
```

Filefield() produces a file upload element that consists of an editable text field and a browse button. By typing in the name of a file on her local disk, or by selecting the browse button and clicking on a file, the user can designate a file to be uploaded when the form is submitted. A single form may contain several file upload fields.

The arguments to filefield() are identical to those for textfield(). See that entry for the complete list. The exception is -value, which, though recognized, currently has no effect on the display of the field. This is a restriction enforced by browsers in order to discourage malicious Web authors from creating forms that automatically upload users' private files.

File uploads only work correctly when the element is part of a fill-out form that uses the multipart/form-data encoding. You can create this either by calling start_multipart_form(), or by passing start_form() an -enctype argument of $CGI::MULTIPART.

See "File Uploads" in Chapter Three, *Advanced Tricks*, for more details, as well as the entries for param(), uploadInfo(), and tmpFileName().

## hidden()

**Simple form:**

```
print $q->hidden('veggies','okra','cabbage','broccoli');
```

**Named argument form:**

```
print $q->hidden(-name=>'veggies',
                 -value=>['okra','cabbage','broccoli']);
```

Hidden() produces a text field form element that cannot be seen by the user. It is useful for passing state variable information from one invocation of the script to the next. In the simple form, you call it with the name of the hidden field followed by one or more values to be incorporated into the form. In the named argument version, you provide it with -name and -value arguments.

- ***-name*** Sets the name of the hidden field. This name will become the CGI parameter name when the form is submitted.
- ***-override, -force*** This argument overrides the sticky behavior of fill-out form elements. If set to a nonzero value, -override forces the hidden field to contain the contents provided by the -value argument, even if a CGI parameter with the same name as the list already exists. -Override and -force can be used interchangeably.
- ***-value, -values, -default*** Sets the value(s) of the hidden field. You may provide a single scalar value, or an array reference containing multiple values. Note that hidden fields are sticky, just as all other form elements are. If there is already a CGI parameter with the same name as the hidden field, the existing value will take precedence over the contents of -value. This behavior can be changed with -override. For convenience, the arguments -value, -values, and -default can be used interchangeably.

If you call hidden() without any -value argument, the value will be taken out of the current CGI parameter list. This makes it simple to store the entire script state inside the form using a loop like this one:

```
foreach $param ($q->param) {
     print $q->hidden($param);
}
```

## image_button()

```
print $q->image_button(-name=>'map',
                       -src=>'/images/NYNY.gif',
                       -align=>'MIDDLE');
```

Image_button() produces an inline image that doubles as a form submission button. When clicked, the form is submitted and the (x,y) coordinates of the click appear as CGI parameters along with data from other elements in the form. To recover the click coordinates, look for CGI parameters named button_name.x and button_name.y, where button_name is the name of the button specified in the -name argument. (In the preceding example, the click coordinates can be found in the parameters map.x and map.y.)

The HTML produced by this function can only be used within a fill-out form.

- ***-align*** Specifies the alignment of the image. The values are identical to those used for ordinary inline images and can be any of LEFT, RIGHT, TOP, TEXTTOP, MIDDLE, ABSMIDDLE, BOTTOM, BASELINE, and ABSBOTTOM.
- ***-alt*** Creates alternative text to be displayed in browsers that cannot display inline images (or that have image loading turned off).
- ***-height*** Sets the height of the image, allowing the browser to render the page more rapidly. *See also* -width.
- ***-name*** Sets the name of the image button. This name will become the base CGI parameter name when the button is pressed.
- ***-src*** Specifies the URL of the image to be displayed. This may be a GIF or JPEG image on any server, local or remote.
- ***-width*** Sets the width of the image, allowing the browser to render the page more rapidly. *See also* -height.

This function also accommodates nonstandard <IMG> attributes such as BORDER, CONTROLS, DYNSRC, HSPACE, LOOP, LOWSRC, START, and VSPACE. Just use an argument named after the attribute you want (as in -loop).

---

**NOTE:**
**Despite the documentation in older versions of CGI.pm, JavaScript does not currently allow you to assign an -onClick handler to image buttons.**

---

## isindex()

```
print $q->isindex('http://www.some.site/cgi-bin/search');
```

Declare the document to be a searchable index, and use the indicated CGI script as the search engine. This function is now rarely used. If no argument is provided, your own script is called when the user performs a search.

## password_field()

**Simple form:**

```
print $q->password_field('passwd');
```

**Named argument form:**

```
print $q->password_field(-name=>'passwd',
                         -value=>'xyzzy',
                         -size=>50,
                         -maxlength=>80);
```

Password_field() produces an editable text field that displays stars when the user enters text. It is intended to prevent passwords from being intercepted by people looking over the user's shoulder, but does not otherwise guarantee secrecy. (Among other things, the information is sent as plain text across the network, making it vulnerable to packet sniffing.) This function is otherwise identical in every respect to textfield(). *See also* textfield() for the full list of arguments.

This element is only allowed within a fill-out form.

## popup_menu()

```
print $q->popup_menu(-name=>'pick_one',
                     -values=>['eenie','meenie','minie'],
                     -default=>'meenie',
```

```
-labels=>{'eenie'=>'one',
          'meenie'=>'two',
          'minie'=>'three'});
```

The popup_menu() function creates a popup menu form element (internally, by creating a set of <SELECT> and <OPTION> tags). You can adjust the appearance of the menu items and the item initially selected when the menu is displayed.

- ***-default*** Sets the item to be selected when the popup menu first displays. The value of this argument must be a string that matches one of the menu items defined by -values. Because of form stickiness, the actual selected menu item may be different from the one you request if there already exists a CGI parameter with the same name as the popup menu. If no default item is provided, the popup menu will be displayed with the first item selected.
- ***-labels*** Sets the human-readable labels for each menu item. By default, the menu item values provided in -values are used both for menu display and to pass the selected item back to your script when the form is submitted. -Labels allows you to change this behavior. The argument should point to a hash reference in which the keys are the menu items (from -values) and the values are the labels to be displayed to the user. In the example at the beginning of this entry, the CGI parameter returned to your script is one of "eenie," "meenie," or "minie," but the menu items the user sees are "one," "two," and "three."
- ***-name*** Sets the name of the field. This name will become the CGI parameter name when the form is submitted. Any combination of characters is allowed, including whitespace and control characters, but simple names are recommended.
- ***-onBlur, -onChange, -onFocus*** These three arguments set the JavaScript event handlers for the corresponding events. See "JavaScript-Enhanced Pages" in Chapter Three, *Advanced Tricks*.
- ***-override, -force*** This argument overrides the sticky behavior of fill-out form elements. If set to a nonzero value, -override forces

the menu to display with the -default item selected, even if a CGI parameter with the same name as the menu already exists. -Force is a synonym provided for your convenience.

- ***-value, -values*** This argument sets the menu items (-value and -values are synonymous). The argument should point to a list reference containing a series of strings. Each string becomes a menu item. When the form is submitted, the currently selected item is transmitted to your script as a CGI parameter whose name is the name of the popup menu, and whose value is the value of the selected menu item. In CGI.pm 2.38 and higher, you may use a hash reference as the value of this argument, in which case, the keys of the hash will be used as the CGI parameter values, and the values are used as the human-readable labels. However, this format does not allow you to specify the order in which the menu items appear.

  If you see warnings from your script about the use of -values being ambiguous, use the alternate -value argument, place the entire argument in quotes, or change the capitalization to -Values.

## radio_group()

```
%labels = ('eenie'=>'please',
           'meenie'=>'stop',
           'minie'=>'that');
print $q->radio_group(-name=>'pick_one',
                      -values=>['eenie','meenie','minie','moe'],
                      -default=>'meenie',
                      -linebreak=>1,
                      -labels=>\%labels);
```

The radio_group() function creates a set of radio buttons all linked by a common name. In a scalar context, the function returns a string containing the properly formatted HTML tags. In an array context, the function returns a list of radio button elements which you can then manipulate in whatever way you like (such as incorporating it into a table in order to control the layout).

The HTML tags returned by this function are only valid when placed within a fill-out form.

- ***-columns, -cols*** If this argument is present, the radio buttons will be placed in a neatly formatted HTML 3.2 table with the number of columns indicated. This argument must point to a positive integer. *See also* -rows, -rowheaders, and -colheaders. -Columns is a synonym for -cols, provided for your convenience.
- ***-colheaders*** If you use the -columns or -rows arguments, -colheaders can be used to create headings for the table columns; otherwise, it is ignored. The argument should point to an array reference containing the column headers.
- ***-default*** Sets the radio button to be selected when the group is first displayed. If not provided, the first button on the list will be selected. The value of this argument must be a string that matches one of the checkboxes defined by -value. Because of form stickiness, the actual radio button that is selected may be different from the one you request if there already exists a CGI parameter with the same name as the group.
- ***-labels*** Sets the human-readable label displayed next to each checkbox. By default, the radio button values provided in -values are used for this purpose, but you can override this behavior by providing a -labels argument pointing to a hash reference. The hash keys are the checkbox values (from -values), and the values are the labels to be displayed to the user. In the example at the beginning of this entry, the checkboxes will return values of "eenie," "meenie," "minie," or "moe" to your script, but will display "please," "stop," and "that" next to the first three buttons. Because no label is defined for moe, the raw value is displayed next to the fourth button.
- ***-linebreak*** Ordinarily, the radio buttons will be displayed as a long horizontal row that word-wraps at the end of the line along with

other HTML elements. By providing an argument of -linebreak with a nonzero value, you can change this behavior so that the line breaks are placed between each button, causing them to display as a vertical list down the left margin of the page. You can also surround the list with other HTML elements, such as a centering directive, in order to tweak the formatting further.

- ***-name*** Sets the name of the radio button group. This name will become the CGI parameter name when the form is submitted.
- ***-nolabels*** Suppresses the display of labels next to the buttons if set to a nonzero value. You may want to do this if the buttons are being used to select cells in tables or inline images.
- ***-onClick*** Sets a JavaScript event handler to be called when any of the buttons in the group are clicked. See "JavaScript-Enhanced Pages" in Chapter Three, *Advanced Tricks*.
- ***-override, -force*** This argument overrides the sticky behavior of fill-out form elements. If set to a nonzero value, -override forces the checkbox to display with the -default item selected, even if a CGI parameter with the same name as the list already exists. -Force is a synonym provided for your convenience.
- ***-rows*** If this argument is present, the checkboxes will be placed in an HTML 3.2 table with the number of rows indicated. This argument must point to a positive integer. *See also* -columns, -rowheaders, and -colheaders.
- ***-rowheaders*** If you use the -columns or -rows arguments, this argument can be used to create headings for the table rows; otherwise, it is ignored. The argument should point to an array reference containing the row headers.
- ***-value, -values*** Sets the values of each radio button in the group (-value and -values are synonymous). The argument should point to an array reference containing a series of strings. Each string becomes the value of a different button. When the form is submitted, the currently checked members are transmitted to your script as a CGI parameter whose name is the name of the group, and

whose value is the selected member. In CGI.pm 2.38 and higher, you may use a hash reference as the value of this argument, in which case, the keys of the hash will be used as the CGI parameter values, and the values are used as the human readable button labels. However, this format does not allow you to specify the order in which the radio buttons appear. If you see warnings from your script about the use of -values being ambiguous, use the alternate -value argument, place the entire argument in quotes, or change the capitalization to -Values.

## reset()

```
print $q->reset('Undo');
```

The reset() function creates a form reset button. When the user presses the button, the browser will undo all the changes the user has made to the form and return it to its original state. The single argument is the human-readable label to print on the top of the button. The HTML returned by reset() is only valid within a fill-out form.

Unlike other form elements, the contents of reset() are never transmitted to your script. It is handled completely internally by the browser. Hence, there is need for -name or -value arguments. Note that reset() only restores the form to its state when it was last loaded. It does *not* restore fill-out forms to their default states. To do this, see the defaults() function.

## scrolling_list()

```
%labels = ('eenie'=>'ouch',
           'meenie'=>'that',
```

```
            'minie'=>'tickles');
print $q->scrolling_list(-name=>'pick_some',
                         -values=>['eenie','meenie','minie','moe'],
                         -default=>['eenie','moe'],
                         -size=>5,
                         -multiple=>1,
                         -labels=>\%labels);
```

The scrolling_field() function creates a scrolling listbox form element (internally, by creating a set of <SELECT> and <OPTION> tags). You can adjust the appearance of the list, its contents, and the items initially selected.

- ***-default, -defaults*** Sets the item(s) to be selected when the list first displays (none by default). The value of this argument must be a string that matches one of the menu items defined by -values. To select multiple items, pass a reference to an array of strings. Because of form stickiness, the actual selected items may be different from the one you request if there already exists a CGI parameter with the same name as the list. The synonym -defaults is provided for your convenience.
- ***-labels*** Sets the human-readable labels for each list. By default, the values provided in -values are used both for display purposes and to pass the selected items back to your script when the form is submitted. -Labels allows you to change this behavior. The argument should point to a hash reference in which the keys are the list items (from -values), and the values are the labels to be displayed to the user. In the example at the beginning of this entry, the CGI parameter returned to your script is one of "eenie," "meenie," "minie," or "moe," but the menu items the user sees are "ouch," "that," and "tickles." Because no label is provided for moe, it is displayed as is.
- ***-multiple*** Controls whether the user can select more than one item at a time. If absent or zero, only one item can be selected.

If set to a nonzero value, multiple items can be selected simultaneously.

- ***-name*** Sets the name of the list. This name will become the CGI parameter name when the form is submitted.
- ***-onBlur, -onChange, -onFocus*** These three arguments set the JavaScript event handlers for the corresponding events. See "JavaScript-Enhanced Pages" in Chapter Three, *Advanced Tricks*.
- ***-override, -force*** This argument overrides the sticky behavior of fill-out form elements. If set to a nonzero value, -override forces the list to display with the -default items selected, even if a CGI parameter with the same name as the list already exists. -Force is a synonym provided for your convenience.
- ***-size*** Sets the length of the list. If the list contains more items than can be displayed at once, a vertical scrollbar will allow the user to scroll to see more entries. This argument must be a positive integer. If not provided, the list will default to a length equal to the number of items it contains.
- ***-value, -values*** Sets the list items (-value and -values are synonymous). The argument should point to a list reference containing a series of strings. Each string becomes an item. When the form is submitted, the currently selected items are transmitted to your script as a CGI parameter whose name is the name of the popup menu, and whose value is the value of the selected items. If multiple list items are selected, param() will return the selected items as an array. In CGI.pm 2.38 and higher, you may use a hash reference as the value of this argument, in which case, the keys of the hash will be used as the CGI parameter values, and the values are used as the human-readable list labels. However, this format does not allow you to specify the order in which the list items appear. If you see warnings from your script about the use of -values being ambiguous, use the alternate -value argument, place the entire argument in quotes, or change the capitalization to -Values.

## start_form(), startform()

```
print $q->start_form();
print $q->start_form(-method=>POST,
                     -action=>'/cgi-bin/process_form');
```

The start_form() and startform() functions (the names are synonymous) create the <FORM> tag for beginning an HTML fill-out form. In most cases, no arguments are necessary. The tag will default in such a way that the browser will submit the contents of the form back to your script using the POST method. You can customize this behavior using the following arguments:

- ***-action*** Sets the URL of the script to receive the contents of the fill-out form when it is submitted. The default is the current script.
- ***-enctype*** Sets the way that the browser encodes the information in the fill-out form before submitting it to your script. There are two options:

  **application/x-www-form-urlencoded** This is the type of encoding used by all browsers prior to Netscape 2.0. It is compatible with many CGI scripts and is suitable for short fields containing text data. For your convenience, CGI.pm stores the name of this encoding type in $CGI::URL_ENCODED.

  **multipart/form-data** This is the newer type of encoding introduced by Netscape 2.0. It is suitable for forms that contain very large fields or that are intended for transferring binary data. Most importantly, it enables the file upload feature of Netscape 2.0 forms. For your convenience, CGI.pm stores the name of this encoding type in $CGI::MULTIPART.

  Forms that use this type of encoding are not easily interpreted by CGI scripts unless they use CGI.pm or another library that knows how to handle them. Unless you are using the file upload feature, there is no particular reason to use this type of encoding.

  See also start_multipart_form() described later in this chapter.

- ***-method*** Sets the HTTP method to use for transmitting the contents of the fill-out form to the Web server as a CGI parameter list. The value of this argument can be the string GET, in which case, the CGI parameters are appended to the script's URL; or POST, in which case, the parameters are sent to the script's standard input. Because many Web servers silently truncate URLs to certain maximum characters, the POST method is highly recommended (as well as being the default).
- **-name** Gives the fill-out form a name. This is only used by browsers that understand JavaScript or other scripting languages, and gives the interpreted code a handle with which to manipulate the fill-out form. Because of JavaScript limitations, the name must consist entirely of printable characters; whitespace is forbidden. If provided by a browser that is not JavaScript compatible, this argument will be ignored.
- ***-onSubmit*** Provides a JavaScript or VBScript event handler to be called when the user presses the submit button. This handler is given a chance to review the contents of the fill-out form and return true if the submission is to be allowed. The submission is canceled if the handler returns false.
- ***-target*** The name of a frame (preexisting or new). When the fill-out form is submitted, the output from the script that is called will be directed into the named frame. This argument only works with frame-enabled browsers.

## start_html()

### Simple form:

```
print $q->start_html('Secrets of the Pyramids');
```

### Named argument form:

```
print $q->start_html(-title=>'Secrets of the Pyramids',
                     -author=>'fred@capricorn.org',
```

```
-base=>'true',
-meta=>{'keywords'=>'pharoah secret mummy',
        'copyright'=>'1996 King Tut'},
-style=>{'src'=>'/styles/style1.css'},
-print_dtd=>1,
-bgcolor=>'blue');
```

This function returns the top part of an HTML document, including the <HEAD>, <TITLE>, and <META> sections. It leaves an opening <BODY> tag at the end. After printing the string returned by start_html(), you are expected to create a valid HTML document. When you are finished, you should call end_html() to produce the closing </BODY> and </HTML> tags.

In the simple form, start_html() accepts a single argument that indicates the title of the document. If the title is empty, "Untitled Document" is assumed. In many cases, the simple form is all you will need. The named argument form of the call recognizes the following arguments:

- ***-author*** The author of the page, usually in the form of an e-mail address. This information will be incorporated into the <LINK REV="MADE"> tag that some HTML publishing systems use to establish authorship information.
- ***-base*** If set to a true (nonzero) value, this argument tells start_html() to create a <BASE> tag containing the URL of the script. This helps browsers resolve relative URLs if the documents created by this script are ever moved from one server to another. This feature is most often used in conjunction with -target in order to name a default frame in which to load all hypertext links from this document. *See also* -xbase.
- ***-dtd*** Precedes the <HTML> tag with an SGML document type definition (DTD). The presence of a DTD allows HTML pages to be viewed and edited with certain high-end SGML editors, and is ignored by most browsers. In addition, several HTML validators

use the DTD to check documents for syntactic correctness. Unfortunately, the DTD confuses a few poorly written browsers, including the America Online browser, so this feature is turned off by default. You may provide a value of 1 to provide a default DTD that promises HTML 2.0 compliance, or provide your own correctly formatted DTD. For example:

```
print $q->start_html(-dtd=>'-//W3C//DTD HTML 3.2//EN');
```

A fairly complete list of valid DTDs can be found at ugweb.cs.ualberta.ca/~gerald/validate/lib/catalog.

The function default_dtd() allows you to change the default DTD, as shown previously.

- ***-meta*** Defines one or more <META> tags for passing meta-information to browsers and Web-roving robots. Pass this parameter a reference to an associative array containing key/value pairs to be incorporated into an HTML <META> tag. In the example at the beginning of this section, the following HTML is created:

```
<META NAME="keywords" CONTENT="pharoah secret mummy">
<META NAME="copyright" CONTENT="1996 King Tut">
```

There is no support for the HTTP-EQUIV type of <META> tag. This is because you can modify the HTTP header directly with the header() function:

```
print header(-Refresh=>'10; URL=http://www.capricorn.com');
```

- ***-onLoad*** Provides a JavaScript event handler to be called when the HTML page is loaded. See "JavaScript-Enhanced Pages" in Chapter Three, *Advanced Tricks*, and the -script, -noScript, and -onUnload arguments.
- ***-onUnload*** Provides a JavaScript event handler to be called when the HTML page is unloaded (which happens just before the page is closed or replaced by another document). See "JavaScript-Enhanced Pages" in Chapter Three, *Advanced Tricks*, and the -script, -noScript, and -onLoad arguments.

- ***-noScript*** Provides some HTML code for the browser to display when it can't (or won't) run JavaScript or one of the other scripting languages. *See also* the -script argument.
- ***-script*** Adds a set of JavaScript or VBScript declarations to the HTML header (see JavaScript-Enhanced Pages in Chapter 3). The value of this argument may either be a simple string, in which case, the JavaScript code is incorporated directly into the HTML document, or a hash reference. In the latter case, start_html() looks for keys named -code, -src, and -language. The contents of -code are taken to be scripting statements and incorporated directly into the page as in the simple string case. -Src, if present, is taken to be the URL of an external document that holds JavaScript statements. If used together, the statements in -code are appended to those in the external document. -Language can be used to change the scripting language the browser uses. Possible values include JavaScript, JScript (Microsoft's version of JavaScript), VBScript, and PerlScript (an embedded Perl interpreter provided by the ActiveWare company, www.activeware.com). Not all browsers support all scripting languages. For example:

```
print $q->start_html(-title=>'Scripted CGI',
                     -script=>{
                         -language=>'JavaScript',
                         -src=>'/jscript/utils.js',
                         -code=>'alert("Page Loaded")'
                         }
                       );
```

- There is no need to protect the JavaScript code with HTML comment characters. Start_html() does this automatically to avoid problems when older browsers try to display pages containing JavaScript. *See also* the -noScript, -onLoad, and -onUnload arguments.

- ***-style*** Defines a cascading stylesheet for the document (see "Fancy HTML Formatting" in Chapter Three, *Advanced Tricks*, for details). This argument may point either to a simple string, in which case the string is assumed to contain the definition of the entire style sheet, or to a hash reference. In the latter case, start_html() will look for keys named -code and/or -src. The contents of -code will be incorporated directly into the document as in the simple string case. The contents of -src are taken to be a URL of the document holding the actual stylesheet. Either key can be used individually, or both together, as shown here:

```
print $q->start_html(-title=>'CGI with Style',
                     -style=>{
                          -src=>'/styles/style1.css',
                          -code=>'H1 {color: red}'
                          }
                     );
```

  There is no need to place HTML comment characters around stylesheets incorporated directly into the page. Start_html() does this for you, guaranteeing that older browsers will not be confused.
- ***-title*** The title of the page. This serves both as the name of the window displayed by the browser and the title of the bookmark entry if the user adds the document to her bookmarks file.
- ***-xbase*** This argument allows you to create a <BASE> tag that points to some other location (such as a different Web site). All partial URLs referred to by this document will be resolved relative to the URL pointed to by this argument. This argument can be used in conjunction with -target to set the default frame in which to load relative URLs.

### Other Arguments

In addition to the arguments listed here, any other arguments that you provide will be turned into like-named HTML attributes and incorporated into the HTML <BODY> tag. Commonly used attributes include:

- ***-background*** Sets the background image (wallpaper) for the page. This must be the URL to a GIF or JPEG image somewhere on the Web, preferably a small image that tiles well.
- ***-bgcolor*** Sets the background color of the page. You may provide a named color, such as blue, from the list of 16 defined by the original IBM PC VGA color adaptor, or provide a RGB triple in the form #RRGGBB, where RR, GG, and BB are the red, green, and blue components of the color in hexadecimal.
- ***-link, -vlink, -alink*** Sets the color of hypertext links. -Link affects links that have not yet been visited by the user, -vlink affects links that have been visited in previous browsing sessions, and -alink affects links that have been visited in the current session. You may provide a named color or an RGB triple. *See also* -bgcolor.
- ***-text*** Sets the color of normal text. You may provide a named color or an RGB triple. *See also* -bgcolor.

## start_multipart_form()

```
print $q->start_multipart_form();
```

This function is identical in all respects to start_form() except that it defaults to an encoding type of multipart/form data. You should call this function for any fill-out forms that will contain file upload fields.

## submit()

**Simple form:**

```
print $q->submit('Send Form');
```

**Named argument form:**

```
print $q->submit(-name=>'action',
                 -value=>'Send Form');
```

The submit() function creates a form submission button. When the user presses this button, the current contents of the form will be bundled up and transmitted to the script. In the simple form, the single argument is the human-readable label to print on top of the button. With the named argument form, you can give the button a name and a unique value, allowing you to distinguish which of several buttons was used to submit the form.

The HTML tag returned by this function is only valid when placed within a fill-out form.

- ***-name*** Sets the name of the button. This name will become the CGI parameter name when the form is submitted. If no -value argument is provided, the name also becomes the human-readable label.
- ***-onClick*** Sets a JavaScript event handler to be called when the button is clicked. After calling the event handler, the form will be submitted. If you would like to intercept the submission and possibly prevent it from occurring, you should provide an -onSubmit handler to the start_form() function. See the entry for start_form(), as well as the section on "JavaScript-Enhanced Pages" in Chapter Three, *Advanced Tricks*.
- ***-value, -label*** Sets the value of the button. This becomes the value of the CGI parameter when the form is submitted. It is also used to set the human-readable label printed on top of the button. If neither a -name or a -value argument is provided, the label defaults to Submit Query. The function also recognizes -label as a synonym -value.

## textarea()

### Simple form:

```
print $q->textarea('favorite_poem');
```

**Named argument form:**

```
print $q->textarea(-name=>'favorite_poem',
                   -value=>'Quoth the raven, "Nevermore."',
                   -rows=>10,
                   -cols=>50,
                   -wrap=>physical);
```

This function produces a large, multiline text edit field. It is only valid within a fill-out form. The simple form of the function names the field, but does not otherwise change the default appearance (which varies from browser to browser). The named argument form allows you to customize the field's appearance.

- ***-cols, -columns*** Sets the width of the field in characters. A horizontal scrollbar allows the user to enter wider lines if necessary (and if -wrap is off). This argument must point to a positive integer. -Columns is a synonym for -cols.
- ***-name*** Sets the name of the field. This name will become the CGI parameter name when the form is submitted. Any combination of characters is allowed, including whitespace and control characters, but simple names are recommended.
- ***-onChange, -onFocus, -onBlur, -onSelect*** These arguments point to JavaScript event handlers for the indicated events. See "JavaScript-Enhanced Pages" in Chapter Three, *Advanced Tricks*.
- ***-rows*** Sets the height of the field in rows. A vertical scrollbar will allow the user to enter more text, if necessary. This argument must point to a positive integer.
- ***-override, -force*** This argument overrides the sticky behavior of fill-out form elements. If set to a nonzero value, -override forces the text field to display the contents of -value, even if a CGI parameter with the same name as the field already exists. -Force is a synonym provided for your convenience.

- ***-value, -default*** Sets the default starting contents of the field. Any string value is acceptable. Because of the sticky nature of form elements, the string pointed to by this argument is only used if a like-named CGI parameter does not already exist. Use -override to change this behavior. -Default is a synonym for -value.
- ***-wrap*** Sets the WRAP attribute. It can be one of "off," "physical," or "virtual." If "off," word-wrapping only occurs in the field when the user presses the Enter key. The contents of the field are transmitted to your script with line breaks inserted exactly as they were displayed to the user. If "physical," word-wrapping occurs automatically when text exceeds the width of the field, and the text is transmitted to your script as if the user had actually transmitted it that way. If "virtual," word-wrapping occurs automatically when text exceeds the width of the field, but the contents of the field are transmitted to your script as a single unbroken line of text (unless the user inserts a line break manually). The WRAP attribute may not be recognized by some older browsers. *See also* textfield(), filefield(), and password_field().

## textfield()

**Positional form:**

```
print $q->textfield('favorite_color');
```

**Named argument form:**

```
print $q->textfield(-name=>'favorite_color',
                    -value=>'chartreuse',
                    -size=>50,
                    -maxlength=>80);
```

This function produces a one-line text entry field (internally it creates the appropriate <INPUT> HTML tag). It is only valid within a fill-out form. In the simple form of the function, the single argument is the name of the text field. The named argument calling style allows you extensive control over the appearance of the field.

- ***-maxLength*** Puts an upper limit on the number of characters the user can enter in the field. The browser will refuse to accept any characters in excess of this upper bound. This argument must be a positive integer. The default is to allow the user to enter any number of characters.

  Note that using this argument will not prevent users from submitting CGI parameters to your script that are much larger than the limit. They need only create their own fill-out forms and point them at your script.
- ***-name*** Sets the name of the field. This name will become the CGI parameter name when the form is submitted. Any combination of characters is allowed, including whitespace and control characters, but simple names are recommended.
- ***-onChange, -onFocus, -onBlur, -onSelect*** These arguments point to JavaScript event handlers for the indicated events. See "JavaScript-Enhanced Pages" in Chapter Three, *Advanced Tricks*.
- ***-override, -force*** This argument overrides the sticky behavior of fill-out form elements. If set to a nonzero value, -override forces the text field to display the contents of -value, even if a CGI parameter with the same name as the field already exists. -Force is a synonym provided for your convenience.
- ***-size*** Sets the width of the text field, in characters. If the user enters more characters than this, the field will scroll to accommodate. Any positive integer value is acceptable, but values greater than 80 generally exceed the browser window width.
- ***-value, -default*** Set the default starting contents of the field (both -value and -default are synonymous). Any string value is acceptable. Because of the sticky nature of form elements, the string pointed to by this argument is only used if a like-named CGI parameter does

not already exist. Use -override to change this behavior. *See also* password_field(), textarea(), and filefield().

## HTML Shortcuts

The HTML shortcut functions produce an HTML tag and, optionally, a closing tag. You can control the text between the opening and closing tags, the tag attributes, or specify that the tag be distributed across the members of a list. The syntax is summarized in Table 2.1 of Chapter Two, *CGI.pm Basics*. HTML shortcuts also nest inside each other naturally.

It is important to realize that the HTML shortcuts do all their work by obeying simple syntax rules. There is no deep understanding of HTML inside CGI.pm. In fact, the HTML shortcuts are all generated automatically from a single internal subroutine named _generate_tag_func() (some day for amusement, try to figure out how this function works). CGI.pm will let you do things that are forbidden by the HTML specification, such as placing a <P> paragraph tag within an <A> anchor tag. It will also allow you to misspell attributes, or even to use attributes that do not belong in a tag. You may catch these problems by running the output of your script through an HTML validation program, such as *htmlchek* (uts.cc.utexas.edu/~churchh/htmlchek.html).

The advantage of this design is that you can keep up with new HTML extensions without waiting for another version of CGI.pm to be released. (Has Microsoft just added a SLOWMOTION attribute to the <IMG> tag? No problem!) You can even add new HTML tags just by importing them in the use statement.

The following is a listing of HTML shortcuts and their most commonly used attributes. The function-oriented interface is shown in the examples because the HTML shortcuts are more frequently used this way. The standard HTML 2 tags can be imported from the :html2 set, the HTML 3 tags from the :html3 set, and a few of the Netscape extensions in the :netscape set (many of which are part of the proposed HTML 4.0 standard). There is not a Microsoft extension set (as of version 2.38), but there might be by the time you read this. Only the :html2 set is imported automatically when you use the :standard group. If you need to import another set, that fact is noted in the description.

Some of the more obscure attributes and tags have been glossed over. For a comprehensive listing, see any of the excellent HTML reference guides on the market, such as *HTML, The Definitive Guide,* by Chuck Musciano and Bill Kennedy (O'Reilly & Associates, 1996), or *HTML 4.0 Sourcebook* by Ian Graham (John Wiley & Sons, 1998). Also be aware that the -class attribute, which assigns a cascading stylesheet style to a tag, can be used in any HTML tag. In this section, the -class attribute is only shown associated with those tags where it is most frequently used.

## a()

```
print a({-href=>'http://somewhere.else/'},
              "Jump to Land O' Fred");
print a({-name=>'ch01'},
          h1("Chapter 1"));
```

Create an <A> anchor tag. Frequently used attributes:

- ***-href*** The URL toload, when used as a hypertext link.
- ***-name*** The name of the location in the document, when used as a destination anchor.
- ***-onClick*** A JavaScript event handler to be called when the user clicks the link (JavaScript-savvy browsers only; see "JavaScript-Enhanced Pages" in Chapter Three, *Advanced Tricks*).
- ***-onMouseOver*** A JavaScript event handler to be called when the mouse passes over the link.
- ***-target*** A window target to load the destination into when operating with a frames-savvy browser (see "Frames" in Chapter Three, *Advanced Tricks*).

## address()

```
print address("Fred Webmaster");
```

Create an <ADDRESS> tag for the *address* logical style. Frequently used attributes:

- ***-class*** Sets the style to the named subclass in cascading stylesheet-savvy browsers (see "Fancy HTML Formatting" in Chapter Three, *Advanced Tricks*).

## applet() (:html3 group)

```
print applet({-code=>'spider',
              -codebase=>'http://your.site/applets/',
              -width=>300,
              -height=>200},
               Param({-name=>'speed',-value=>'fast'}),
               Param({-name=>'font',-value=>'Times'})
             );
```

This function produces an <APPLET> tag suitable for embedding Java applets. Typically, an applet tag will contain multiple calls to Param() (not param()—notice the capitalization differences) to set various applet runtime options. Attributes include:

- ***-align*** The alignment of the applet on the page. Values include LEFT, RIGHT, and CENTER.
- ***-alt*** Some alternate text to display if the Java interpreter is deactivated.
- ***-code*** The name of the Java class file to load, minus the .class or .jar extension.
- ***-codebase*** The URL at which the browser can find the Java class file. If not provided, the browser will attempt to fetch the class file

from the same directory in which your script resides, which is unlikely to be successful.

- ***-height*** The height to allocate on the page for the applet, in pixels.
- ***-hspace*** Additional horizontal space, in pixels, to put between the applet and the text that flows around it when the applet has been anchored to the right or left margin with -align.
- ***-name*** A name for the applet. This allows JavaScript functions to manipulate the applet in various ways.
- ***-vspace*** Additional vertical space, in pixels, to put between the applet and the text that flows around it when the applet has been anchored to the right or left margin with -align.
- ***-width*** The width to allocate for the applet, in pixels.

## b()

```
print "Don't ",b("do")," that!";
```

Create a <B> tag for the bold physical style.

## base()

Set the base URL for the document. This function is deprecated. Use the -base or -xbase arguments in start_html() instead.

## basefont() (*:html3*)

```
print basefont({-size=>5});
```

Set the size of the base font. Relative font size changes elsewhere in the document (see font()) are based on this value. Required attribute:

- ***-size*** The size of the font, an integer between 1 and 7.

## big() (:netscape group)

```
print "I am ",big("bigger")," than you.";
```

Create a <BIG> tag, causing the text inside to be increased in size.

## blink() (:netscape group)

```
print "I am ",blink("very annoying")," don't you think?";
```

Create blinking text, annoying everyone who views your page.

## body()

Create an HTML <BODY> section. This is deprecated. Use start_html() instead.

## br()

```
print "Don't be broken",br,"hearted.";
```

Create a <BR> tag, causing a line break. Frequently used attributes:

- ***-clear*** Control the break relative to inline images anchored to the right or left margins. May be one of RIGHT, LEFT, or ALL to cause the text to break until it is clear of images on the right, on the left, or both sides (Netscape and Internet Explorer only).

## caption() (*:html3*)

This function creates a table caption, and should only be nested within a table. See the description of table() for a code example. Attributes include:

- ***-align*** Specify the position of the caption relative to the table. This attribute is recognized by both Microsoft and Netscape browsers, but unfortunately, they do not quite agree on its meaning. With Netscape browsers, this attribute controls the vertical position of the caption relative to the table. Possible values are TOP and BOTTOM to place the caption at the top or bottom of the table, respectively. With Internet Explorer, this attribute controls the horizontal position of the caption relative to the page and must be one of LEFT, RIGHT, and CENTER. The vertical position of the caption is controlled with -valign.
- ***-valign*** In Internet Explorer only, this attribute controls the vertical placement of the caption and can be one of TOP or BOTTOM.

## center() (:netscape group)

```
print center("Old King Cole was a merry old soul.");
```

Center the given text. May contain paragraphs and other large sections.

## cite()

```
print cite("Das Kapital")," by Karl Marx";
```

Create text in the logical "citation" style, usually a proportional italic font.

## code()

```
print "Help!  I keep getting the message: ",
      code('core dumped'),"!";
```

Create text in the logical code style, usually a monospaced font.

## dd()

```
print dl(
         dt('Paranoia'),
         dd("An occupational hazard."),
         dt('Schizophrenia'),
         dd("I'm in two minds about it.")
        );
```

Create the definition part of a definition list. *See also* dt() and dl().

## dfn()

```
print "Set TERM to ",dfn('vt102')," and you're all set.";
```

Create text in the logical definition style. Rarely used.

## div() (:html3 group)

```
print div({-align=>RIGHT},
          "Old King Cole was a merry old soul.");
```

Enclose its contents in a <DIV> tag, usually to apply an alignment attribute to a section of text. Frequently used attributes:

- ***-align*** Control the text alignment of its contents. Valid values are LEFT, RIGHT, and CENTER.

## dl()

```
print dl(
         dt('Index'),
         dd("Something that indexers make"),
```

```
        dt('Table of Contents'),
        dd("Something that authors make")
    );
```

Create a definition list (<DD>). *See also* the dd() and dt() functions. Frequently used attributes:

- ***-compact*** If this attribute is present, the list will be compacted to take as little vertical space as possible. This attribute should be given as {-compact=>"}. This tells CGI.pm to include the attribute as COMPACT rather than COMPACT="something".

## dt()

```
print dl(
        dt('Okra'),
        dd("A slimy vegetable."),
        dt('Kale'),
        dd("A broad-leafed vegetable.")
    );
```

Create the term part of a definition list. *See also* dd() and dt().

## em()

```
print "You've been at that for ",em('hours!');
```

Create logically emphatic text that is usually rendered in an italic font.

## font() (*:netscape* group)

```
print "This is ",font({-color=>'red'}),"red")," text.";
```

Temporarily change the font size, face, or color in Netscape and Netscape-compatible browsers. Frequently used attributes:

- ***-color*** Set the font color, either using the named form (red) or the RGB hexadecimal form (#RRGGBB).
- ***-face*** Set the text face (Internet Explorer only). You should provide a list of faces that the user's machine might support. For example:

```
font({-face=>"New York, Times Roman, Times New Roman"},
      "One of these must work!");
```

- ***-size*** Sets the font size, either as an absolute number from 1 to 7 (default 3), or as a relative size from the base font. For example, +2 will make the font two steps larger than the default. *See also* basefont().

## form()

Creates an HTML fill-out form section. This function is deprecated. Use start_form() instead.

## frame() (*:netscape* group)

```
frameset({-cols=>'50%,50%'},
      frame({-name=>'left',-src=>'/cgi-bin/do_frame/left'}),
      frame({-name=>'right',-src=>'/cgi-bin/do_frame/right'})
   );
```

Define a frame for use in frame-enabled browsers. *See also* frameset() and noframes(). Commonly used attributes:

- ***-marginheight*** The distance between the contents of the frame and the top and bottom borders, in pixels. The value of this attribute should be a positive integer.

- ***-marginwidth*** The distance between the contents of the frame and the left and right borders, in pixels. The value of this attribute should be a positive integer.
- ***-name*** The name of this frame so that it can be referred to in the -target attribute of header(), start_html(), a(), and start_form().
- ***-noresize*** If specified, the frame will be made unresizable; otherwise, the user will be able to change its geometry by clicking the frame boundary and dragging. You should use this attribute in this way {-noresize=>"} because the corresponding HTML attribute ordinarily does not take an argument.
- ***-scrolling*** Specifies the type of scrollbars allowed in the frame. Possible values include: "yes," to force scrollbars; "no," to suppress scrollbars; and "auto," to let the browser decide when scrollbars are needed. If not specified, the default is "auto."
- ***-src*** Specifies the URL of the document to load into the frame. The URL can be a CGI script, as shown in the previous example, or a static HTML document.

## frameset() (*:netscape* group)

```
frameset({-cols=>'50%,50%'},
     frame({-name=>'left',-src=>'/cgi-bin/do_frame/left'}),
     frame({-name=>'right',-src=>'/cgi-bin/do_frame/right'})
  );
```

Creates a <FRAMESET> for a frame-enabled browser. When creating a frameset document, do not call start_html(); just write out the HTTP header and the frameset definition. Only Netscape and compatible browsers can currently handle frames. *See also* frame() and noframes(). Commonly used attributes:

- ***-cols*** The number and width of columns in the frame set. This is frequently given as a list of percentages, but other forms are allowed as well. For details, see a recent HTML reference guide.
- ***-rows*** The number and width of rows in the frame set. This is frequently given as a list of percentages, but other forms are allowed as well. See a recent HTML reference guide for details.

## h1(), h2(), h3()...

```
print h1("Dawning of a New Day");
```

Creates a level 1 to 6 header. Frequently used attributes:

- ***-align*** Sets the alignment of the header. Possible values are LEFT, RIGHT, and CENTER.
- ***-class*** Sets the style to the named subclass in cascading stylesheet-savvy browsers (see "Fancy HTML Formatting" in Chapter Three, *Advanced Tricks*).

## head()

Creates an HTML <HEAD> section. This function is deprecated. Use start_html() instead.

## html()

Creates an <HTML> section. This is deprecated. Use start_html() instead.

## hr()

```
print hr({-width=>"50%"});
```

Create a horizontal rule. Netscape-compatible browsers recognize a number of optional attributes:

- ***-align*** Sets the alignment of the rule on the page. Possible values are LEFT, RIGHT, and CENTER.
- ***-noshade*** Indicates that this rule should not have 3D shading, but should be rendered as a plain line. Because this attribute ordinarily does not have an argument, you should pass it to the function like this: hr({-noshade=>''});
- ***-size*** The vertical size of the rules, expressed in pixels.
- ***-width*** The horizontal width of the rule, expressed either in pixels, or as a percentage of the page width.

## i()

```
print "Did she say ",i('Homo sapiens'),"?";
```

Creates an <I> tag for the italic physical style.

## img()

```
print img({-src=>'/images/starburst.gif',
           -align=>LEFT,
           -alt=>'starburst'});
```

Creates an inline image <IMG> tag. The following standard and nonstandard attributes are accepted:

- ***-align*** Controls the alignment of the image relative to the page text. The HTML standard recognizes three alignments, TOP, MIDDLE, and BOTTOM. Netscape browsers also recognize TEXTTOP, ABSMIDDLE, BASELINE, and ABSBOTTOM. See an HTML reference for a description of what these alignments do. Netscape and Internet Explorer also recognize the image alignments LEFT and RIGHT. These anchor the image to the left and right margins of the page, respectively, in such a way that text flows around them.

- ***-alt*** Provides some descriptive text to display when the browser is unable to display the image or the user has turned automatic image loading off.
- ***-border*** Put a colored border around the image (Netscape and Internet Explorer only). The value of this attribute should be a positive integer indicating the thickness of the border in pixels. A value of 0 removes the border entirely, even if there is a hypertext link surrounding it.
- ***-height, -width*** Sets the height and width of the image, in pixels. Specifying these values can speed up the rendering of the page, because the browser does not have to wait until the image is loaded. You can scale the image at will by providing dimensions that are larger or smaller than the true image size.
- ***-hspace*** When the image is anchored to the right or left margin, this controls the amount of horizontal space between the image and the text that flows around it.
- ***-ismap*** This attribute tells the browser to treat the image as a clickable image map. You should provide this attribute with an empty string, since the ISMAP attribute does not usually take an argument. See the -usemap attribute, as well as the image_button() fill-out form element.
- ***-src*** Provides the browser with the URL source of the image. This attribute is required.
- ***-lowsrc*** This Netscape-specific extension provides the URL of a low-resolution image to display while the final image is loading. It can speed up the perceived performance of the page.
- ***-vspace*** When the image is anchored to the right or left margin, this controls the amount of vertical space between the image and the text that flows around it.

- ***-usemap*** This attribute points to the URL of a client-side image map to use to process clicks on the image. It is only valid when used in combination with the -ismap attribute, and only then when used with a browser that understands client-side image maps. *See also* the image_button() attribute.

## input()

Create an <INPUT> tag for use in fill-out forms. This function is deprecated. Use the more specific (and more powerful) textfield(), filefield(), password_field(), button(), checkbox(), checkbox_group(), radio_group(), submit(), imagebutton(), and reset() functions instead.

## kbd()

```
print "Don't forget to press the ",kbd('enter')," key.";
```

Create text with the keyboard logical style (<KBD>).

## li()

```
@epigrams = ('Look both ways before crossing the street.'
             'A penny saved is a penny earned.',
             'A stitch in time saves nine.',
             'Epigrams are for the birds.');
print "If I've told you once, I've told you a thousand times:",
      ol(
         li(\@epigrams);
         );
```

Create the list item for an ordered or unordered list. The ability to distribute the tag across all members of an array reference is frequently used with this tag, as shown in the preceding example. *See also* ol() and ul(). Frequently used attributes include:

- ***-type*** Sets the bullet type of the item in unordered lists. Possible values include disc, circle, and square (Netscape and compatibles only).
- ***-value*** Sets the numeric value of the list item in ordered lists. This will reset the count to the indicated value for the item and all items beneath it. The value of this argument is usually a positive integer, but letters and roman numerals are also accepted for ordered lists numbered in this way (Netscape and compatibles only).

## Link()

Creates a <LINK> tag for use within the HTML header. If you want to use this to establish author information, it is easier to use the -author argument in the start_html() function. Note that the initial letter is capitalized to avoid collision with Perl's link operator.

## ol()

```
print ol({-type=A},
         li(['kale','cabbage','okra'])
         );
```

Starts an ordered list (numbered or lettered). *See also* li(). Frequently used attributes include:

- ***-compact*** If this attribute is present, the list will be compacted to take as little vertical space as possible. This attribute should be given as {-compact=>''}. This tells CGI.pm to include the attribute as COMPACT rather than COMPACT="something"

- ***-start*** The starting number or letter for the first item on the list (Netscape and compatible browsers only). Ordinarily an integer, but you can use a letter or a roman numeral if appropriate for the list type.
- ***-type*** The list type (Netscape and compatible browsers only). It can be: "1," for a numbered list; "A," for a list starting with the sequence A, B, C; "a," for a list starting with a sequence of lowercase letters; "I," for a list numbered with roman numerals; or "i," for a list numbered with lowercase roman numerals.

## p()

```
print p("This is a complete paragraph");
print p({-align=>center},"This is a centered paragraph");
print "I don't like it here.",p,"I want to be somewhere else.";
```

Creates a <P> paragraph tag. Paragraphs can either enclose the text of a paragraph, as shown in the first example, or be used to separate two blocks of text, as shown in the third. Paragraph attributes, such as ALIGN, will apply to the entire text contained within. Frequently used attributes:

- ***-align*** Sets the alignment of the text. Possible values are LEFT, RIGHT, and CENTER.
- ***-class*** Sets the style to the named subclass in cascading stylesheet-savvy browsers (see "Fancy HTML Formatting" in Chapter Three, *Advanced Tricks*).

## Param() (*:html3* group)

Provides runtime parameters for Java applets. This function is only valid in the context of an <APPLET> section. See the description of applet() for a complete code example.

Note the capitalization. The function is called Param() to avoid collision with the standard param() function. Valid attributes are:

- ***-name*** Specifies the run-time parameter's name.
- ***-value*** Specifies the run-time parameter's value.

## pre()

```
print "When I say",pre(<<END),"I mean it!"
2! + 3! > 5!
END
```

Creates a block of preformatted text set in a monospaced (typewriter) font. Frequently used attributes:

- ***-width*** Advise the browser of the length of the longest line in the block of text. The browser may use this information to choose a font of the right size, or it may not.

## samp()

```
print samp("Floating point exception (core dumped)");
```

Create text in the sample logical style. This is supposed to be used for example computer output, but is rarely seen.

## Select()

Creates a <SELECT> tag for creating selection lists in fill-out forms. Note that the initial letter is capitalized to avoid collision with Perl's built-in select operator. This hardly matters because Select() is deprecated. Use the more specific (and much more powerful) popup_menu() and scrolling_list() functions instead.

## small() (*:netscape* group)

```
print "I am much ",small('smaller')," than you."
```

Reduces the size of the text by some amount.

## strong()

```
print strong("Hurry!"),
      " The hyenas have gotten into the bird bath again!";
```

Creates text with the strong logical style. Usually rendered in boldfaced text.

## sup() (*:html3* group)

```
print "E = mc",sup(2);
```

Create superscripted text.

## table() (*:html3* group)

```
print
        table({-border=>''},
        caption(strong('When Should You Eat Your Vegetables?')),
             Tr({-align=>CENTER,-valign=>TOP},
                [
                th(['','Breakfast','Lunch','Dinner'])),
```

```
          th('Tomatoes'),td(['no','yes','yes'])),
          th('Broccoli'),td(['no','no','yes'])),
          th('Onions'),td(['yes','yes','yes']))
        ]
    );
```

The table() function creates HTML 3.2 tables. *See also* Tr(), th(), and caption(). There are a large number of attributes for adjusting all aspects of the table's appearance:

- ***-align*** Controls the alignment of the table as a whole on the page. Possible values are LEFT and RIGHT to anchor the table to the left and right margins, respectively. To center the table on the page, place it within a center() or div({-align=>CENTER}) function.
- ***-bgcolor*** Sets the background color of the table (Internet Explorer only). Refer to the description of color specifications in start_html().
- ***-border*** Sets the presence and width of the table border. You may supply an empty string (" ") or an undefined value to get the default border, or give a positive integer to obtain borders of increasing width. A value of 0 supresses the border.
- ***-bordercolor*** Sets the color of the border (Internet Explorer only).
- ***-bordercolordark*** Sets the color of the border shadow (Internet Explorer only).
- ***-bordercolorlight*** Sets the color of the border highlight (Internet Explorer only).
- ***-cellpadding*** Sets the number of pixels of padding to put between the contents of each cell and the edge of the cell. This should be a positive integer.
- ***-cellspacing*** Specifies the number of pixels to separate each cell by.
- ***-hspace*** Adds some additional horizontal space between the table and the text flowing around it. Only relevant when the table is

anchored to the left or right margin using -align. This attribute should be a positive integer.

- ***-vspace*** Adds some additional vertical space between the table and the text flowing around it. Only relevant when the table is anchored to the left or right margin using -align. This attribute should be a positive integer.
- ***-width*** Sets the width of the table as a whole. This attribute can be expressed as an absolute number, in which it is taken as the width in pixels, or as a percentage, in which case it is taken as a percentage of the page width.

## td() (*:html3* group)

This function creates a table data cell <TD> tag and may only be used in the context of a table definition. See the definition of table() for a complete code example.

The ability of an HTML shortcut function to distribute the tag across all members of a list reference is handy for table headers. For example, you can create an entire row of a table with the line:

```
$top_row = Tr(td(['mittens','Fleece Mittens',
                  'CYM941','$29.95']));
```

Td() accepts a large number of attributes for controlling the appearance of the cell:

- ***-align*** Controls the alignment of all the text in the cell. Possible values are LEFT, RIGHT, and CENTER and have the usual meanings.
- ***-bgcolor*** Sets the background color for all cells in this row (Internet Explorer only). Both the named and RGB types of color specification are accepted.

- ***-bordercolor, -bordercolorlight, -bordercolordark*** Sets the color of the row color, its highlight, and its shadow (Internet Explorer only). See the equivalent attributes in table() for a description.
- ***-colspan*** Controls how many columns this cell should span. You may provide any integer up to the total number of columns in the cell. The default is 1.
- ***-nowrap*** If present, this attribute will suppress word-wrap in the cell. Because the attribute does not usually have an argument, you should provide an empty string as an argument (as in td({-wrap=>''})).
- ***-rowspan*** Controls how many rows this cell should span. You may provide any integer up to the total number of rows in the cell. The default is 1.
- ***-valign*** Sets the vertical alignment of all text in the row. Values are TOP, CENTER, and BOTTOM. Netscape also recognizes a BASELINE alignment, which aligns the cell contents to the top line of text in other cells in the row.
- ***-width*** Sets the width of this cell, either as an absolute number of pixels, or as a percentage of the table's width.

## th() (*:html3* group)

This function creates a table header cell <TH> tag and may only be used in the context of a table definition. See the definition of table() for a complete code example.

The ability of an HTML shortcut function to distribute the tag across all members of a list reference is handy for table headers. For example, you can create the entire top row of a table with the line:

```
$top_row = Tr(th(['Item','Description','Catalog','Price']));
```

Th() shares with td() a large number of attributes for controlling the appearance of the cell. See the description of td() for the complete list.

## title()

Sets the title of the document. This function is deprecated. Use start_html()'s -title argument instead.

## Tr() (:html3 group)

This function defines a table row <TR> tag and may only be used in the context of a table definition. Note that the initial letter is capitalized to avoid collision with the Perl tr/// operator. See the definition of table() for a complete code example.

The ability of an HTML shortcut function to distribute the tag across all members of a list reference is frequently used with Tr(), as this fragment illustrates:

```
@rows = (th('Word') . td('Definition'));
foreach (sort keys %dictionary) {
   push(@rows,th($_) . td($dictionary{$_}));
}
print table(Tr(\@rows));
```

Tr() recognizes a large number of formatting attributes:

- ***-align*** Controls the alignment of all the text in the row. Possible values are LEFT, RIGHT, and CENTER and have the usual meanings.
- ***-bgcolor*** Sets the background color for all cells in this row (Internet Explorer only). Both the named and RGB types of color specification are accepted.

- ***-bordercolor, -bordercolorlight, -bordercolordark*** Sets the color of the row color, its highlight, and its shadow. See the equivalent attributes in table().
- ***-valign*** Sets the vertical alignment of all text in the row. Values are TOP, CENTER, and BOTTOM. Netscape also recognizes a BASE-LINE alignment, which aligns the cell contents to the top line of text in other cells in the row.

## tt()

```
print "I don't think he is human ",
      tt("because he talks like a robot.");
```

Put the enclosed text in a monospaced (typewriter) font.

## ul()

```
print ul({-type=disc},
         li(['kale','cabbage','okra'])
        );
```

Start an unordered (bulleted) list. *See also* li(). Frequently used attributes include:

- ***-compact*** If this attribute is present, the list will be compacted to take as little vertical space as possible. This attribute should be given as {-compact=>''}. This tells CGI.pm to include the attribute as a bare attribute name, rather than an attribute/value pair.
- ***-type*** The bullet type (Netscape and compatible browsers only). It can be "disc" for a solid disc, "circle" for an open circle, or "square" for an open square.

### var()

```
print "Enter your name as ",var('last, first'),'.';
```

Renders text in the variable logical style. Usually used for syntactic placeholders that users are supposed to replace by whatever is appropriate.

## cgi-lib Compatibility Functions

These functions are provided for compatibility with older scripts that use cgi-lib.pl and are intended to ease the upgrade path. They are not recommended for use in new scripts. You must import these functions by using the :cgi-lib group.

### ReadParse()

```
use CGI qw/:cgi-lib/;
ReadParse();
print "The price of your purchase is $in{price}.\n";
```

When you call ReadParse(), CGI.pm creates an associative array named %in that contains the named CGI parameters. Multivalued parameters are separated by \0 characters in exactly the same way cgi-lib.pl does it. The function result is the number of parameters parsed. You can use this to quickly determine whether the script was passed any CGI parameters when it was called.

You may pass ReadParse() a variable glob in order to parse the parameters into a different associative array. For example:

```
ReadParse(*Q);
@partners = split("\0",$Q{'golf_partners'});
```

The associative array created by the function contains a special key named "CGI," which returns the CGI query object itself:

```
ReadParse();
$q = $in{CGI};
print $q->textfield(-name=>'wow',
                    -value=>'does this really work?');
```

This allows you to add the more interesting features of CGI.pm to your old scripts without rewriting them completely. As an added benefit, the %in variable is actually tied to the CGI object. Changing the CGI object using param() will dynamically change %in, and vice versa.

Cgi-lib.pl's @in and $in variables are not supported, nor is the file upload interface.

## HtmlTop()

```
print HtmlTop();
```

This function returns the top of an HTML file, from the <HTML> tag to <BODY>.

## HtmlBot()

```
print HtmlTop();
```

This function returns the bottom of an HTML file, the </BODY> and </HTML> tags.

## MethGet()

Returns a true value if the HTTP request method is GET.

## MethPost()

Returns a true value if the HTTP request method is POST.

## PrintHeader()

```
print PrintHeader();
```

This function returns an HTTP header appropriate for an HTML document.

## SplitParam()

```
ReadParse();
@buddies = SplitParam($in{'golf_buddies'});
```

Given the type of packed multivalued parameter retrieved by ReadParse(), splits it into its component pieces and returns the array.

Appendix A

# Frequently Asked Questions

This is a list of frequently asked questions about CGI.pm.

1. *When I run a script from the command line, it says "offline mode: enter name=value pairs on standard input." What do I do now?*

   This is a prompt to enter some CGI parameters for the purposes of debugging. You can now type in some parameters like this:

   ```
   first_name=Fred
   last_name=Flintstone
   city=Bedrock
   ```

   End the list by typing a control-D (or control-Z on DOS/Windows systems).

   If you want to run a CGI script from a script or batch file, and do not want this behavior, just pass it an empty parameter list like this:

   ```
   my_script.pl ''
   ```

   This will work on UNIX systems:

   ```
   my_script.pl </dev/null
   ```

On versions of CGI.pm 2.38 and greater, you can turn off debugging entirely by importing the -noDebug pragma.

2. *I can't retrieve the name of the uploaded file using the* param() *method.*
   Make sure that you are creating the fill-out form using *start_multipart_form()* or by specifying multipart/form-data as the encoding type. Also remember that the remote user has to cooperate. Older versions of Netscape and Internet Explorer cannot do file upload.
3. *When users accidentally try to upload a directory name, the browser hangs.*
   I do not know why browsers let users upload directories, but this seems to happen with astonishing regularity. Older versions of CGI.pm will hang when this happens, but newer versions will abort. You will see a malformed, multipart POST message in your server error log.
4. *I can read the name of the uploaded file, but can't retrieve the data.*
   First check that you have told CGI.pm to use the multipart/form-data scheme. If it still is not working, there may be a problem with the temporary files that CGI.pm needs to create in order to read in the—potentially very large—uploaded files. Internally, CGI.pm tries to create temporary files with names similar to "CGITemp123456" in a temporary directory. To find a suitable directory, it first looks for /usr/tmp, then for /tmp, then for directories suitable for Windows and Macintosh systems. If it can't find any of these directories, it tries for the current directory, which is usually the directory that the script resides in.
   If you are on a nonstandard system you may need to modify CGI.pm to point at a suitable temporary directory. This directory must be writable by the user ID under which the server runs (usually nobody), and must have sufficient capacity to handle large file uploads. Open up CGI.pm, and find:

```
package TempFile;
  foreach ('/usr/tmp','/tmp') {
    do {$TMPDIRECTORY = $_; last} if -w $_;
}
```

Modify the *foreach()* line to include the directories that you would like to store temporary files in.

5. *On Windows systems, the temporary file is never deleted, but hangs around in \temp, taking up space.*
   Be sure to close the filehandle before your program exits.
6. *When uploading large files over an SSL connection, the upload aborts or hangs halfway through.*
   This is reported to be a problem with Netscape's implementation of SSL on several of its servers, and affects both SSL versions 2.0 and 3.0. Switching to a different server, such as Stronghold or IIS, appears to fix the problem.
7. *When users press the Back button, the same page is loaded, not the previous one.*
   Some browsers get confused when processing multipart forms. If the script generates different pages for the form and the results, pressing the Back button does not always return you to the previous page; instead, the browser reloads the current page.
   A workaround for this is to use additional path information to trick Netscape into thinking that the form and the response have different URLs. I recommend giving each form a sequence number and bumping the sequence up by one each time the form is accessed:

```
my($s) = $q->path_info=~/(\d+)/; #fetch sequence
$s++;  #bump it up
# Trick browser into thinking it's got a new script:
print $q->start_form(-action=>$q->script_name . "/$s");
```

8. *I can't find the temporary file that CGI.pm creates during file upload.*
   You are encouraged to copy the data into your own file by reading from the filehandle that CGI.pm provides for you. In the future, there may not be a temporary file at all, just a pipe. However, for now, if you really want to get at the temp file, you can retrieve its path using the tmpFileName() method. Be sure to move the temporary file elsewhere in the file system if you do not want it to be automatically deleted when CGI.pm exits.
9. *What is the relationship of CGI.pm with the CGI::* modules? With CGI-Lite?*
   The CGI::* modules (including CGI::Base, CGI::BasePlus, CGI::Form, CGI::Request) were an attempt to make CGI scripting completely object-oriented and modular. However, performance was poor, and the object-oriented approach was not as popular as it might have been, so this effort was put on hold. I am now working to merge the best parts of CGI.pm and the CGI::* modules with LWP, Gisle Aas's client-side library for Web robots.
   CGI-Lite is an object-oriented CGI library written by Shishir Gundavaram. It is small and lightweight. It does not have all the functionality of CGI.pm, but it loads and runs slightly faster. I was not involved in its development.
10. *My scripts don't run correctly with Microsoft Internet Information Server!*
    If you are using the DLL version of the ActiveWare port of Perl5, try using the external Perl interpreter (see Chapter One, *Getting Started with CGI.pm*, for details). The DLL version plays several tricks with the CGI environment that are problematic for any CGI program, and those that use CGI.pm are no exception.
    If you rely on the additional path information, you may have to redesign your script. Several versions of IIS set the additional path information incorrectly, and Microsoft has shown no interest in fixing this bug.

# Appendix B

# Using the Companion Web Site

This book's companion Web site is where you'll find the full source code for CGI.pm, its online documentation, code updates, and working downloadable versions of all the examples in the book.

You can use any Web browser to access the site. Even older browsers that don't know about newer innovations, like stylesheets, DHTML, or frames, will work. However, you will of course need a browser that supports these features in order to run any examples that demonstrate them.

Point your Web browser at www.wiley.com/compbooks/stein. From the main page you'll find links to three major sections: the code archive, online documentation, and source code examples.

## The Code Archive

Here you'll find a directory containing the current distribution of CGI.pm and archival copies of previous versions. You'll also find beta release versions of the software that aren't available anywhere else.

The current version of CGI.pm can always be found by downloading a file named CGI.pm-current.*xxxxx*, where *xxxxx* is a file extension indicating the archive type. If you are using a UNIX system, look for the extension tar.gz to find a distribution that has been archived with the tar command and compressed using the GNU gzip program. Windows users should look for CGI.pm-current.zip, which is an archive created by the WinZip program. Macintosh users should look for the extension sea.hqx, a version that should be uncompressed with the UnStuffIt program.

In the event that you don't have one of these archive programs, here's a list of places you can download them:

- **tar**

  ftp://prep.ai.mit.edu/pub/gnu/tar-1.12.shar.gz

- **gzip**

  ftp://prep.ai.mit.edu/pub/gnu/gzip-1.2.4.shar (UNIX version)

  ftp://prep.ai.mit.edu/pub/gnu/gzip-1.2.4.msdos.exe (DOS/Windows version)

- **WinZip**

  ftp://ftp.digital.com/pub/micro/pc/simtelnet/win95/compress/wz32v63.exe

- **UnStuffIt**

  ftp://mirror.apple.com/mirrors/Info-Mac.Archive/cmp/unstuffit-307.hqx

Older versions of the software can be found in a directory named old, and beta versions in a directory named beta. As always, you should be a bit wary of beta releases because they're likely to contain bugs. If you find any, please let me know.

# The Online Documentation

Follow the link labeled Online Documentation to find copies of the CGI, CGI::Push, CGI::Fast, CGI::Apache, and CGI::Cookie manual pages. Copies of these documents are also part of the distribution. It's up to you whether you prefer to read the documentation online or on your own machine.

In the online documentation section you'll also find a link to errata. This contains errata for this book, and notices of feature updates and bug fixes in CGI.pm itself. You might want to check back here every month or so to find out what's new with the module. As a bonus, you'll also find links to other modules I have written or think are of special interest to CGI scripters.

# Source Code Examples

Pointers to every source code example in this book (except for a few trivial one-liners) can be found on this section. Each example has two links, one to its source code, and one to the script itself. Select the source code link to view the text of the script and download a copy of its text (choose Save As... from your browser's file menu). The other link allows you to take the script out for a whirl. You can run it and watch how it responds to different kinds of input.

# Hardware Requirements

To use CGI.pm, your system must meet the following requirements:

**RAM.** 8 Megabytes.

**Hard Drive Space.** 17 Megabytes.

**Peripherals.** CGI-supported Web server.

## User Assistance and Information

The software accompanying this book is being provided as is without warranty or support of any kind. Should you require basic installation assistance, or if your media is defective, please call our product support number at (212) 850-6194 weekdays between 9 A.M. and 4 P.M. Eastern Standard Time. Or, we can be reached via e-mail at: **wprtusw@wiley.com.**

To place additional orders or to request information about other Wiley products, please call (800) 879-4539.

# Index

## D

## T

## X